TREASURY OF WOMEN SAINTS

Treasury of Women Saints

Ronda De Sola Chervin

CHARIS

Servant Publications
Ann Arbor, Michigan

Copyright © 1991 by Ronda De Sola Chervin
All rights reserved.

Published by Servant Publications
P.O. Box 8617
Ann Arbor, Michigan 48107

Acknowledgments are listed in the last appendix.

Cover design by Michael Andaloro

99   10   9   8   7   6   5

Printed in the United States of America
ISBN 0-89283-707-1

Library of Congress Cataloging-in-Publication Data

Chervin, Ronda.
   Treasury of Women Saints / by Ronda Chervin.
      p.   cm.
   Includes bibliographical references.
   ISBN 0-89283-707-1
   1. Christian women saints–Biography.   2. Christian women
saints–Meditations.   1. Title.
   BX4656.C48   1991
   282'.092'2–dc20   91-13626

Dedicated to Charles Rich
who taught me
to love the Saints

Contents

Part Six: Sinners Turned Saints

Introduction

"THERE IS ONLY ONE TRAGEDY, not to have been a saint," wrote French author Léon Bloy. How many saints through the ages have been nourished not only by Holy Communion and Scripture, but also by contact with living saints and the reading of the lives of past saints!

Certainly the saints in heaven, whose lives we read and who read our lives and intercede for us as we make our own journeys toward eternity, play a great part in our spirituality. At baptism and confirmation we are given a saint to be our patron. Daily Mass-goers follow the annual feast days of the saints. Others see films about the most famous of them.

The goal of *Treasury of Women Saints* is to acquaint Christians with the stories of many of these women, some familiar, all fascinating. Since my conversion from an atheistic background thirty years ago, it has been my practice to read the lives of the saints as spiritual nourishment nightly. It is a joy to tell their tales once more, and to inspire readers of these short accounts to read longer biographies. The women saints with whom I had not been acquainted became new friends in heaven, each one's story illustrating gospel truths with a new slant.

A separate book about *women* saints is of special value in our times when so many Catholic women are undergoing identity crises about their role in the church and society. The true dignity of women, well shown by Pope John Paul II in his Apostolic Exhortation on the Dignity and Role of Women, consists precisely in the love of God for each of us made in his divine image and likeness. Women saints clearly exemplify how great a woman can become if she confides her destiny totally to the God of infinite love and providential care. Real self-love, as the saints demonstrate, comes from doing "something beautiful for God," as Mother Teresa of Calcutta has said, in one form or another, at every moment of our lives.

The many differences between the women saints of country, era, lifestyle, and vocation provide models to which every contemporary woman, desiring complete union with Christ, can relate fruitfully. The imitation of the saints does not mean any kind of slavish following of exterior details or even specific interior attitudes. As a spiritual director of mine once said when I was asking him to make me into another Catherine of Siena, "God already has St. Catherine, now he wants St. Ronda." What we want to imitate in the saints is their love, their zeal, their intimacy with God, their astounding courage, their forgiveness, and their compassion.

The women saints are wonderful comrades, foremothers, and sisters to us all, whatever our sex. It is hoped that *Treasury of Women Saints* will also be read by men who need as much as women to be guided by the light that emanates from holy women. It is said that women in general teach men how to love. How much more is this true of women in intimate touch with divine love!

PRACTICAL USES OF THIS BOOK

The format of *Treasury of Women Saints* is a bit different from standard reference books on the saints. Lives are arranged by the categories of: young saints, motherly saints, martyrs, prophetic saints, interior women of the Spirit, and sinners turned saints. There is an alphabetical index at the end of the book. I have also followed the lead of Joan Carroll

Cruz's fine book *Secular Saints,* by having an index of the particular type of sufferings endured by the saints so that a reader with a particular cross might quickly be able to find holy friends who went through the same difficulties.

The categories I have chosen—young saints, mothers, martyrs, prophets, interior women of the Spirit, and penitents—are, of course, not mutually exclusive. St. Thérèse of Lisieux could certainly be included under interior women rather than under young saints, but I chose to add her to the young saints because I think that her youth is a real part of her charm. All women saints had a deep interior life, but with some this was the main aspect of their holiness, whereas others, such as Blessed Marie of the Incarnation, seem to me to be energized as much by their motherliness toward the needy than by their beautiful mystical experiences, and so I have included her as a motherly saint.

By young saints I mean ones who died at twenty-five or younger. I put them first, imagining that the book may be read by mothers and daughters together and that young people might be drawn to follow the saints of other categories if they first are led to identify with saints of their own age levels.

I designate certain saints as motherly because it seems to me that it is the neediness, poverty, illness, and misery of others that touched their hearts the most. Their inner prayer lives inspired them with Christ's own love for the most helpless.

Of the martyrs, I have included only those who actually died because of their insistence on not betraying the creed. Ones designated as martyrs by dying for moral uprightness, such as St. Maria Goretti, I have usually listed under young saints.

By the more unusual title of prophetic saints I refer to women whose holiness was very public because they were actual prophets of future calamities or were recognized as speaking for God. This category also includes founders of religious orders who had to deal with many persecutions in trying to bring about new forms of religious life, or women who had to stand up heroically and witness verbally to abuses of church or society, or those whose main charism strikes me as creatively initiating new things in the church.

By interior women of the Spirit I mean primarily those with a contemplative vocation whether they be cloistered, married, or single. The word mystical often used in my descriptions means simply a felt presence of God in any form, whether it be a gentle touch of love, words from God audible or impressed into the heart, visions, levitations, or the stigmata.

It should be noted that although the Virgin Mary is our perfect saint, intercessor, and model, she has not been included because there are many lengthy books about her already. A cursory treatment would be too unsatisfying to undertake or to read.

The penitential saints may unnerve some readers, for their penances may seem so extreme as to be repulsive. It should be noted that these women who had given themselves to mortal sin in the past felt a much greater need for healing through reparation than a saint whose sins are more in the nature of defects than of purposely chosen offenses against God. The main motive for penance, however, was to join with Christ in suffering for the sins of the world, as expiation. They were aware of both the heinousness of sin and the goodness of God. Saints who received this purity of heart understood the evil of sin and longed to suffer for it with Christ as a sacrifice for the purification of the church.

I end the story of each saint with some reflections of my own concerning how the charism of the particular saint can be related to problems of our times. This is followed by a prayer composed by myself, or, when possible, by lines from the writings of the saint or from a eulogy of her life written by an admirer.

Many readers will want to use this treasury as a daily devotional, reading an entry each day. The life applications and the prayers and meditations, which have been provided in the "For Your Life" and "Prayer-Meditation" sections, are ideally suited to such an approach. After reading the biographical sketch of a particular saint, the reader could enter into a devotional time of reflection and prayer, asking the Lord, "How does this saint's life apply to my own? What is the message I can take with me throughout my day?"

WHAT IS SAINTLINESS?

The Catholic church has always taught the universal call to holiness (Vatican II, *Lumen Gentium*). Sainthood has been defined in many ways. Heroic love of God and neighbor is one standard description. More lyrically, a saint is one who loves God passionately and is ready to do anything that seems to be God's will regardless of personal sacrifice. The saint is one who has taken seriously the words of Jesus, Our Lord, "Be you perfect, as your heavenly Father is perfect" (Mt 5:38). Perfection does not mean the absence of all weaknesses, visible and hidden, but rather a love for God and others so graced that temptations to sin and defects are under the control of the Holy Spirit bringing forth good fruit. All this is crowned by joy in the Holy Spirit, full of hope in the promise of eternal blessedness.

More technically, a saint is one officially canonized by the Roman Catholic church, in recent centuries after long investigation and discernment to protect the faithful from taking as a model anyone not worthy of veneration. The steps in canonization are as follows: after the death of an apparently holy Catholic, an investigation takes place at the diocesan level. If the bishop thinks that, indeed, there is nothing in the life of the candidate that would rule out future canonization and much to commend the proposal, a cause is introduced in Rome where a special commission starts gathering evidence. When it is determined, after careful analysis, including whatever can be presented against him or her by the so-called devil's advocate, that the person so merits, he or she is declared a servant of God and can be called Venerable. The next step is beatification when it is ascertained that the holy woman or man is worthy of honor because her or his life manifests heroic love of God and neighbor and also because the elevation of the saintly person to heaven without the need for purgation seems to be confirmed by God himself in the form of at least one miracle proven to be beyond all possible natural explanation. Canonization follows further supernatural manifestations of a miraculous nature. In *Treasury of Women Saints*, I have included some whose causes have been introduced, whom I dub "holy ladies in waiting," but most are beatified, and/or canonized saints. Those not yet beatified are not to be *venerated* by the faithful, although one can ask them to intercede for us.

My closing prayer for myself and all readers for this introduction is taken from St. Paul's letter to the Ephesians (Eph 3:14—21):

For this reason I bow my knees before the Father, from whom every family in heaven and on earth is named, that according to the riches of his glory he may grant you to be strengthened with might through his Spirit in the inner man, and that Christ may dwell in your hearts through faith; that you, being rooted and grounded in love, may have power to comprehend with all the saints what is the breadth and length and height and depth, and to know the love of Christ which surpasses knowledge, that you may be filled with all the fullness of God. Now to him who by the power at work within us is able to do far more abundantly than all that we ask or think, to him be glory in the church and in Christ Jesus for all generations, forever and ever. Amen.

Part One

Young Saints

1 ✠

St. Dymphna
sixth century[1]

St. Dymphna, of sixth-century Ireland, is the patroness of those afflicted with nervous and mental disorders. Her short life, exotic in its setting, is terrifyingly modern in its implications.

Dymphna, like her mother, was both beautiful and devout. Her father, however, was a pagan king. Tutored by a pious Christian laywoman and a priest, Dymphna grew in grace and wisdom and early decided to consecrate herself to Jesus with a vow of chastity.

When her mother died, Dymphna's father was deeply grieved, but was counseled to find a second wife. As in a fairy tale, he sent messengers to many countries to seek out a woman as lovely as his first wife. When these returned saying that no one could be found as charming as his own daughter, the king decided to cease his search and incestuously marry Dymphna!

The young girl's priest advisor counseled her to flee from Ireland to the present city of Antwerp, Belgium. From there they fled further to the little town of Gheel. When the king learned of this mutiny, he set out himself with his retinue in search of his daughter. When persuasion failed to make Dymphna yield to his designs, the enraged king had the head of her priest advisor severed from his body. When Dymphna continued to resist, her father drew a dagger from his belt and struck off the head of his beautiful fifteen-year-old daughter.

The relics of the two martyrs are venerated to this day. Many miraculous healings are attributed to them.

Gradually more and more cures of mental illness were attributed to St. Dymphna. Her relics were applied to persons coming on pilgrimage from great distances. There is an infirmary in the town of Gheel for the mentally disordered. After some time with the sisters at the institution, the inmates are placed with families in the area who accept them into their homes with great tenderness. A League of St. Dymphna founded in Ohio offers many spiritual benefits for persons afflicted with mental illness.

For Your Life

At times of mental stress, many of us feel abandoned by God, by family, and friends. Yet God has a special concern for the weak, and inability to cope can be an opening to greater reliance on supernatural help. Like the townspeople of Gheel, Belgium, we should care for the mentally ill in our midst.

Unfortunately, in our times, there also is a rise in the frequency of incest. Often children are afraid to resist the overtures of parents or an older sibling. A victim of incest should be encouraged to report the matter to school, state, and church counselors. We should pray for those tempted by this horrific sin.

Prayer-Meditation

Heavenly God, you have willed that St. Dymphna should be invoked as the patroness of nervous and mental diseases. We beg you through your servant, St. Dymphna, who sealed with her blood the love she had for you, to grant relief to those in our midst who suffer from mental affictions and nervous disorders. Through Christ our Lord. Amen.

2 ✠

St. Patricia
early centuries[2]

St. Patricia was part of the imperial family of Constantinople. She wished to remain a consecrated virgin, but her family wanted her to marry. To avoid their plans, Patricia fled to Rome, where she took her vows. When she returned to Constantinople, she gave away all her possessions to the poor and then went back to Naples, Italy, where she died not long after. The many miracles attributed to praying at her grave led to canonization. She is considered one of the patrons of Naples.

For Your Life

Very often family members have different ideas for the future of their children than what God has designed. Sometimes we are called to let go of our children so that they may be free to find their own destiny, trusting that God loves them infinitely more than we do.

Prayer-Meditation

Through the intercession of St. Patricia, may parents be freed from undue anxiety about their children. Through Christ our Lord. Amen.

3 ✠

St. Arthelais

d. around A.D. 560[3]

*L*iving in Constantinople during the reign of Emperor Justinian in the sixth century, was Arthelais, a lovely daughter of the Pro-Consul. When she reached marriagable age, the emperor, hearing of her great beauty, asked her father to give the girl to him as a concubine.

With the help of her father, Arthelais fled with servants to Dalmatia. There they were attacked by robbers, but Arthelais was released miraculously. They continued their journey to Benevenuto to the home of her uncle. Arthelais, on arrival, made an act of thanksgiving by walking barefoot to the Church of Our Lady. After her victorious escape, she devoted herself to prayer and fasting. She died of fever at sixteen.

For Your Life

The story of Arthelais illustrates the way in which everything creaturely, even God-given beauty, can become a source of problems. Many young girls wish they were as beautiful as film or rock stars, yet these same glamorous women often suffer from deep feelings of inferiority because they know they are valued only for their looks and not for their true selves. Through prayer and daring, Arthelais was able to avoid the fate of becoming a sex-object for life. May all young girls ask the Virgin Mary to protect them from dehumanizing, lustful schemes.

Prayer-Meditation

St. Arthelais, intercede for Christian girls that they may prefer beauty in the Spirit to vanity, and avoid men motivated by lust. May these same boys and men be led by the Holy Spirit to understand the beauty of chastity in marriage and celibacy. Through Christ our Lord. Amen.

4 ✠

St. Edith of Wilton
c. A.D. 962-984[4]

In the times of St. Edith it was not uncommon for children to be brought up in monasteries. Edith, daughter of King Edgar, was swiftly removed to Wilton Abbey, England, right after her birth. This startling move is sometimes attributed to some scandal connected with her conception. Therefore, Edith did not know the world and come to forsake it, but had never known life outside the monastery when she made her vows.

At her religious profession at age fifteen, her parents gave lots of gold and jewelry to the monastery as a dowry. Edith continued to live at the monastery, now under obedience to her own mother, who shortly after Edith's profession renounced the world and became the abbess of Wilton! Even though she came from such noble lineage and was the daughter of the abbess, Edith insisted on doing ordinary housework. Various members of the royal family died, and the nobility in power asked Edith to leave the monastery and become queen, but she insisted on remaining a nun. When Edith built a church at Wilton, the archbishop, St. Dunstan, came to dedicate it. He wept during the Mass because it was revealed to him in his prayers that Edith would soon die, whereas he would be forced to remain on earth longer. Forty-three days later, Edith died suddenly.

For Your Life

Some insist that only after lots of worldly experience can someone discern authentically about life in a monastery or convent. The story of St. Edith shows this need not be the case. Young girls who sense a vocation to become religious sisters should be close to those already leading this life so that they can experience it firsthand.

Prayer-Meditation

Through the prayers of St. Edith of Wilton may religious vocations increasingly be discerned so those who are so called may enter a life dedicated to contemplative prayer for the salvation of souls and the greater glory of God. Through Christ our Lord. Amen.

5 ✠

St. Godelieve
c. 1049-1070 [5]

St. Godelieve was born in 1049 in Belgium to noble parents. As a child she was known to be holy, especially because of her loving care for the poor. She wanted to become a cloistered nun, but one suitor, Bertolf, used his political influence to get the beautiful girl as his bride.

After the wedding Godelieve and Bertolf journeyed to his hometown. Godelieve's mother-in-law treated her brutally because she had wanted her son to marry another. She had the poor young wife confined to a cell with hardly any food. Her husband went along with his mother in this treatment, claiming that Godelieve was an unworthy wife.

Finally Godelieve escaped to her father's house, and he

reported the outrage to the bishop. When confronted, Bertolf promised to treat his wife better in the future, but this proved to be a false commitment. He went off on a trip, arranging beforehand that she be drowned by his servants. Thus young Godelieve ended her life of only twenty-one years.

This nightmarish story has an unexpected ending. When Bertolf married once more, he had a daughter who was born blind. When her eyes were washed in the water from the pool where Godelieve had been drowned, she was miraculously healed of her blindness. This event so affected Bertolf that he confessed to the murder of Godelieve and entered a monastery where he lived a life of penance. Many other miracles were confirmed from praying near the relics of this poor, battered, young woman. A Benedictine abbey was built at the request of her husband, which has become a place of pilgrimage. She is an intercessor for peace in families.

For Your Life

It is impossible to read the story of Godelieve and Bertolf without shuddering at the evil deeds of this once so ardent suitor. It reminds us today of women being treated violently by men who once claimed to love them. What is extraordinary about the story, however, is the fact that even a person so entrapped by sin as was St. Godelieve's husband, could receive the grace not only to repent but to decide on a life of holy penance and prayer. May St. Godelieve teach us never to give up on any human being, but instead to pray for his or her conversion.

Prayer-Meditation

St. Godelieve, intercede for all persons undergoing marital strife, especially those most in need of deliverance from domestic violence. May the perpetrators of such violence repent and be healed and restored to right living. Through Christ our Lord. Amen.

6 ✠

Blessed Margaret of Louvain
c. 1207-1225[6]

M argaret was a maid and waitress at an inn in Louvain. She was devoted to housing all who sought shelter, even if they could not pay. She was nicknamed "proud Margaret" because she refused to flirt with the male guests.

When the innkeeper and his wife decided to enter religious life, they sold the inn, intending to donate the money to the religious houses they would enter. Just before they left, some thieves came to steal the money. When the innkeepers resisted, they were murdered. When Margaret came upon them, they offered her clemency if she would conceal their crime. When she refused, they murdered her also, throwing her body into a nearby river. Angels' voices brought the townspeople to the scene, and her body was buried. This was followed by many miracles for those coming to venerate her memory and ask for her intercession. She was beatified as a virgin martyr in 1905.

For Your Life

In our times, theft backed up by murderous threats is all too common. Let us pray for all those who are tempted to steal for any reason, especially to support expensive addictions. May they be healed of the causes of their sinful lifestyles.

Prayer-Meditation

"There are different kinds of martyrdom, namely innocence, as in Abel; uprightness in the Prophets as in St. John the Baptist; love of law, as in the Maccabees; confession of the Faith, as in the Apostles. For all these different causes Christ the Lamb is said to have been slain from the beginning of the world."[7]

7 ✠

St. Rose of Viterbo
c. 1235-1252[8]

*B*orn of a poor family in Viterbo, Italy, Rose showed remarkable spiritual maturity. At the age of seven she asked to live in a small room alone so she could pray. Later she became a Third Order Franciscan but lived at home because in a vision the Virgin Mary told her to stay with the family to be a witness.

Being courageous, when the excommunicated Emperor Frederick came to occupy Viterbo, this twelve-year-old girl told the people not to submit to him but to rebel and oust his garrison. This intervention gave Rose courage for her later vocation of preaching in public to the people. Her continued boldness, however, led to the banishment of her whole family.

When Rose's family returned after the death of Frederick, the young girl tried to enter an order but was refused, probably because they were afraid of having such a troublemaker among them. Instead she led a contemplative life at home until 1252 when she died at seventeen. Rose of Viterbo was canonized in 1457. Her body is incorrupt and venerated at the monastery that had refused her entrance!

It is a mistake to imagine that young people cannot receive supernatural gifts and exhibit extraordinary valor. Sometimes they can be more fearless than their elders by following the clear light of truth rather than worldly maxims of prudence. Rose's short life illustrates that God can inspire a person with a desire for a certain way of life which he means to fulfill in an interior way. We should not be fixated on externals but instead on love of God.

Prayer-Meditation

St. Rose of Viterbo, valiant saint, intercede for all young people that they, like you, may lead lives of prayer and witness courageously to the truth. Through Christ our Lord. Amen.

8 ✠

St. Hedwig of Poland
1371-1399[9]

Born in 1371, Jadwiga, known in Anglo-Saxon countries as Hedwig, was the daughter of King Louis of Poland. When Hedwig was thirteen, since there was no male heir, she was made sovereign. Hedwig was reported to have been beautiful, wise, and devout.

Hedwig had been betrothed to William, Duke of Austria, at nine years of age, and she had come to love him. Unfortunately the ruling Polish Diet had other plans for the young princess, involving a more advantageous political marriage. William tried to elope with Hedwig, but failed, and Hedwig decided to sacrifice her love for William out of duty as a queen.

The suitor the Polish court desired for Hedwig was Jagiello, a prince of Lithuania. Jagiello was a pagan but he agreed to be baptized and have his whole kingdom baptized along with him if only he could be wed to Hedwig. What is more, he agreed to pay off Duke William for so great a loss.

When Hedwig agreed to this plan for the sake of her country and the church, she covered herself with a thick black veil and went to the Cathedral of Kracow to pray for resignation at the loss of her beloved William. Then she left her veil over the crucifix to symbolize her acceptance of this heavy cross.

Jagiello was true to his word. He was baptized himself and had all his people brought into the faith. Hedwig was a true Christian queen, devoted to just laws for the poor, generous alms, and the advancement of education. The marriage was happy, for Hedwig was able to pacify her jealous, willful husband. She and her first-born daughter died in childbirth. Hedwig is a greatly revered saint, especially in Poland.

For Your Life

Not for such dramatic world-shaking reasons, but for other lesser causes, a girl may find that it is impossible to be married to the man she loves the most. This can lead to desperation and the conviction that no other man can content her. The story of St. Hedwig indicates the contrary. Goodness can improve an unromantic marriage and render it happy and holy.

Prayer-Meditation

St. Hedwig, intercede for all who are prevented from marrying the person of their choice. Pray for all marriages that are in some way a second choice for one of the spouses, that they may be blessed. Intercede also for mothers during the delivery of their babies. Through Christ our Lord. Amen.

9 ✠

St. Germaine de Pibrac
c. 1579-1601[10]

Germaine's mother died when she was a toddler in Toulouse, France. Little Germaine had a birth defect, a withered hand. When her father remarried, Germaine's life-long story of suffering began, for her stepmother despised her as a cripple. She thought of Germaine as a liability, since she would be less useful for housework and heavy field work without full use of both hands.

Banished to the stable and clothed in rags, Germaine's only food was table scraps. As the stepmother's burdens grew with each new baby, she took to lashing out at Germaine with sarcasm, ridicule, beatings, and false accusations. In her sorrow, Germaine had recourse to God in prayer, praying the Rosary on a knotted piece of string. Since she could not read, she could not benefit from written prayers.

Germaine's prayer was blessed with many supernatural graces. Soon the villagers were astounded to hear beautiful music coming from the barn where Germaine slept. When they entered, they saw her surrounded by light in a trance of rapture.

By day, Germaine tended the sheep and spun wool, but when the bells rang for Mass, she would leave the sheep to her guardian angel and go. One day, during a storm, the river overflowed, blocking Germaine's path to church. Before the eyes of the villagers, God parted the river for Germaine. After the Mass, Germaine taught the children and the beggars about the love of God.

One winter day Germaine's stepmother was beating her until Germaine collapsed. As she fell, her apron opened to reveal spring flowers. This miracle finally opened up the heart of Germaine's cruel stepmother who repented and invited Germaine to come back and live with them in the main house. She was happy that her prayers for her stepmother had finally been answered, but she preferred the simplicity and solitude of her life in the stable.

For Your Life

The life of St. Germaine reads like a holy pastoral elegy: an illiterate peasant girl reaches the heights of divine wisdom without schooling. Pause to think about the idol-worship of education going on during our day. Some parents even limit family size in order to guarantee having sufficient savings to send their one or two children to expensive universities where many end up losing their most precious gift, the faith.

Prayer-Meditation

From the prayer of St. Germaine: "O Lord, I am not worthy of you. Come in my heart and soul and mind, guide my every thought, word, and deed."[11]

10 ✠

Blessed Kateri Tekakwitha
1656-1679[12]

*I*n 1656 an Indian girl was born to a war-chief and a Christian near the Mohawk River in upstate New York. Her name was Tekakwitha which means "putting things in order." Tekakwitha's father, a Mohawk, had married Kahenta, her mother, during the conquest of her Algonquin tribe. Kahenta had found the Christian God through the Jesuits. She kept her faith a secret among the pagan Mohawks by praying with another captive Christian woman.

When she was four, Tekakwitha's entire family died of smallpox. The girl was taken care of by Anastasia, her mother's Christian friend. As a result of the epidemic, Tekakwitha was left with a pocked face, poor eyes, and weakened legs. These marks isolated her from the other Mohawk women, but readied her for the joy of finding Christ who loved her unconditionally. Although marriage was valued highly in the tribe, even before her baptism Tekakwitha refused to be given in marriage.

Joy came into the Indian maiden's life when a treaty between the French and the Iroquois allowed French Jesuits to come to the village and preach. Secretly it was arranged that Tekakwitha be baptized with the name Kateri (Catherine) and take instructions. After her commitment to the faith, she was scorned and persecuted by her people, all the while having to wait on others hand and foot. Finally a Jesuit priest suggested she escape to Canada to live with other Christians.

In spite of threats to kill her, Kateri made her way safely to St. Lawrence where she spent her time helping the aged and sick and teaching the children. To go to Mass, she had to arise at four in the morning and walk barefoot even in the snow. In spite of her marked face and weak body, everyone thought she radiated spiritual beauty. Kateri died at twenty-three and recently has been beatified.

For Your Life

Physical beauty is so prized among girls and women that those less favored by nature or marred by illness have difficulty believing that anyone could delight in them and find them lovable. Yet God can inspire others to love one of his creations, and once seeing her virtues, to delight also in her physical presence. Even non-Christians have come to see ultimate beauty in the loving face of aged Mother Teresa of Calcutta. If we strive to unite ourselves with God and neighbor in Christian love, we will always be welcome wherever we go.

Prayer-Meditation

Blessed Kateri, intercede for your people, so many of whom suffer from alienation and poverty. Pray also for girls and women who feel themselves to be ugly, that they may find the secret of true beauty in the Holy Spirit. Through Christ our Lord. Amen.

11 ✠

St. Thérèse of Lisieux
1873-1897[13]

Among the most beloved saints of all time is Thérèse of Lisieux, often called "The Little Flower." Born in Alençon, France, to parents whose holiness is now being considered worthy of canonization, Thérèse was the youngest daughter, adored by everyone in the family, including her four sisters who all became nuns.

The death of the mother of Thérèse when she was only four years old was traumatic. She clung to her older sisters and women relatives. When her favorite sister entered the Carmelite Order, Thérèse had what some would term a nervous breakdown. Her illness was overcome by a vision of the infant Jesus.

This supernatural experience imprinted on the soul of the girl a great devotion to the Holy Child Jesus and a spirituality of childlike faith. On a pilgrimage to Rome, although primed to be respectful and quiet, Thérèse burst forth with pleas to the pope to give her permission to enter Carmel early at age fifteen. Finally, a little later, she was admitted. Although little Thérèse was much loved by the Sisters, her Carmelite experience was filled with interior trials and aridity. The fact that her beloved father was paralyzed with a stroke and endured a mental breakdown as well was further cause for heroic sufferings. She would have liked to leave her enclosure to comfort him in his agony, but since she was a cloistered nun, it was not allowed in those days.

So mature was the soul of this young girl, she was made novice mistress in her early twenties. What she taught the other nuns and later the world through her autobiographical account was how to offer up minute annoyances and difficulties. She surrendered these to Christ and to intercession for the church, especially for missionary priests. She claimed this was a little way that small souls without the stamina of a St. Teresa of Avila and other prophetic saints could use to become holy and to please Jesus.

After a most painful death at age twenty-four, the account of her life—sent out first only to other Carmelites and later published—caused her to be loved and admired all over the world. What is more, as she had promised, showers of roses, in the form of supernatural phenomena and special graces, seemed proof indeed that the infant Jesus loved little Thérèse abundantly and wished to affirm by miracles the efficacy of her "little way." Because of the profusion of roses that are sent as a sign to those who ask for the prayers of St. Thérèse, she is considered the patroness of flower-venders.

For Your Life

When reading the dramatic lives of some saints, we may think that our circumstances and talents are so different that we can never imitate these heroines. St. Thérèse of Lisieux teaches us that we can be united with God by offering him each moment of our daily lives. That simple offering can be a means to the holiness for which we long.

Prayer-Meditation

From a letter of St. Thérèse of Lisieux: "Sometimes, when I read spiritual treatises... my poor little mind soon grows weary, I close the learned book, which leaves my head splitting and my heart parched, and I take the Holy Scriptures. Then all seems luminous, a single word opens up infinite horizons to my soul.... I see that it is enough to realize one's nothingness, and give oneself wholly, like a child, into the arms of the good God.... I rejoiced to be little because 'only children, and those who are like them, will be admitted to the heavenly banquet.' "[14]

12 ✠

St. Clelia Barbieri

1847-1870[15]

A recently canonized saint, Clelia Barbieri, was born in 1847 in Emilia, near Bologna, Italy. There was a lot of anti-clericalism in Italy during her life and it took courage to become a catechist. Clelia's dream was to gather other young women together with her to form an order devoted to a contemplative, but also apostolic, life. She wanted to spread the truths of the faith, particularly to youth. The order that was formed is called the Minims of Our Lady of Sorrows. She is the youngest founder in the history of the church!

St. Clelia's spirituality was characterized by a fire of love in her heart for Jesus and his truths. She was especially devoted to the Eucharist. This explains why she could do so much in such a short life of only twenty-three years. Clelia died very young, collapsing suddenly as if consumed by the inner fire of love for Jesus that burned within her.

For Your Life

As John Paul II proclaimed in his homily at the time of her canonization: "Her life illustrates that holiness is a work of divine grace, not of strategy and human culture."[16] It also shows how the family and the parish can nourish aspirations to holiness. Devotional prayer, the sacraments, and the basic teachings of the faith are not dead in our times. They are the fundamental source of holiness on which spirituality has to be grounded in order to bring forth good fruit.

Prayer-Meditation

From the words of St. Clelia: "Lord, open your heart and throw forth flames of love, and with these flames, enkindle my heart. Make me burn with love."[17]

13 ✠

Blessed Elizabeth of the Trinity
1880-1906[18]

*E*lizabeth Catez was born in 1880 to a French military family. Shortly after her birth they moved to the city of Dijon. Although considered to be a little devil as a tot and capable of terrible rages as a young girl, her fiery qualities were gradually channeled by breeding and grace so that by young adulthood she was enchanting, vivacious, and tender.

Elizabeth became an accomplished pianist. Musical analogies enliven her later spiritual writings, for harmony in all was the hallmark of her interior peace. Young Elizabeth loved everything that was beautiful and great, especially nature.

What made her so different from many girls with the same natural gifts was a spirituality of intense inner listening which began with her First Holy Communion. Her prayer life grew in depth. At fourteen she felt impelled by the Holy Spirit to consecrate her life to Jesus in a vow of perpetual virginity.

Later her widowed mother tried to interest her in accepting one of her many suitors, but even though Elizabeth described herself as coquettish, her deepest desire was to live for Jesus as a Carmelite. One of her sensitive suitors remarked to another admirer of Elizabeth: "No, she is not for us."

Named Elizabeth of the Trinity at the Carmel of Dijon, her interior life was characterized most by the felt presence of the Three Persons of the Trinity indwelling in her soul. She died only six years after her entry into the convent.

The writings of Elizabeth, published after her death, are studded with scriptural reflections and with the spirit of praise. She called herself "Praise of Glory" and considered it to be her vocation to offer continual praise for the glory of God.

For Your Life

Young girls afraid that being religious could mean losing out on the fun of youth will take heart from reading about Elizabeth. Instead of repressing her natural gifts, Elizabeth allowed the Holy Spirit to transfigure them so that her laughter and happiness in friendship would never be marred by vulgarity or sin. Extremely popular with women and men alike, she saved her most intimate love for Jesus.

Prayer-Meditation

From writings of St. Elizabeth of the Trinity: "'A Praise of Glory' is a soul of silence that remains like a lyre under the mysterious touch of the Holy Spirit so that He may draw from it divine harmonies; it knows that suffering is a string that produces still more beautiful sounds; so it loves to see this string on its instrument that it may more delightfully move the heart of God."[19]

14 ✠

St. Maria Goretti
1890-1902[20]

The life of Maria Goretti, starker than that of the heroines in Italian operas, began in Corinaldo in the Apennine mountains in 1890. She was born into a farming family living in poverty. She had an older brother and two younger brothers and two smaller sisters, all of whom she would take care of by her mother's side. Her mother, Assunta, was so poor that her only dowry was a picture of the Madonna. Yet, she was a strong and spiritual woman.

When it became clear there was no way to make a living farming in their district, the family migrated to the Pontine marshes as tenant farmers. They were accompanied by a friend, Serenelli, and his fourteen-year-old son Alessandro, whose mother had died. This boy had become worldly when sent as a lad to work with the sailors at the waterfront of Ancona. The two families lived in an old barn separated into small rooms, with the cherished Madonna centrally placed for their family Rosary.

Maria, as the oldest girl, shared the chores in taking care of nine people. In place of education, Maria, who could neither read nor write, was taught about Jesus and Mary, virtue and sin, and that it was better to die than to commit a mortal sin.

When Maria was nine, her beloved father died suddenly. Her mother was carrying their sixth child. At twelve, Maria received her First Communion. Villagers viewed her as a good and holy child, full of unselfishness. Meanwhile Alessandro began to feel attracted to the graceful young girl living in the same house. He told her he would kill her if she told her mother about his attempts to induce her into sexual sin. On July 5, 1902, Maria was alone minding the baby when Alessandro came home suddenly from the field. He sharpened a knife and insisted that Maria come into the house from the landing where she was sewing. When she refused, he dragged her inside the kitchen. She protested that he would go to hell, while she sobbed and tried to cover her body. He gagged her and, enraged that he could not take her sexually, stabbed her fourteen times.

After twenty hours of terrible pain, Maria made her final confession and prepared to meet the Lord. As she breathed her last, she said, "I forgive Alessandro, I forgive him with all my heart, and I want him to be with me in heaven." In prison Alessandro was given thirty years instead of a life-sentence, since he was a minor. After receiving visions of Maria from heaven forgiving him, Alessandro repented. He was released at age forty-five and went to serve the monks of a Capuchin monastery.

For Your Life

In the life of every Christian there come times when fidelity to the moral commandments of Christ entails heroic suffering. In the direct confrontation depicted here between good and evil, we are invited to renew our own pledge that we will never choose sin regardless of the pain that may result. Rape has become a common crime in our days. Even as we work to block such acts, may we show forth Christ's forgiving love for rapists just as Maria Goretti did.

Prayer-Meditation

St. Maria Goretti, we pray that you may intercede for us to be chaste. Help us to fight against our pornographic culture. Help us to radiate true love for all and never to indulge in any fantasies, words, or acts manifesting lust. We pray for the healing of all victims of rape and for forgiveness and new life in Christ for all who have forced others into sexual sin. Through Christ our Lord. Amen.

15 ✝

Laura Vicuna
1891-1904[21]

*T*he short life of Laura Vicuna of Chile, at the turn of the twentieth century, was long enough to let her become a heroic model for young girls in similar predicaments.

Laura's father was a soldier of the noble class in Chile. He died when Laura was only three years old, just after the birth of her little sister. Bereft of support, the mother entered into a relationship with an owner of a large ranch, Señor Mora. He offered to pay for the care and schooling of her children at a Salesian boarding school if Mercedes became his mistress. At school Laura learned about the Christian faith. She was a lively, friendly girl who helped the younger children with their tasks and acted like a mother to them, combing their hair and mending their clothing.

By the time she was eight, on summer vacation, Laura came to realize the nature of her mother's life. Laura noticed that her mother did not receive the sacraments. She began to pray fervently for her mother. The drunken lover of Mercedes liked to try to kiss and hug the young daughter as well. Over time the advances of her mother's lover to Laura became more and more violent to the point where she had to hide. As revenge for Laura's refusal to accept his sexual demands, Señor Mora cancelled her tuition at the school. The Sisters offered to take her for free.

At the time of her confirmation at twelve years old, Laura offered her life in prayer for the intention of the conversion of her mother. When Laura was sent home from the boarding school because of illness, Mercedes recognized the danger to her daughter from Señor Mora and moved out of town. The enraged man followed them, and with threats of violence, demanded that they return. Laura walked out the door. But Señor Mora followed her out and whipped and kicked her. He placed her on his horse and prepared to leave. Seeing townspeople coming to her rescue, he then threw her back into the street. After a week, on January 22, 1904, Laura died from the violence to which she had been subjected. Her parting words were: "Mama, I'm dying, but I'm happy to offer my life for you. I asked our Lord for this."[22] Immediately after her daughter's death Mercedes made a good confession and returned to the faith.

For Your Life

Many young girls live with parents or relatives whose way of life is not only sinful but dangerous to the whole family. The tale of Laura Vicuna can give them courage to believe that prayer can lead to the ultimate conversion of family members whose tragic behavior patterns continue to hurt them.

Prayer-Meditation

Holy Mary, Mother of all purity, we pray that through the life and prayers of Laura Vicuna many may be turned away from lust and violence. May they be healed of any temptations that might have come from being hurt themselves by their own parents. May the victims of such sins have the strength to remove themselves from the homes of such destructive persons and find shelter and safety elsewhere. Through Christ our Lord. Amen.

16 ✠

Blessed Teresa of the Andes
1900-1919[23]

One of the most recently canonized saints is the charming Blessed Teresa of the Andes, a Carmelite nun of Chile. Teresa, called Juanita before entering Carmel, was the daughter of a well-to-do family with seven children. She had a happy childhood, surrounded by love and Christian piety. The death of a beloved grandfather left Juanita with a sad sense of how all things pass away. This increased her inclination toward religion. At the same time, however, she had her faults, especially, as she herself reports, vanity and irritability.

At age six she was taken to daily Mass by her mother and aunt. She liked to talk to Mary, the Mother of God, about her joys and sorrows, begging her to help her control her temper. At her First Communion, Juanita felt that she had become fused to Jesus who spoke to her in her heart thereafter at every Communion. Holy Communion and adoration became the joy of her life.

Often ill, Juanita saw her early brushes with death as a way to come closer to God through suffering. Our Lord had told her, "If you want to be like me, then take up your cross with love and joy."[24]

Juanita's deep piety was nourished at school where she studied with the Sisters of the Sacred Heart. She was often put in charge of the younger children. She also loved sports: swimming, horseback riding, and tennis. Playing piano and singing added to her childhood happiness. "It is such a joy when I awaken to salute God by singing,"[25] she told one of her brothers.

At fifteen she wanted to pursue a religious vocation. She

chose Carmel because she wanted to be close to Christ as a victim-soul, especially to intercede for priests.[26] While at boarding school with the Sacred Heart Sisters, with whom she maintained a close friendship, Juanita started writing an *Intimate Diary* at the request of her spiritual director, Mother Rios. This she continued during her short stay before her early death at the Carmel of Los Andes near Santiago. She chose that particular Carmelite monastery because it was so poor, with neither electricity nor running water.

Just before entering the Carmel, Juanita went through a dark night in her soul where she lost the sense of Jesus always close to her. But upon entering the community at the age of nineteen, the greatest joy flooded her heart. She exercised quite a wide apostolate from within the walls by means of prayer and letters to all her friends. In 1920 it was discovered that Sister Teresa was a victim of incurable typhus. She died within three weeks. To the astonishment of her family, everyone who had known their Juanita-Teresa proclaimed that she was a new saint. She was beatified by Pope John Paul II in 1989.

For Your Life

Blessed Teresa of the Andes is most well known for her joy in the Lord. She thought of God as infinite joy. Let us lift our own hearts above our worries and tears and let God bring us a taste of his joy.

Prayer-Meditation

From the *Intimate Diary of Teresa of the Andes*: "Fifteen is a most dangerous age for a young girl because it is her entrance into the tempetuous sea of the world. But now that I am fifteen years old, Jesus has taken command of my ship and has protected it from encountering other vessels. He has kept me in solitude with Himself. Consequently, my heart, by knowing this Captain, has fallen under the spell of His love, and here keeps me captive. Oh, how I love this prison and this wonderful king... and how I love this Captain who amid the waves of the ocean does not allow me to suffer shipwreck."[27]

17 ✠

Margaret Sinclair
1900-1925 [28]

A young Scotswoman of our century, whose cause has been introduced in Rome, Margaret Sinclair was born in Edinburgh at the turn of the century. Margaret was part of a devout Catholic family with six children. The family descended from Irish immigrants who had sought refuge in Scotland from religious persecution and famine in their own land.

At the parish school, Margaret is remembered as being bright and fond of sports, especially running and swimming. At fourteen, she began to work at a furniture factory nine hours a day. In spite of this busy schedule, Margaret always attended daily Mass. At lunch time she liked to visit the Blessed Sacrament and to read the lives of the saints. She also loved to dance.

A crisis arose when a young man whom she had helped return to the faith wanted to marry her. He swore he would kill himself if she refused him. This proposal made it plain to her how much she wanted to join a religious order, instead of getting married. Her desire was to be a Poor Clare Sister and to serve as an extern-Sister—one who relates to the outside world so that the choir Sisters can be free to pray without interruption. Margaret greatly enjoyed her life of work, prayer, and communal recreation.

All this was to come to an end very soon, however, because Margaret was diagnosed as having tuberculosis. During her illness, she experienced terrible loneliness and feelings of abandonment. Yet it is said that she always smiled and never complained as she offered her pain for the conversion of sinners. During this time, God came to her assistance by sending special interior graces. On November 24, 1925, she died uttering this prayer: "Jesus, Mary, and Joseph, I give you my heart and my soul." It is said that Margaret's charming spiritual beauty was remembered by all who knew her. A priest friend wrote a small pamphlet about her life. This publication, after only five years of circulation, led to her cause being advanced for beatification and canonization.

For Your Life

It is not unusual for family members or friends to try to pressure a young person against his or her will to adopt a course in life that will satisfy wishes of their own. It is important for each of us to seek, instead, the will of God, which often corresponds to the deepest desires of our own hearts.

Prayer-Meditation

May God send us the grace he gave to Margaret Sinclair to find our true place in life where we can best express love of God and neighbor. Through Christ our Lord. Amen.

18 ✠

Venerable Jacinta Marto
1910-1920[29]

Jacinta Marto was born in the village of Aljustrel, Fatima, in Portugal, in 1910. She was the seventh child of Manuel Pedro and Olimpia de Jesus dos Santos, farmers and pious Christians. At that time there was no formal schooling and what Jacinta learned was from the family and the catechism classes taught by her aunt, María Rosa dos Santos.

From early childhood Jacinta was a girl who loved prayer, obedience, and good friends. She was a vivacious, joyful little girl who loved to play and dance. Her faults, before her experiences of the apparitions of the Blessed Virgin at Fatima, had to do with being domineering, pouty, and possessive. These were to be eradicated as she grew in humility, penance, and generosity after the famous visions.

Jacinta's main daily chore was to help Francisco, her older brother, pasture the flock in the company of their cousin, Lucia. It was in 1916 when Jacinta was six years old that the three children first saw an angel who asked them to pray and do penance for sin and to obtain through prayer the graces of conversion for many.

The beautiful, dramatic story of the apparitions of Fatima, made familiar through films, books, and magazine articles, began on May 13, 1917 when Jacinta, Francisco, and Lucia saw the Virgin Mary at Cova da Iria in the fields near Fatima. After hearing Mary requesting prayers and sacrifices, Jacinta consecrated her life to God and entered into a life of continual prayer, seeking silence and solitude. She spoke of a fire of love for Christ crucified that burned in her heart, and she would weep on hearing about his passion. She liked to hide in church to be close to the Eucharist. She venerated Mary, constantly honoring her through praying the Rosary.

Jacinta endured the suffering of ridicule and denunciation by those who thought the vision was fraudulent. She was beaten and put into prison by those who wanted to put a stop to the growing public interest in the apparition. With great courage this little girl refused to be cajoled by the bribes of city authorities who wanted her to say that the visions were false, or who wanted to worm out of the children the "secrets" that Mary gave them to hold in their hearts.

As a means of penance Jacinta became even more obedient to her parents and older siblings. She gave her own food to the poor and limited the drinking of water, so necessary in the summer heat of Fatima. All these sacrifices she offered for the conversion of sinners.

In 1918 she became sick with a bronchial ailment and was moved away to a hospital. She knew she was dying and that it would be her greatest penance to have to die alone without the beloved company of her family. She abandoned herself to the will of God and died in 1920, alone, in the hospital at Lisbon. In 1989 her heroic virtues were recognized and she was declared by Rome to be venerable. Many believe that the conversion of Russia will come about because of the prayers and sacrifices offered in response to Our Lady's exhortations at Fatima.

For Your Life

Some think that living the Christian faith is only possible for adults and that little children should be given unrestrained freedom with little religious training. The life of holy Jacinta and her companions shows us how much good can be done for the church and the world by the humble prayers of the young. Parents can help their children to grow in holiness by reading them stories and showing them videos of the story of Fatima, and by encouraging them to offer daily prayers and sacrifices for the sins they see all around them.

In honor of Our Lady of Fatima, all Catholics who feel so called, can pray the Rosary every day and often repeat the aspiration, "Jesus, Mary, Joseph, I love you, save souls." Through Christ our Lord. Amen.

19 ✠

Blessed Maria Gabriella
1914-1939[30]

B lessed Maria Gabriella is called the saint of unity because she offered her life in the cause of ecumenism, based on a passage of the Gospel of St. John where Jesus expresses his longing that "all may be one" (Jn 17:11).

Maria Sagheddu was the daughter of a shepherd of Sardinia, Italy, born into a family that was familiar with the sorrows of death. Two of her siblings had died before she was born, and her father died when she was but three. She never studied further than the sixth grade. Maria was not a childhood saint, being rather rebellious, angry, critical, and stubborn.

A decisive moment of conversion for Maria came when her favorite sister died. At this point Maria surrendered herself to Christ and under spiritual direction joined the famous Catholic Action Movement, dedicating herself to catechetics, helping the elderly, and deep prayer. At twenty-one Maria left her home and entered a Trappistine monastery near

Rome dedicated to St. Joseph, strongly informed by the new current of interest in ecumenism. In 1938, Maria offered herself as a victim-soul for the cause of unity among Christian churches. Soon afterwards her offering was sealed by the affliction of pulmonary tuberculosis which destroyed her body within fifteen months. She had never been sick before making this offering.

The beatification of Sister Maria Gabriella was attended by representatives of Anglican, Lutheran, Episcopalian, and Orthodox churches.

For Your Life

At the time of Vatican II there was a great deal of grass-roots excitement about the possibility of the reunification of the divided Christian churches. There is a Prayer for Unity Octave in the Catholic church. But many have begun to lose heart and no longer pray with fervent expectation for unity with their separated brothers and sisters. May the story of Blessed Maria Gabriella rekindle our desire for this great cause.

Prayer-Meditation

Blessed Maria Gabriella, you chose to exemplify the Scripture, "In my own flesh I fill up what is lacking in the sufferings of Christ for the sake of his body, the Church" (Col 1:24). You offered yourself as a victim-soul for Jesus' sufferings that his church which is divided might be one. May your intercession from heaven bring about the unity so important for a common Christian witness against the evils of our times. Through Christ our Lord. Amen.

20 ✠

Blessed Antonia Mesina
1919-1935[31]

*B*orn in 1919 to a military family of ten children, Antonia was a lively, playful, obedient, and affectionate child as well as a good student. At age ten she joined the Catholic Action youth group. When her mother became very ill, Antonia took over all the chores of the large family. In carrying out laundering, cooking, and care of younger children, she was always joyful and tender.

In 1935 at sixteen she went off with a friend to the forest to gather wood. On the way they met a teen-age boy from the school. This boy grabbed Antonia, who tried to flee. When she resisted his rape attempt, Antonia was knocked down and battered with a rock. She died shortly afterwards. Her attacker was sentenced to death. Antonia Mesina was beatified by Pope John Paul II in 1987.

For Your Life

Quite a number of children in larger families bear the weight of bringing up the younger ones—especially if both parents work. If they are as cheerful as Antonia, they can make the youth of their younger brothers and sisters into a magic time of happiness. If, instead, they become domineering, petty, or harsh, they can make the childhood of these same siblings seem like a nightmare. Taking care of the young while still young oneself is a good preparation for marriage and family.

Blessed Antonia, intercede for young people called upon to help raise their younger brothers and sisters, that they may be given a joyful, yet firm, spirit. Through Christ our Lord. Amen.

21 ✠

Venerable Maria Teresa Quevedo
1930-1950[32]

Maria Teresa was the third child of a doctor living in Spain just at the time of the fall of the Spanish monarchy. At an early age Maria Teresa dedicated herself to Our Lady. She was described by her mother as a "bundle of happiness... pretty, but terribly self-willed."[33] This stubbornness took the form of refusing to do what she didn't like, such as eating foods that didn't appeal to her. Later she realized how patient her family had been with these outbursts. However, after her First Communion, she changed out of love for the Virgin Mary, offering each little sacrifice of her day as a gift to her.

Although she disliked school work, she was a delightful girl who got along with everyone. She was president of her class, voted best dressed, and captain of the basketball team. She enjoyed dancing and bullfights, and later going to parties and fast driving! At a school retreat when Maria Teresa was eleven, she decided that she wanted to become a saint. The form this took was one that fit in with the normal life of a young girl. For example, when she lost the tennis championship she was sure to win, she realized that this was a gift of humility from Our Lady.

In 1947 Maria Teresa entered the Carmelite Order. Like Thérèse of Lisieux, her life in Carmel was not marked by spectacular events, but rather by small sacrifices made with great love. In 1950 she contracted tubercular meningitis with treatments involving sixty-four spinal taps. It was recognized that she could not long survive. Maria Teresa, however, was most cheerful, sure that she could do more good in heaven than on earth. At the moment of death she smiled suddenly and proclaimed, "How beautiful, O Mary, how beautiful you are."[34] For her grieving mother she won by her prayers the grace of resignation. Her beatification is expected.

For Your Life

When a child or young person is afflicted with a terminal illness, the members of the family very often fall into despair, sometimes accusing God of acting unjustly. The life of Maria Teresa Quevedo, so perfect and complete, can help us to understand that rather than long life on earth, holiness is the only goal worth pursuing. Maria Teresa's happy, fun-loving youth can show us that sanctity is not only for reclusive personalities but for anyone who wants to respond with all her or his heart to God's love.

Prayer-Meditation

Dear Venerable Maria Teresa, intercede for all those who will die at a young age and for their grieving families. Pray that they may trust God and be granted a sign from God that their young are happy in his loving hands, and that if they persevere in God's grace, they will one day be reunited. Through Christ our Lord. Amen.

22 ✠

Blessed Pierina Morosini
1931-1957[35]

Pierina was the eldest child and only daughter in a family of ten children born on a farm near Bergamo, Italy. She spent her time helping her mother, and after school, learning how to sew and work on the cotton mill to help with family finances. On her way to work each day, Pierina went to an early Mass before the factory opened at six in the morning. While sewing, she seemed always to be in union with God rather than chatting aimlessly with the other workers.

Pierina was part of Catholic Action, a movement vital to the youth of her time. Soon she became the leader of her youth group. She longed to become a missionary nun but had to renounce this plan in order to help her family. Instead Pierina took private vows of poverty, chastity, and obedience. Her favorite story of holiness was the life of Maria Goretti. She loved this saint so much that she journeyed to Rome to celebrate her beatification.

In 1957 when she was twenty-six, on the way home from work through the woods, she was raped and beaten to death with a rock by a young man. A huge crowd of people came to her funeral, calling her the new Maria Goretti. She was beatified by Pope John Paul II in 1987.

For Your Life

We tend to consider a long life to be a sign of God's blessing and a violently shortened life to be a tragedy. Pierina was not of this mind. She thought, instead, of Maria Goretti as glorious in being willing to die as a witness to the virtue of chastity. Let us ask for the grace to be willing to live and die for the faith, with God's perfect or permissive will determining the day and the hour of our death.

Prayer-Meditation

Blessed Pierina, we ask you to intercede for young adults today that they may, like you, devote themselves to love of God and generous work, not for the sake of amassing luxury items, but toward the support of their families and those most in need. Through Christ our Lord. Amen.

Part Two

Motherly Saints

23 ✠

St. Anne
first century [1]

M any mothers and grandmothers can identify with St.
Anne, mother of Mary and grandmother of Jesus.
According to tradition, St. Anne, as spouse of Joachim,
bridged the Old and New Testaments. She belonged to the
House of David and lived in Bethlehem.

Most of what we learn of her comes from the *Apocryphal
Gospel of the Birth of Mary*. Although this book was not
accepted into the canon of Scripture, it is of great antiquity
and can give us a glimpse of her life. The very fact that our
Lord had a grandmother and grandfather highlights the important historical aspect of our religion. Jesus is a person
with an historical lineage.

Anne's way of life included hard work. Her house was
simple, with a flat roof, the rocks of the mountains forming
the rear wall. Study of the Law and the Prophets and daily
prayer was part of family tradition. Like any Jewish maiden
she would hope for marriage, maternity, and also yearn for
the Messiah who would come to save Israel.

The name, Anne, signifies "grace." The name of her future
husband, Joachim, means "preparation for the Savior." He
was from the tribe of Judah from which the promised
Messiah would issue forth. Anne was barren before Mary's
birth. An angel came and announced that her only daughter,
born late in life, was to be consecrated to the Lord, dwell in
the temple, and ultimately bring forth the Son of God, the
Savior. Some think that Mary was born in Jerusalem but also
lived in Nazareth. Possibly Joachim and Anne had two
dwellings. Most reliable sources [2] think that St. Anne presented Mary in the temple at an early age and left her there

41

to be educated. Yet this seclusion would not preclude being educated also by her mother at times. According to the customs of the time, Mary would have returned to her home at Nazareth when she reached marriageable age, at about fourteen. She was betrothed to Joseph, who—according to some traditions—was her cousin.

It is up to us to imagine how events described in the Gospel of St. Luke might have affected Anne. Even if Anne believed that her daughter was destined to be the mother of the Messiah, she would be terrified of reactions of the townspeople to the pregnancy. They would have expected greater restraint from an engaged woman and could have stoned Mary, had not Joseph protected her. Imagine also a grandmother's horror of reports of the massacre of the innocents after the birth of Jesus and of their flight to Egypt.

It is thought that Anne became a widow shortly after the birth of her grandson. We can imagine Anne's joy at the return of the young couple after their exile, accompanied by their wondrous son. We can guess how marvelous must have been the thoughts of Anne about the future of this child! Although we know nothing about the date of Anne's death, she is depicted in religious art on her deathbed surrounded by Mary, the boy Jesus, and other relatives.

Paintings and statues of St. Anne, as well as churches dedicated to her, can be found all over the world. It is said that during her life on earth, Anne ministered to the sick, and many healing miracles are attributed to her intercession, particularly at the shrine of St. Anne de Beaupré near Quebec, Canada, and in Eastern Rite Churches. She is the patroness of housewives.

For Your Life

Grandmothers can play an enormous role in the religious education of their grandchildren. They usually have much more time than mothers and can use part of visits to teach the children how to pray, to read them the Bible and lives of the saints, and to show them religious videos.

St. Anne also gives us a model of holy widowhood. A modern-day woman may also be consoled at the death of her husband by praying to Jesus, Mary, and Joseph. Many find widowhood an opening to fruitful ministries previously closed to them because of lack of time.

Prayer-Meditation

From the words of Mary at the Annunciation, "Behold the handmaid of the Lord, be it done unto me according to thy Word.... Behold, all generations shall call me blessed" (Lk 1:38). St. Anne, pray for the Jewish people that all of them may know your grandson as their Savior. Intercede for the barren and for widows that they may not lose faith. Through Christ our Lord. Amen.

24 ✠

St. Elizabeth
first century[3]

Elizabeth was a kinswoman of Mary, the mother of Jesus. She was the wife of Zachary, who was a priest. As is described in Scripture (Lk 1:6), they were "both righteous before God, walking in all the commandments and ordinances of the Lord." When they had given up hope of conceiving a child, an angel came to Zachary to tell him that they would have a son who would be filled with the Holy Spirit and who would be instrumental in bringing the people to repentance.

Mary went to Elizabeth after the Annunciation to help in her childbearing and, no doubt, to enjoy the communion of another woman of faith who had been gifted with a miraculous pregnancy. John, who would later be called "the Baptist," leaped in the womb of Elizabeth, as if sensing the presence of Jesus in Mary's womb. The fact that Mary uttered the beautiful praise prayer called "the Magnificat" to Elizabeth, shows how much she trusted in Elizabeth's holy discernment.

For Your Life

St. Elizabeth's intercession can be invoked by women who have difficulty conceiving children and also by older parents. The relationship between St. Elizabeth and Mary gives us a model of Christian friendship between women. Let us greet each other when we meet by praising God rather than beginning a visit with idle talk.

Prayer-Meditation

May St. Elizabeth share with us her love and friendship with Mary. In this way, may we come to appreciate more Our Lady's tender love and her desire to be our friend. Through Christ our Lord. Amen.

25 ✠

St. Martha
first century[4]

St. Martha appears in Scripture (Lk 10 and Jn 11-12) as the sister of Mary and Lazarus of the town of Bethany, not far from Jerusalem. The three were disciples of Jesus, whom he loved as friends. It is thought that Martha was the eldest and had care of the household. Although it seems that she wasn't a mother herself, she certainly was a motherly saint in the way she provided personal care and hospitality for others.

In Scripture Jesus chides Martha for being too busy about many things whereas her sister Mary knew that only one thing was necessary—intimate, personal love for the Lord (Lk 10:41). It is sometimes thought that Jesus did not appreciate the loving-kindness that she showed him by way of hospitality. It is more realistic to surmise that Jesus was pleased, indeed, by Martha's solicitude, but wanted to direct her further by suggesting that she put contemplation first. St. Martha is the patroness of cooks and dietitians.

We get a glimpse of Martha again when Lazarus, her brother, died. She rushed out to find Jesus, acknowledging that life and death were in his hands since he was "the Christ, the Son of God" (Jn 11:27). Thus, Martha was truly gifted by the Spirit, for it is precisely in the face of death that so many are tempted to disbelieve in the power of Christ to save. Notice that Martha's confession of faith came even before the resurrection!

For Your Life

Too many Catholic women and men suffer from the defect Jesus found in St. Martha—in her expression of her great and holy love of the Lord, she placed too much emphasis on serving him with her hands and feet and not enough in quiet meditation on his words and immersion in his real presence. One apt contemporary adage runs, "If you are too busy to pray, you are too busy!"

Prayer-Meditation

St. Martha, teach us to recognize Jesus as the Lord of life and death and to trust that as he raised Lazarus, he will also raise each of us and our loved ones on the last day. Through Christ our Lord. Amen.

26 ✠

St. Monica

A.D. 331-387[5]

One of the most beloved motherly saints of all times is St. Monica of North Africa, mother of the famous St. Augustine of Hippo, one of the preeminent doctors of the church. When Monica, brought up as a Christian, reached marriageable age, she was wedded to Patricius, who was wealthy, but a pagan and given to ill-temper and lust. In those days many such men battered their wives. Patricius did not, because Monica was so good-tempered herself. Monica endured his ways because she thought to convert him through her example. She believed as St. Paul wrote: "The unbelieving husband is consecrated through his wife" (1 Cor 7:14). After a long time, Patricius was baptized and died shortly afterwards.

Monica and Patricius had three children, including Augustine, a precocious but wild youth, for whom Monica prayed incessantly. Augustine thought his mother's advice ridiculous. It was with great anguish that she finally refused to him the hospitality of the family home, so dissolute had he become. Then St. Monica had a vision of Augustine converted. She was advised by bishops that the son of so many tears could not perish, and to talk more to God about Augustine than to Augustine about God.

A heart-rending incident took place when Augustine had decided to leave for Rome without his mother. Monica rushed to the ship to come along and influence him toward the Christian faith. To get rid of her, Augustine pretended that there was plenty of time before sailing and then took off without her. Undaunted, Monica followed him, trying to arrange a good marriage for him as a substitute for his long-time mistress with whom he had conceived a son. It is a sign of Augustine's pro-life sensibilities even as a pagan that he named this child, born out of wedlock, Adeodatus, "gift of God." To Monica's great joy, however, Augustine was moved by tremendous graces (see the *Confessions of St. Augustine*), and he decided to become a celibate.

After the baptism of Augustine, Monica became a motherly figure to his disciples gathered around him for philosophical and religious discussions. By this time he understood that his mother's wisdom, far from being ridiculous, was remarkably pertinent. Just before she died at fifty-six, the mother and son had a joint mystical experience of God while overlooking the sea of Ostia. After her death, Augustine wept bitterly, thinking of all the pain he had caused her. St. Monica's relics are cherished in the Church of St. Augustine in Rome. Her feast-day is August 27, the day before that of St. Augustine.

For Your Life

Mothers and fathers of wayward youth are sometimes tempted to give up on them and treat them almost like strangers. St. Monica's example of incessant prayer should inspire us to offer our children to the mercy of the Christ who loves them even more than we do.

Prayer-Meditation

St. Monica, intercede for our children and for us that we may not give up hope, even when our children stray far from God. Through Christ our Lord. Amen.

27 ✠

St. Nonna
c. A.D. 374[6]

St. Nonna was a Christian, married to Gregory, a law-maker of Nazianzus who was a member of a sect. After their marriage Gregory converted and became a saint. Their three children became saints! Their eldest son was Gregory, doctor of the church. Gorgonia, his sister, and Caesarius, his brother and a physician, completed the trio.

Nonna was beloved by her children for being both saintly in prayer and good works, outside and inside her home. As her son Gregory wrote in his eulogy: "While some women exalt in the management of their households and others in piety—for it is difficult to achieve both, she nevertheless surpassed all in both. She increased the resources of her household by her care and practical foresight.... She devoted herself to God... as though removed from household cares."[7] St. Nonna died in old age a few months after her husband.

For Your Life

The example of St. Nonna and her husband is but one of quite a number in the lives of the saints concerning inter-religious marriages that lead to the conversion of the non-Christian spouse. Often it is the holiness of the wife that converts her husband.

Some women who are very prayerful use their piety as an excuse to avoid annoying household chores. Some who are very efficient at household duties use that as an excuse to avoid offering quality time to God. St. Nonna can teach us to combine practical goodness with spirituality.

From the eulogy of his parents by St. Gregory of Nazianzen: "They have been one in honor, one in mind, one in soul, and their bond no less a union of virtue and intimacy with God than of the flesh... they have been fairly and justly apportioned to the two sexes. He is the ornament of men, she of women, and not only an ornament but also a pattern of virtue."[8]

28 ✠

St. Gorgonia
c. A.D. 372[9]

S t. Gorgonia was born to a whole family of saints: St. Gregory Nazianzus was her father, and St. Nonna, her mother. We know of Gorgonia mostly from her eulogy delivered by St. Gregory Nazianzen, one of her brothers. Her other brother was St. Caesarius.

Gorgonia married Vitalian, a man of Iconium. She had three children, after which she consecrated herself to God with the blessing of her husband. Gorgonia was a model to her children of family virtues, including modesty of dress, good counsel to friends, and hospitality to the needy.

Once when ill with fevers, partial paralysis, and intermittent comas which no doctor could cure, she went to church and placed her head on the altar and claimed she would stay there until she was healed. When she received Holy Communion that day she was totally healed. She died in A.D. 374.

For Your Life

We know from psychology what a great impression parents make on their children. From a mother's only slight attachment to vanity or to greed, a child may be imprinted for life with much worse versions of these same traits. The story of two generations of saints in one family can inspire us to aim not only for goodness but for 100 percent holiness. Instant healings are rare, but the story of St. Gorgonia's insistent plea for a cure that she might continue on with her good works could inspire us to greater intercession for our own healing and that of others.

Prayer-Meditation

From the eulogy of St. Gregory Nazianzen for his sister Gorgonia: "She was never adorned with gold or... with spiral curls.... Hers were no costly, flowing, diaphanous robes, hers no brilliant and beautiful gems.... While familiar with external ornaments of women, she recognized none more precious than her own character and the splendor which lies within."[10]

29 ✠

St. Matilda
A.D. 895-968[11]

L ike many little girls of her time from devout noble families, Matilda was brought up in the convent. She lived in
Erfurt, Germany, with her grandmother, a nun, as her guide.
Since she was pious, educated, and lovely, she was sought in
marriage by Henry, son of Duke Otto of Saxony. Henry
sought remarriage after the annulment of his first spousal
bond to a woman who wanted to live in a convent!

Henry and Matilda fell deeply in love with each other.
Although overly-involved in hunting, sports, and war,
Henry was also charming and handsome. Their marriage
was a happy one. While Henry, who soon became king of
Germany, was off to battle, Matilda prayed ardently for his
safety. As a legacy from her monastic childhood, she persevered in simplicity and was a loving mother even to her servants. Together the king and queen worked for better laws
for the people. They had five children, many of whom entered positions of influence in church and state.

When Henry died suddenly, Matilda gave away her jewelry and renounced the world. She still lived at court, but
dressed simply and ate sparingly. Unfortunately, her son,
Otto, did not agree with her values and began to audit all
she gave away and spied on her donations. Soon her other
son, Henry, joined his brother in this mistrust. To avoid conflict, Matilda gave up her rights of inheritance and left for the
countryside.

When many ills and disasters befell Germany, Matilda's
daughter-in-law decided that God was displeased with the
treatment of saintly Matilda, and begged her to return. This
she did, forgiving her sons and continuing in good works for

the poor, including paying debts and sheltering the homeless.

Henry died, but her son, Otto, became the holy Roman emperor and her son, Bruno, Archbishop of Cologne. St. Matilda died in A.D. 968, asking the nuns with whom she was staying to give away everything but her burial robe.

For Your Life

The story of St. Matilda illustrates many truths of life and of the faith. First of all, we witness a king whose first marriage was annulled by the church. Nonetheless, his second marriage was fruitful and happy. We see that even though Matilda's older sons were at odds with her, she was willing to forgive them and return to their court. We see that her goodness made a deep impression on her daughter-in-law, contrary to the opinion that mothers-in-law and daughters-in-law can never get along. With God all things are possible!

Prayer-Meditation

St. Matilda, please pray for happier marriages and better relationships between older and younger members of the same family. Through Christ our Lord. Amen.

30 ✠

St. Adelaide
A.D. 931-999 [12]

A delaide, princess of Burgundy, was betrothed at age two to Lothaire, who would become king of Italy. After their wedding, when her husband was assassinated, the enemy party wanted her to remarry into their family. When

Adelaide refused, she was brutalized and kept in near solitary confinement in the castle of Garda from which she was saved by a priest who dug a passage for her. Adelaide hid in the woods until rescued.

When Otto of Germany invaded Italy, he married Adelaide to consolidate his power. They bore five children. After her second husband's death, her son reigned, but her daughter-in-law resented her, and Adelaide left for her brother's house in Vienna. Eventually her son admitted his fault and was reconciled. Finally after several other deaths in the family, Adelaide herself became the regent of Italy. She was revered for her forgiveness of enemies, founding of monasteries, and attempts to convert pagans. St. Adelaide died at sixty-eight in A.D. 999.

For Your Life

Life with in-laws, even if you are a queen, can be difficult. The saints, often victims of family friction caused by others, were always ready to forgive. Many returned from places to which they had been banished and continued to lead fruitful lives of service to God and neighbor. In times of difficulty with family, repeat this thought: "I shall always forgive and forget in union with Jesus who forgave his enemies for much worse evils."

Prayer-Meditation

St. Adelaide, intercede for extended families who allow strife to divide them. Ask God to help with forgiveness and reconciliation. Through Christ our Lord. Amen.

31 ✠

Blessed Ida of Boulogne
d. 1113 [13]

Born to French nobility and married at seventeen to Count Eustace II of Boulogne, Blessed Ida devoted herself to good works and to the building of churches. Ida raised her three sons to be pious, virtuous, and generous.

When widowed, she sold all her properties and gave them as alms to the poor and for the building of monasteries. St. Anselm of Normandy, who later would become the Archbishop of Canterbury, was her spiritual director. Later Blessed Ida supported the Crusade to Jerusalem and two of her sons, Godfrey and Baldwin, became kings of Jerusalem. She died in A.D. 709 and was compared by a chronicler to the good wife of Proverbs (Prv 31:10-31).

For Your Life

Some activists contrast the supposed luxury of building beautiful churches and monasteries with the more pressing need to minister to the poor. Blessed Ida valued both love of God and love of neighbor and manifested this by a dual apostolate of glorifying God in church architecture and also caring for the needy. Many of the devotees of the monasteries Ida had built probably were the very poor people she helped in other ways.

Prayer-Meditation

From a letter of St. Anselm to Blessed Ida: "You have bestowed so many and so great kindnesses upon men... coming to our monastery or traveling from it, that it would be wearisome to you if we were to send you messages and letters of thanks for them all; nor have we anything with which to reward you as you deserve. So we commend you to God, we make Him our agent between you and us. All that you do is done for Him; so may He reward you for us, for Him, you do so much."[14]

32 ✠

Blessed Joan of Aza
d. 1190 [15]

*B*lessed Joan was the mother of St. Dominic. She lived near Old Castile, Spain, and was happily married to Don Felix de Guzman. Joan was a charming and intelligent woman who was known for visiting the poor and the sick. After caring for the household, she would devote her spare time to prayer, sometimes through the whole night.

Joan and Felix had four children, three sons who became priests, and a daughter from whose marriage came two Dominicans. After these children were settled in life, the couple longed for another son to be their heir. Joan went to a monastery and made a novena to have still another child. She received a vision and a voice saying she would become a mother again and that this son would be a great light for the church and a crusader against heretics. Subsequently she had a dream of her son, who became St. Dominic, as a black and white dog holding a torch in his mouth—now a symbol of the Dominican Order, whose members wear black and white habits. Because of this dream, they are also sometimes called "Domini Canes"—watchdogs of the Lord.

When Dominic was born, his parents offered him to the service of God. Joan died toward the end of the twelfth century. She was beatified on her own merits in 1828.

For Your Life

Even those who schedule a definite prayer time through attending daily Mass, meditation on Scripture, other devotions, or quiet prayer, find that some days there is no time out from pressing duties. Sometimes, as in the case of Blessed Joan, the Holy Spirit will awaken someone in the middle of the night and let that be a time of resting in his arms. Let us always be open to some new way the Spirit might wish to reach us.

Some parents wish to have more children for worldly reasons. Sometimes this takes the form of discrimination against a child's gender. Instead, we should offer our children to God, as did Blessed Joan, and let him lead them as he wishes.

Prayer-Meditation

Blessed Joan, intercede for parents that they may be happy with the children God sends and eager to have as many as they can take care of lovingly in their particular circumstances. Through Christ our Lord. Amen.

33 ✠

St. Elizabeth of Hungary
1207-1231[16]

The story of St. Elizabeth of Hungary is one of the favorites of many Catholic married couples because of the tenderness of the love between Elizabeth and her husband. Elizabeth's story begins in a fairy tale fashion. As an infant she was betrothed to Louis of Thuringia. At four years old she was taken in procession to Thuringia to be prepared for her future court life. The people of the Thuringian court ridiculed and tormented the small girl for her serious ways and fervent prayer. To her rescue came the prince, Louis, who loved his future wife from the very start with great tenderness and admiration. Together they dreamed of great deeds that they could do for Christ when they grew up.

Elizabeth and Louis were married when he was twenty-one and she fourteen. They were extremely happy and shared their love for Christ with each other in prayer. During the night when Elizabeth prayed, she would always hold the hand of her sleeping husband. When he left for a journey, she would follow his retinue as long as she could, weeping as he left and rejoicing on his return.

Elizabeth and Louis had three children, one of them the Blessed Gertrude. Elizabeth became the first Germanic member of the third order of St. Francis. During famines she gave away the store of grain to the poor. She built a hospital for the ill and fed them with her own hands, as well as giving food to some nine hundred people who came to her gate each day. Perhaps it is for this reason that she is considered the patroness of bakers.

When Louis died in a crusade, Elizabeth screamed with pain for days. Louis' relatives were now able to banish this saintly woman with her children, lest she do more harm to their worldly aspirations. So poor was she now that she had to beg food for her children. Later her relations at the court asked her pardon and let her come back and continue her hospices for the sick and poor. She died at twenty-four in 1231.

For Your Life

It is sometimes imagined that only those consecrated to God with vows of poverty, chastity, and obedience can become great saints. The life of St. Elizabeth and her husband shows that love for one another itself glorifies God, so that a holy marital love, far from being an obstacle, can become a wonderful ladder of love to Christ. May the lives of married Christians emulate those of Elizabeth and Louis.

Prayer-Meditation

St. Elizabeth of Hungary, intercede for all those about to enter the marriage covenant, that their marriages may be filled with love and beauty as was yours. Through Christ our Lord. Amen.

34 ✠

Blessed Zedislava Berka
1210-1252[17]

Born in the early thirteenth century in a Christian family on the borders of Mongolia in Bohemia, young Zedislava was taught by her mother to minister every day to the poor at the castle gate by means of application of medicinal herbs and the giving of alms. The young girl was beloved for her sweetness and charm as she went among a warlike people.

In spite of Zedislava's reluctance, her parents married her to a soldier in command of a castle on the frontier. She gave birth to four children. A worldly man, her husband wanted her to dress luxuriously and attend the numerous banquets he enjoyed. Prayerful and inward, Zedislava objected to the demands of her husband, but she managed to spiritualize all the sacrifices that resulted from her role in life. On one occasion her husband was furious with her for bringing a repulsive beggar into the castle. When he went to investigate for himself, in place of the beggar he found the figure of Christ crucified!

Zedislava also embraced with great delight the possibilities that opened up to her when some Polish missionaries introduced her to the newly-founded Third Order of St. Dominic. Her husband agreed to build a hostel for pilgrims and refugees from Tartar battles, and to give her more and more time for other ministries such as visiting prisoners, obtaining pardons for them, and teaching catechism to the children of the castle servants. When financing the building of a church, Zedislava expressed her own enthusiasm for the project by carrying heavy boards herself in the night so that no one would find out and stop her.

After her death, her husband saw a vision of her soul in

glory and this inspired him to convert from his worldly lifestyle.

For Your Life

It often happens that one spouse in a marriage is deeply Christian; whereas, the other lives more in compromise with cultural values of the time. Blessed Zedislava teaches us that it is possible to become holy in spite of exterior circumstances. Perseverance in prayer can eventually lead the less Christian spouse to allow for many ministries and even be converted in the end.

Prayer-Meditation

Blessed Zedislava, intercede for all wives of difficult husbands that they may practice gentle persuasion while finding ways to follow the Spirit in their good works. Through Christ our Lord. Amen.

35 ✠

St. Notburga
1264-1313[18]

While not a mother herself, St. Notburga is one of the patronesses of domestic work. She came from a poor home in Austria and was sent at age eighteen to be a servant of a German count. There she worked in the kitchen, but gave all the leftovers to the poor. The count's wife began to object, wanting all the extras to go to feed the swine rather than the poor. Notburga complied for awhile, but then, noting that the pigs seemed fine without it, went back to giving the scraps to the poor. For this reason she was fired.

Next Notburga went to work in the fields. Once she stopped work to go to Saturday vespers. Her master objected. To win the argument, Notburga threw her sickle into the air. It remained suspended, to the amazement of many who saw this miracle. After the death of the count's wife, Notburga was begged to return to her former employer, the count. He attributed all his misfortunes to his wife's refusal to share with the poor. In the church where St. Notburga's relics are on view, many miracles have occurred, especially in answer to petitions for the poor.

For Your Life

Many Christians have revived the Old Testament practice of tithing, giving a tenth of their income to the church for its maintenance and works for the poor, as well as to particular initiatives for helping the needy. Yet many other Christians will be upbraided at the judgment for living in relative luxury, while they neglected their own parish and did not provide for the needs of the poor—unless they change and repent.

Prayer-Meditation

St. Notburga, give to us a willingness to accomplish our menial tasks with love and joy and to practice generosity as a key Christian virtue. Through Christ our Lord. Amen.

36 ✠

Blessed Margaret of Castello
d. 1320[19]

Margaret was the first child of a brave and renowned Italian military man of the town of Metola, Italy, and his wife Emilia. They were horrified when Margaret was born: blind, lame, dwarfed, and hunchbacked. So distressed were the parents, they kept the birth secret, giving the child to a servant who arranged for her baptism. Yet in later life, Margaret herself was a loving mother to the sick, dying, and imprisoned, in spite of her rejection by her own parents.

Margaret was probably one of the most unwanted babies ever. Yet undaunted by her exile and misfortunes, Margaret liked to retire to the chapel to pray. Her father, afraid that as she grew up she might reveal herself as his child, decided that since she was so pious he would have her walled up into a church in the forest, out of sight and mind. This was a practice of mature anchorites, but scarcely a suitable home for a young child. The walled-up cell, with only slits for Holy Communion and necessities, was freezing in the winter and suffocating in the summer. Nonetheless, with the help of her sympathetic chaplain, Margaret began to grow into a true contemplative. To the amazement of the chaplain, Margaret began to add voluntary fasting to all her involuntary miseries.

When Margaret was twenty, she was taken to a church at Castello where there were rumors of miraculous cures. When her parents realized that there was no miracle for Margaret, they simply abandoned her in the church to fend for herself.

Although disabled, Margaret was very resourceful. She joined herself to some beggars and learned how to live in this way, until gradually poor people started taking her into their homes. Soon they realized that there was a saintly person among them, capable of calming family quarrels and changing the atmosphere of their lives for the better.

When her fame for holiness grew, she was taken into a monastery. In spite of her infirmities she was most industrious and helpful. This did not compensate, however, for a disadvantage the other sisters found in having Margaret among them. This so unwanted woman desperately wanted to keep the rule to the letter, in contrast to the laxity that had grown up in that convent. So they sent her off, claiming that she was an impossible eccentric, not a saint at all.

After this blow, Margaret became a Third Order Dominican, going about with the other women of this order ministering to the sick, the dying, and prisoners in jail. One imprisoned scoffer was converted when he saw Blessed Margaret levitate off the floor in prayer for him. In order to fulfill her Dominican vocation, she learned all the Psalms by heart. She claimed that although blind, she could see Christ during the Mass.

Many miracles of healing were attributed to Margaret during her life and many more afterwards. She died at thirty-three and was beatified in 1609. Her body is still incorrupt and can be seen behind glass in the chapel of the School for the Blind in Castello, Italy. The feast-day of Blessed Margaret is April 13.

For Your Life

It is remarkable to note how motherly Blessed Margaret was herself in her care for others in spite of her deep rejection by her own mother and father. Her life also indicates clearly that those unwanted by their parents are always greatly wanted by God.

Like all the totally blind who live in goodness and hope, Margaret's only sights were supernatural: the glory of God shining on us "through a glass darkly" (1 Cor 13:12) on earth and in full splendor in heaven.

Blessed Margaret, intercede for the pro-life movement of our time, that unwanted babies may not be aborted, that those with disabilities will be cherished and nurtured, and that the lives of the terminally ill will be protected and respected. Through Christ our Lord. Amen.

37 ✠

St. Elizabeth of Portugal
1271-1336[20]

The daughter of a king and princess, whose great aunt was St. Elizabeth of Hungary, Elizabeth of Portugal was a sweet, virtuous girl who by eight had begun to fast. At twelve she married Denis, king of Portugal. Although not of the same ardent faith, Denis allowed Elizabeth to use her time for prayer and good works.

Elizabeth was especially interested in helping the poor, pilgrims, and the sick. She founded hospitals and orphanages. Meanwhile, however, her husband was becoming more sinful as she became more saintly. With amazing charity Elizabeth took care of his illegitimate children, and at the end of his life he repented for all his sins.

After the death of Denis, Elizabeth lived as a Third Order Franciscan near a convent of Poor Clares she had founded. She also acted often as a peacemaker during fratricidal wars. She died while reconciling two enemies.

For Your Life

Christian love has no boundaries. A queen who might have been imperious and arrogant instead is found tending the poor and even the children of her husband's adulterous relationships. Let us pray for the grace to be motherly toward anyone who needs us.

Prayer-Meditation

St. Elizabeth of Portugal, help us to overcome all anger and resentment, especially against family members who have wronged us, to become as forgiving as you were. Through Christ our Lord. Amen.

38 ✠
St. Zita
thirteenth century [21]

St. Zita was born into a poor and very devout home in Italy in the thirteenth century. One of her sisters became a nun, and a brother was a hermit. As a child she was exceedingly obedient, always responding immediately to any directive that her mother told her would be pleasing to God.

At the age of twelve, Zita, who would become the patroness of domestic workers, was sent to work as a servant to a family in the weaving business. Zita used to pray during the night and rise early to attend the first Mass of the day. She distributed much of her own food to the poor and invited beggars to sleep in her bed. The life of Zita was far from tranquil, since her fellow-servants despised her way of life and resented her rejection of their curses and immoral suggestions. Once she defended herself against a potential rapist by scratching his face. The other servants tried to get her into trouble with her employers, but eventually Zita was exonerated and admired for her goodness and hard work. Once when the head of the household came to inspect food-stores which Zita had given away secretly to the poor, the bin of beans was miraculously replenished. Another time when she had given her employer's fur coat to a poor person, an angelic figure came to the door to return it, after which he disappeared. In time, the servant became the spiritual adviser of the whole household. She soothed the master in his rages and was given free time to visit the poor, the sick, and the prisoners. She died at sixty, still serving the same family.

For Your Life

Many women resent all menial labor as monotonous and unbearable. Some Christian women like to substitute overly long hours of prayer and meditation for household duties. Many times today, especially when both parents work, justice requires greater sharing of domestic duties among family members, but a certain amount of such work is the lot of most women. It is important to understand such work not only as a result of the fall but also as a natural means of building the kingdom of God and of serving others lovingly.

Prayer-Meditation

From the sayings of St. Zita: "A servant is not good if she is not industrious: work-shy piety in people of our position is sham piety."[22]

39 ✠

Blessed Jacoba
d. A.D. 1273[23]

*J*acoba was a noble Roman lady, the mother of two, who offered hospitality to St. Francis when he came to visit Rome. In return, St. Francis gave her a lamb who followed her each day to Mass and remained by her side while she prayed! It is said that this lamb would awaken her in the morning by bumping her and bleating.

When Jacoba's husband died, she became a Third Order Franciscan. Her sons still needed her, preventing her from entering the Poor Clares. Just before his death St. Francis asked her to come and bury him. Although there was a strict rule that no woman could enter a friary, St. Francis asked her to come in to minister to him. She remained a great friend and benefactress of the order after the death of the founder.

Jacoba died in 1273. She is buried in the Basilica of St. Francis of Assisi.

For Your Life

One of the themes of feminine spirituality in our age is the need of men for the spiritual ministry of women, even when men have consecrated themselves to God in religious life. The special charisms of women are complementary to those of men and cannot simply be replaced by a same-sex friendship. The story of Jacoba and St. Francis shows that even the holiest of men felt a need for the specific Christian friendship of a saintly woman.

Blessed Jacoba, we ask your intercession that saintly women and men would form friendships for the benefit of their spiritual growth and the greater good of the church. Through Christ our Lord. Amen.

40 ✠

Blessed Castora Gabrielli
d. 1391 [24]

Castora was a sweet girl of Gubbio, Italy. Born to a noble family with an uncle who was a bishop, Castora was married to a lawyer who was a violent, angry man. She bore this patiently and spent the time she had after her household duties in prayer, asking for help to bear her cross. Their only son became a devout Christian man. After the death of her husband, Castora became a Third Order Franciscan. Her son agreed to give all their possessions to the poor. She died in 1391.

For Your Life

Some children brought up as Christians would be horrified to see their mother giving away their legacy to poor strangers. Castora's son did not take this attitude but was happy to participate in the good works of his mother. He must have often witnessed his mother being abused and offering this up to God. Surely she might, in good conscience, have fled from such a husband. That is what many Christian counselors would probably recommend today. But her decision to bear up under it must have strengthened her son in patient endurance, although we may question her judgment in staying. May the children of Christian parents today take the best from their elders and reject what is evil.

Prayer-Meditation

Blessed Castora, pray for all victims of family violence. Intercede also for those who inherit wealth that they may rejoice to give to the poor what they, themselves, do not really need. Through Christ our Lord. Amen.

41 ✠
St. Francesca of Rome
1384-1440[25]

*I*n this volume there are many more Franciscan, Dominican, and Carmelite saints than those of the Benedictine family, which is rich in saints, though sometimes they are less well-known. Of these lesser-known but wonderful Benedictine saints is Francesca Romana, a fine example of a wife, mother, saint, and Benedictine.

Francesca was born in Trastevere, a part of the city of Rome. She was well acquainted with the politics of the day which led to the Great Schism[26] and to much turmoil throughout the Christian world. Coming from a noble but pious family, Francesca was brought up in luxury, but also with a sense of the greatness of God. She wanted to become a nun but her parents had planned, instead, a marriage with

Lorenzo Ponziano, who seemed to them a perfect match.

Imagine her surprise when, after her early marriage at thirteen, she discovered that her sister-in-law, with whom she was now living, also longed for a life of prayer and seclusion. The two young wives resolved to live by a rule and to spend all their free time plainly dressed going out to the poor of Rome and to hospitals where they cared for the most repulsive cases. Happily their husbands agreed to their desire to devote themselves to such Christian works at the expense of attending social events. In her marriage there was, it is attested, not a single dispute between them.

After the birth of her first child and the death of her mother-in-law, Francesca was chosen to take over the household. She wished to avoid this, but she obediently agreed and soon made the servants into true brothers and sisters. There are two other children known to have been born to Francesca.

During a plague Francesca and her sister-in-law gave away all the provisions of the house to help the needy, finally begging in the street. During the battles of those times, several times her husband had to escape and her eldest son was taken prisoner, leaving Francesca, her sister-in-law, and her two younger children in a ruined home. During this time her second son died. After his death Francesca saw him in a vision with an archangel telling her of the joys of heaven.

Lorenzo eventually returned from prison, but greatly weakened, lived in retirement and was nursed by Francesca. Her eldest son married a woman who hated Francesca and ridiculed her publicly, but when nursed by her mother-in-law during an illness, she repented and afterwards became her disciple. Understanding the saintly character of his wife, Lorenzo agreed to renounce their sexual life together so that Francesca would be free to start a congregation of Benedictine Sisters. After Lorenzo died, Francesca joined the Sisters. At this point she increased her penitential exercises and spent whole nights in prayer, accompanied by visions and raptures.

Francesca Romana died in 1440 bathed in light and claiming that her angel was beckoning her to follow him. Many miracles took place at her death and afterwards. She was canonized in 1608.

For Your Life

Many married women are now out in the workplace, often by necessity, but sometimes by choice. Since so few mothers are at home, it is a great help, as it was to Francesca, to have a near relative or close friend with whom to share a Christian way of life. Women today, isolated in their homes, might pray to God to send them such a companion so that they can share household duties, prayer, and other good works.

Prayer-Meditation

From the sayings of St. Francesca Romana: "It is most laudable in a married woman to be devout, but she must never forget that she is a housewife. And sometimes she must leave God at the altar to find him in her housekeeping." It is said that once she was interrrupted by her husband five times on the same page of her reading of the office of Our Lady. When she returned to take up her spiritual reading, the letters on the page had turned to gold.[27]

42 ✠

St. Angela Merici
1474-1540 [28]

A ngela Merici, founder of the Ursuline teaching Sisters, was born in Desenzano, a village by the lovely Lago Garda in northern Italy. Through her order, she has mothered many children in Christ. Her very happy childhood among a farm family was disrupted tragically by the sudden deaths of her father and mother. It was at this time that Angela's troubled soul was filled with such an inundation of divine love that she realized she would never be alone, having God as her Father forever. Angela and her sister with whom she shared holy aspirations and practices, moved to the home of a well-to-do uncle. Unexpectedly Angela's sister died also. Bereft once more, Angela begged God for a sign. One day in the fields she saw the sky open and her sister with the Virgin Mary resplendent in glory.

When her dear uncle also died, Angela returned to her childhood home, now as a member of the third order of St. Francis. Other young apostolic women joined her in her work of helping the sick and teaching catechism to the children whose faith she feared would be lost due to the rising tide of humanism. The young women and the children all loved to be with Angela who was so gentle, sweet, and joyful. Soon more and more children came to the house for study and play, and began to bring their parents closer to the sacraments. In those days faith had become so weak that a person was considered fervent who received Holy Communion even once a year! Angela fasted and prayed for anyone in the town who seemed addicted to vice, and many of these suddenly repented and returned to the church.

Asking God what was to be her destiny, Angela was

granted a vision that she would found an order of Sisters in Brescia, a city where she knew a rich family who came to Lago Garda each summer. When this family suffered from the death of a family member, they insisted that Angela come to Brescia to comfort them. While in the city of Brescia Angela began as usual to minister to the sick. But her burning desire was still to find some way to stem the tide of false teaching. "What could a totally uneducated girl do?" she wondered. The Holy Spirit, who knows how to use the simple to confound the wise, illuminated her mind so that she could read in Latin the Book of the Hours. After this miracle, people from all over the city of Brescia, including theologians, came to Angela for answers to their questions and doubts.

Although urged by her followers to begin a teaching order, Angela still felt inadequate for the task. She decided to make a pilgrimage to the Holy Land to seek discernment. To her horror, at the start of the pilgrimage, she was stricken with blindness and not only had to forego the actual sight of the holy places where Jesus walked, taught, and died, but also thought that surely this would remove all possibility of starting a teaching order. However, on the return voyage she was miraculously healed at a shrine in Crete.

On her return she was able to begin the order in her dream. She adopted St. Ursula, martyred for the faith, as the patroness of what would be called the Ursuline Sisters. Angela Merici died in old age in a joyful ecstasy saying, "Into Thy hands I commend my Spirit." Her order spread to France, Canada, the United States, and all over the world.

For Your Life

The death of parents and family can seem devastating, leading to much pain. St. Angela Merici's life helps us to realize that a loving heart always finds those to love and be loved by. Instead of dreading the possibility of death of beloved ones, we should commend them and ourselves to God and await the marvelous designs of his Providence.

From the sayings of St. Angela: "Dearest Sisters, we are the children of the saints. We seek the land to which they have gone and our love is all for our Lord who rules that land. But the road is one of self-denial and suffering. Thus did He, our Beloved, trod the road and drew after Him His lovers. We are among the number. We are sowing now, but when God thinks well we shall reap, if we don't faint."[29] "Do now, do now, what you will wish to have done when your moment comes to die."[30]

43 ✠

St. Louise de Marillac
1591-1660[31]

*B*orn in Paris in 1591, her mother died shortly after her birth. Louise was raised mostly by her father. He was a military courtier, but a very philosophical and literary man, who adored his young daughter. Louise was a shy, sensitive, serious girl, inclined to piety and solitude. When her father realized how intelligent she was, he sent her to a school run by Dominican nuns. The great sorrow of her life was the death of her father when she was but thirteen. Happily, her uncle loved her almost as much and took her into his home.

Louise wished very much to become a cloistered nun, but she was not accepted because she seemed too fragile. The account of the physically arduous long life of Louise afterwards is but one of many instances where a person refused by religious orders for reasons of health lives to confound the world with his or her energetic activities for the sake of the Lord's kingdom.

In 1613 Louise was married, very happily, to Antoine Le

Gras, a court secretary to Marie de Medici. This marriage ushered the shy woman into the French court of that time with all its frivolous social gatherings, luxurious dining, and fancy attire. Intensely disliking such a way of life, the saint spent her time instead in tending the poor and the sick. Soon a group of rich women were attracted by her deep commitment to the poor, not only in financing charitable works but also by participating in them themselves. This was the beginning of the famous Sisters of Charity. Thus Louise became a mother to the poor through the order she founded.

During the long illness of her husband that followed, Louise suffered greatly from sympathy for him. She also became melancholy over the character of her one difficult son. It was the reading of the works of Francis de Sales which helped her to overcome scrupulosity and self-doubt. During this time of transition, Louise had a vision that she was to found a company of women to serve the poor under the leadership of a man she would at first dislike. That man was to be St. Vincent de Paul, and the order would become the Sisters of Charity. At the time Louise's vision was astounding, for it was unheard of to allow women to minister on the streets, outside of the protection of the cloister.

The Sisters of Charity began simply as bands of young women who liked to help St. Vincent de Paul, whom Louise grew to love deeply, on his missions to remote poverty-stricken towns. After Vincent left, groups of women often would be at a loss as to how to continue without his forceful leadership. Having made the acquaintance of Louise and seeing how marvelously she combined piety and prudence, St. Vincent sent her out to consolidate the work he had started.

This meant long difficult trips often by foot in snow, rain, and wind, to towns where there was no resting place better than a primitive hut. Formerly rich, Louise found that devotion to the poor was not only the will of God for her, but also an indirect means of overcoming her morbid self-doubts through such meaningful activity. So wonderful was the mind of Louise de Marillac that when she gave popular talks about the faith to poor women in the villages, men would sneak in and hide so as to listen.

Eventually it became necessary to find a way to train and form the peasant girls who wished to spend their lives tending the sick, teaching the children, taking care of and finding foster homes for abandoned babies, visiting sick prisoners and galley slaves, caring for the insane, and tending the victims of the wars then raging in France. The women called to this work moved into the home of Louise and lived with only yearly vows, devoted to the needs of the poorest of the poor. Louise taught them that the protection of Mary was like a cloister in the midst of the world.

St. Louise died in great pain but also great peace in 1660. St. Vincent, her lifelong companion in the apostolate, a man of austerity not given much to words of affirmation, wrote once to Louise saying: "God alone knows... what He has done in giving you to me. In heaven you will know."[32]

For Your Life

Many of the saints were described as beautiful and charming. Louise is depicted instead as serious and sincere. We should not think of sanctity as a sort of holy glamor, but as the best way to become focused on what really matters most: the love of God and neighbor.

In our times there is the same need to minister to the sick and to teach children. Many widows discern that it is much better to serve others than to brood alone in their homes. Pro-life apostolates of today also may remind us of the work of St. Louise in finding homes for unwanted babies.

Prayer-Meditation

From a letter of St. Louise: "I decided that, if I should be fortunate enough to have to visit the sick, I would try to make them understand... (that) we must offer up all our pain to Him in union with His divine Son.... If there is likelihood of their illness leading to death, I will do my utmost to make them offer up acts of faith and hope and confidence... and I will also try to give them some knowledge of the grandeur, beauty and love of God, and of the joy of possessing Him eternally and of the glory of the blessed."[33]

44 ✠

St. Jeanne de Chantal
1572-1641[34]

*J*eanne de Chantal might well be called a daughterly saint rather than a motherly saint, since the two most important relationships in her life were with fatherly men. Her own father took over her education after her mother died, and St. Francis de Sales took over her spiritual direction after the accidental death of her husband.

Born to a noble family of Burgundian parliamentarians, Jeanne became her father's right-hand daughter, learning much that was out of the range of most young girls. At twenty she married the Baron de Chantal and had a very happy marriage. They had four children. After just eight years of marriage, Jeanne's beloved husband was killed in a hunting accident. The interior experiences Jeanne had at that time were to color her future. Her inordinate, prostrating grief of four month's duration led her to realize the passing nature of things and to attach herself all the more intensely to the Lord Jesus.

The loss of Jeanne's husband was fraught with difficulties. She was persuaded to go to live not with her beloved father but instead with her father-in-law, who could provide more advantages in society for the children. Her life there was terrible because her father-in-law's housekeeper was an insolent, sinful woman who would not allow Jeanne to take over the management of the house. Nonetheless, she spent her free time in loving attention to her children and in wonderful works to the poor, especially in the area of medical help administered by her own hands.

All the while she prayed for a good spiritual director. She was given a vision of the man who could minister to her in this way and found him in the flesh when St. Francis de Sales came to preach in her city. There was an immediate, strong, supernatural bond between the two. St. Francis had also had a vision of Jeanne as the founder for an order in the city where he was the bishop, Annecy. He immediately wrote to her, "It seems to me that God has given me to you. I am assured of this more keenly as each hour passes."[35] The letters of St. Francis de Sales to Jeanne de Chantal are among the most beautiful expressions of spiritual friendship to be preserved.

Although Jeanne was yearning to enter religious life, St. Francis de Sales advised her to wait until her children were older, meanwhile teaching her how to simplify her prayer life, formerly full of particular devotions, so that it might reflect her deepest longings for contemplative union with God. Eventually arrangements were made for the older children, and she was free to found the famous order of the Visitation dedicated to contemplative prayer. This order grew beyond the confines of Annecy, first in France, and then in other countries of the world.

Sometimes it is held against Jeanne that she abandoned her children too early. At the time when she entered the order, her son, an unruly, stubborn teen, even though very suitable, loving arrangements had been made for him, had a temper tantrum and threw himself on the ground in front of the door so that she had to step over him to start her journey. Parents of teenagers might be less scandalized by Jeanne's conduct than her critics and sympathize with her need to give him over to the extended family's provision. In essence, she had postponed for many hard years out of love for him and her other children the life God had willed for her.

Jeanne died in 1641. She was so much loved as a holy woman that she had to press herself against a wall when visiting convents of her order to prevent relic-seekers from snipping off pieces of her habit behind her back!

For Your Life

Many women today still choose to postpone other goals such as career in order to provide loving care for their children at home. Yet this can be very difficult when surrounded by other mothers who decide to pursue career goals while their children are still young. St. Jeanne de Chantal teaches us to prepare for future ministries by growing in love of God in prayer and in love of neighbor precisely by taking care of our children and others we know who are in need of motherly care. (Obviously, how this is approached will depend upon a mother's particular circumstances.) Then we will be better equipped to fulfill some other particular task for the body of Christ.

Prayer-Meditation

From a letter of Jeanne de Chantal to another Sister, describing how to administer the rule in one of the Visitation convents: "Know, my dear sister, that the chief responsibility of our office is to guide the souls that the Son of God has redeemed by His precious blood, not like a mistress of a household or a governess but like a mother and one entrusted with the care of the brides and servants of God. These must be treated with respect and special love...."[36]

45 ✠

Blessed Marie of the Incarnation (Martin)

1599-1672[37]

Marie Guyart was born into a middle-class family of bakers in Tours, France. At age seven Marie was ushered into union with Christ by a dream: "It seemed to me that I was playing some childhood game... I was looking upward when I saw the heavens open and Our Lord Jesus Christ in human form emerge and come toward me.... As this most adorable Majesty approached me, my heart felt on fire with love for him and I started to open my arms to embrace him. Then he, the most beautiful of all the children of men, took me in his arms and with a look full of indescribable sweetness and charm, kissed me with great love and asked me, 'Will you be mine?' I answered, 'Yes.'"[38]

Although somewhat drawn to the life of a nun, she acceded to her parents' judgment that she was made for a practical life as the wife of Claude Martin, a merchant of the city. At eighteen Marie was the mother of a son, but less than a year afterwards her husband died. Having, indeed, a very practical side to her character, Marie did not let her husband's business sink into bankruptcy but decided to rescue it, eventually also administering a carting business on the docks among rough stevedores. Even while watering down the horses, she was able to retain a sense of the presence of God. Out of her prayer life came penetrating insights into the meaning of redemption, the Sacred Heart, the Eucharist, and the Trinity, culminating in the mystical marriage of her own heart with that of Jesus.

In spite of her great love for her son, Marie longed for the religious life. Finally she received permission from her director to entrust her son to the extended family and become an Ursuline teaching Sister. This vocation attracted her because of her great concern for the salvation of souls. At first her son found the loss of his mother devastating, but later he was to become a holy religious himself, deeply united on a mystical level with the heart and soul of his absent mother.

It was the French missionary venture to Canada, prefigured in a mystical dream of a land of great natural beauty, full of forests and mountains shrouded in mist, which liberated Marie from a depression that followed her entrance into the convent. Eventually she was chosen by Jesuit missionaries as the ideal Sister to minister to the Indians of Quebec, Canada.

Her own account of her dangerous passage to Canada and the primitive conditions of life in the Americas is fascinating and inspiring. Consider that the voyage from France to Canada took three months. Once they arrived, they faced conditions of drastic poverty, freezing cold, wars where violent Indian tribes killed her convert Indians, and devastating fires. Only her tremendous love for Christ and an intense motherly love for the Indian people made such a life bearable.

In Canada her daily life included washing and grooming of children, teaching, learning Indian languages, administering the small band of Sisters, dealing with conflicts between the Sisters, and trying to minister within the complexities of colonial existence where often the French soldiers undid the work of the missionaries. These soldiers taught the Indians not the joy of Christ but the thrill of alcohol addiction, so profitable to its merchants. Ultimately most of the work of the Sisters would be in educating the French girls of colonial families.

For Your Life

Many children experience Christ, Mary, the angels, and saints in some personal vision. Sometimes parents regard these as necessarily imaginary. Yet such a memory may return to influence the same child years later at a time of crisis of faith. Without fostering an unhealthy superspiritualism, we should cherish supernatural moments in our lives and in those close to us. Sometimes the type of work we are obliged to perform can seem far from our real talents and these visions. If God could seek out Marie of the Incarnation at the docks among the horses, we should expect to find him also in the most mundane of our own duties.

Prayer-Meditation

From the letters of Blessed Marie of the Incarnation: "People who came to visit us (at the mission school in Canada) could not understand how we could embrace these little orphans, holding them in our laps, when their bodies were heavily smeared with grease (against the cold) and covered only by a small, greasy rag. For us all this was an unimaginable happiness. Thanks to the goodness of God, our vocation and love for the natives never diminished. I carry them all in my heart and try very gently through my prayers to win them for heaven. There is always in my soul a constant desire to give my life for their salvation."[39]

46 ✠

St. Jeanne de Lestonnac
d. 1640[40]

Jeanne was a niece of the famous essayist, Montaigne. Her father was Catholic, her mother veered toward Calvinism. When her mother failed to influence Jeanne toward Protestantism, she treated her badly in revenge. The little girl sought refuge in prayer. When she was seventeen, she married happily, but her husband died leaving her with four children whom she raised.

At the age of forty-seven, Jeanne entered a Cistercian monastery at Toulouse, but her health could not stand the austerities. After only six months she was sent back into the world. At this heart-breaking time, the Lord sent her a supernatural experience concerning an order she was to found— the Congregation of Notre Dame, for the education of girls of every class.

Although many schools were opened with great success, Jeanne was to experience yet another trauma. One of her Sisters invented bad stories about her and was elected as superior in Jeanne's place. Afterwards she treated the founder with cruelty, even battering her. In the end this Sister was so touched by Jeanne's humility and patience, she repented. St. Jeanne de Lestonnac died in 1640. After her death her body emitted sweet fragrances for days, and a blazing light surrounded her.

For Your Life

The extraordinary life of St. Jeanne de Lestonnac contains many lessons for us. First a woman of forty-seven founds a religious order. In our day, when so many women are left widowed in middle-age, quite a number of them are finding themselves with religious vocations. The ill-treatment Jeanne endured at the hands of one of her fellow Sisters is unfortunately mirrored today in some religious houses where there is tremendous friction between conservatives and liberals, with all sorts of petty persecution going on. May patience replace discord, in the spirit of St. Jeanne.

Prayer-Meditation

Through the prayers of St. Jeanne de Lestonnac may all Christian girls receive a good education in secular and religious subjects. May strife between Sisters in religious orders be replaced by understanding and affection. Through Christ our Lord. Amen.

47 ✠

Blessed Marguerite d'Youville
1701-1771[41]

Marie Marguerite was born in Quebec, Canada, the first daughter of six children to parents of French ancestry. As a young girl, Marguerite spent most of her time helping her mother care for the younger ones. When her father died unexpectedly, the large family was without income. They lived as best they could off the land and their mother's needlework.

At eleven, Marguerite was sent off for two years to the Ursuline convent school founded by Blessed Marie of the Incarnation. It was noted how intelligent and peaceful Marguerite was, and also that she was very dignified. These traits remained as she grew into a woman of indomitable strength and purpose. At the Ursuline school Marguerite became more and more devoted to the Sacred Heart. When she founded her own order of nuns, they would always wear over their hearts a silver crucifix with the Sacred Heart image on it.

Along with her strong, responsible characteristics, Marguerite did not shun the fun of feasts and parties characteristic of the French colony, and she considered it natural that she would marry someday, and she did after the family moved to Montreal. Unfortunately Marguerite's arranged marriage to a handsome, wealthy young man turned out tragically. Accustomed to her own family life, full of joy and love, Marguerite found that her mother-in-law was a domineering, sarcastic woman who had no tenderness. After their bright courtship, her husband also became indifferent and unfeeling. He spent most of his time bribing the Indians to trade their furs for liquor, with which he made them so drunk that they had not the will to venture to the usual markets to sell their wares. He himself lost most of the family fortune by gambling.

Added to the troubles with her husband and mother-in-law, poor Marguerite lost one child after another to infant illnesses. The two boys that survived, however, were nurtured in the faith so well by their saintly mother, both became priests. Finally her husband died, leaving Marguerite totally bankrupt and saddled with bad debts. Never reproaching him during their life together and always offering up her trials for the conversion of his soul, Marguerite was now faced with the auction sale of all her goods and the prospect of starting afresh without any money. Resourcefully she opened up a shop and sold her own needlework and other sewing supplies.

During her married years, Marguerite had become close to the Sulpician Fathers who ministered in a church in Quebec. She joined the Confraternity of the Holy Family, dedicated to the care of the poor. More and more, Marguerite felt attracted to corporal works of mercy for the most needy, especially convicted criminals displayed in the stocks in the public squares and destitute old men and women. Under the direction of the Sulpician Fathers she gradually started taking the neediest cases into her own home. Various ladies of the Confraternity attracted by Marguerite's charism of tenderness to the poor began to collaborate. When there were four of them living together with the poor, the Sulpician Fathers formed them into a fledgling order. They lived together under a simple rule, caring for the destitute, and earned money for their own needs through fancy needlework.

All the saints had to endure some kind of persecution. At one time, Marguerite's group was held to blame for drunken Indians who used to loiter on their doorstep, leading the women to be mocked with the name of "the tipsy Sisters." Later they would wear gray habits and call themselves the Gray Nuns because the word *gris* for tipsy could also mean *gris* for gray. Marguerite's Congregation numbered some seven thousand members by the 1970s and can be found in all parts of the world. She was beatified by Pope John XXIII in 1959.

For Your Life

Since even the purest hearts are subject to ridicule, we should be willing to extend ourselves in love for the needy regardless of mockery by the cynical.

Prayer-Meditation

From the daily litany of the Gray Nuns: "Our Father, Who art in heaven, hear the voice of Thy children on earth.... O Father of all eternity, show Thyself our Father.... O Father, Source of all love, multiply our works of charity and render them fruitful into eternal life."[42]

48 ✠

Nano Nagle
1718-1784[43]

Born to a wealthy Irish family, Honora Nagle, nicknamed Nano, still had to live under the conditions of poor Catholics in an Ireland administered by the English and Protestant Irish. Since Catholic schools were forbidden, she was educated in the fields behind tall hedges where the teachers and children could not be seen by the authorities.

As a young woman she was sent to Paris where she and her sister Ann enjoyed its rich cultural and social life. At the death of their father, they were forced to return home and found themselves confronted by growing poverty and squalor caused by confiscation of lands by the anti-Catholic politics of the times. Soldiers would evict Catholic families from their lands and leave them on the open road to starve to death.

Horrified by what she saw, Nano despaired of doing anything in Ireland and thought it would be better to go back to France and enter a convent. But once within the walls, Nano was haunted by scenes of her homeland and longed to do something to help her poor people. A Jesuit spiritual director advised her to work as a laywoman to educate Irish children. This venture would be perilous indeed, for not even faithful Catholics wanted their own to violate laws prohibiting any organized Catholic education. Setting up schools could draw unwelcome attention.

For this reason, when Nano returned to Cork, Ireland, she lived with her well-to-do brother and his wife, but secretly opened a small school in a slum area without implicating her family. After awhile she had two hundred girls studying under her and later opened some schools for boys as well. In her schools the Irish children learned to read, write, and understand their catechism. Eventually her relatives found out about her work and opposed it, fearing persecution from the government. Showering her with insults, they attempted to intimidate her. Then they cut off her funds. Thus this woman of wealthy family was reduced to begging in the streets to support her schools.

By night Nano, herself a victim of chronic tuberculosis, went through the slums helping the poor, finally arriving at her own hut where she spent the night in prayer. Her charity having no bounds, she also started a lay mission society to follow forced Irish migrants who were sent to plantations in the West Indies. There the lay missionaries taught the Irish indigents the Catholic faith.

As time went on, Nano Nagle was able to realize her greatest dream: she founded an order of Sisters who devoted themselves exclusively to educating the poor. Initially called the Sisters of Charitable Instruction of the Sacred Heart of Jesus, today they are known all over the world as the Sisters of the Presentation of the Blessed Virgin Mary. Nano Nagle died at sixty-five in 1784, having served her schools to the end no matter how beset by difficulties and illness. Her cause is being studied for beatification and canonization.

For Your Life

We are often tempted to despair of doing any good because of the ills of the times. Meditating on the difficulties Nano Nagle had to overcome with family and society, surrounded by the most abject poverty, we should take heart and follow the leading of the Holy Spirit. Nothing is impossible with God's grace and direction, even in what seem to be the worst of times.

Prayer-Meditation

From the words of Nano Nagle when a friend thought she was too sick to continue her arduous routine: "I think any little labor I have, the Almighty has given me health to go through it; and if I did not make use of it in his service, he may soon deprive me of it."[44]

49 ✠

St. Julie Billiart
1751-1816[45]

*J*ulie Billiart was the fifth of seven children of a family who ran a linen shop in France in the eighteenth century. As a child her favorite game was playing school, with herself as a teacher. The parish priest, noticing how much she loved religion classes, let her receive Holy Communion early and taught her how to control her temper by means of making short mental prayers.

For a long period Julie became paralyzed, unable to walk. She offered her sufferings to God and began to get a reputation for holiness from the cheerful way she accepted her pain. During the French Revolution, she hid priests in her house. When the revolutionaries wanted to find her and burn her in public, she was hidden in a cart covered with hay and escaped. During this time Julie saw a vision of Christ surrounded by Sisters who were to be her order for the Christian education of girls. She had to accept in faith that somehow, even though she seemed half-dead, from paralysis and other ills, this vision would come to pass.

In 1803 she and a friend started a small religious house. The order was called the Sisters of Notre Dame de Namur, now in many places of the world. A priest who admired Julie made a special novena to the Sacred Heart and then afterwards insisted that the poor woman who had not walked in twenty-three years take a step of faith. After this miraculous cure, Julie founded several schools. She also received the gift of healing. Once twenty-three of the sisters were laid low by typhoid fever. She merely exclaimed, "My children, if you have any faith, arise!" All but four were completely cured. The last year of Julie's life was spent nursing the wounded and feeding the starving after the famous battle of Waterloo. She died in 1816 and was canonized in 1969.

For Your Life

Sometimes we set off to do "something beautiful for God" without being sufficiently holy ourselves. Julie's time as an invalid was a great purification that made her later work much more fruitful. Never begin any work without prayer.

Prayer-Meditation

St. Julie Billiart, intercede for Sisters, lay teachers, and girls in all the schools of your order, and in all Christian schools, that children may grow in holiness day by day as they study. Through Christ our Lord. Amen.

50 ✠

St. Philippine Duchesne
1769-1852[46]

St. Philippine Duchesne, a French missionary to the United States, and a Sister of the Society of the Sacred Heart, was born in Grenoble, France in 1769 to a family of lawyers, businessmen, and politicians. She became a mother to Native Americans, African Americans, and pioneer settlers alike in America in the early 1800s. Philippine was brought up in the manner of most young girls of her class who would one day be wives and mothers. They were educated in religion, morals, reading, writing, literature, and domestic arts. Philippine, whose tastes were always more individualistic and adventuresome than most girls', developed a great admiration for the Jesuit missionaries to the Indians in the New World. At the Visitation school where Philippine studied, she was especially attracted to Eucharistic Adoration and love for the Sacred Heart. Through devotion to prayer, Philippine overcame the natural tendency of a strong character to dominate others. Mildness and charity became her means of harmonizing disparate gifts.

Philippine's parents resisted the desire of their daughter to become a Visitation nun herself. To this opposition, Philippine reacted by living like a nun within her large home, refusing to participate in the social life around her. Finally she went to the Visitation convent and insisted on remaining. During this time she was especially influenced by the life of Blessed Marie of the Incarnation, a woman of prayer, like herself, but devoted to the mission in Canada for the Indians.

The French revolutionaries succeeded at this time in banning all religious vows, and soon Philippine was outside the convent, but always initiating charitable works for the poor, the sick, the dying, and imprisoned priests. Her work for the poor was characterized by recognizing their own dignity, by responding to the presence of Christ within them. Soon she realized that efforts on their behalf should be an entire life-work based on close personal contact.

With this in view, Philippine tried to reopen the Visitation convent, but met with great opposition to her plans, since so many of the former nuns had become accustomed to a more relaxed style. Eventually her small group joined the newly-formed Society of the Sacred Heart. This society was founded by St. Madeleine Sophie Barat for the Catholic education of young women, who lived as boarders in the schools, and also for the teaching of the poor during the day.

Although always extremely active in her works, in prayer she loved to surrender herself in the simplicity of adoring love.

In 1818 at the age of forty-eight, Philippine's great wish to be a missionary was granted. She went with some other Sisters to help with the educational plans of the bishop of a vast territory surrounding Saint Louis, Missouri. There, and as far away as Louisiana, she attempted to found schools mostly for Creole children and pioneer settlers. Philippine was astonished by the prejudice against the African Americans she found in the United States and fought against it. Many were the trials this valiant pioneer was to suffer from within the community and with various ecclesiastical authorities. What enabled her to continue with heroic love of God and neighbor was her strong spirituality.

For Your Life

So often we plan ahead for our lives, assuming that if our desires are good God will arrange everything our way. The life of St. Philippine shows how circuitous the route is that leads to the fulfillment of our heart's desires. We are called not give up our deepest wishes, but to serve in whatever way circumstances demand, meanwhile letting God mold us into the person he can use in the way he wills. Our motto should not be "my will be done!" but "thy will be done!"

Prayer-Meditation

From the letters of St. Philippine: "The voyage (to America) and the trials ahead will never be as great as the help I may confidently expect from him."[47]

51 ✠

St. Elizabeth Seton
1774-1821[48]

A native American saint, Elizabeth Seton was a remark-ably lovable, motherly woman as well as a courageous convert and founder. Born in New York City to a prominent Episcopalian family, little Elizabeth lost her mother early in life. She was very attached to her father, a doctor, and used to accompany him on trips to Ellis Island to help the sick, poor immigrants. She was a very devout church woman, loving to pray, and living from Sunday to Sunday for her spiritual sustenance.

Elizabeth married a charming young businessman and had five beloved children. Into this happy scene came, however, one disaster after another. First was the failure of her husband's business which left them bankrupt, and then her husband's illness. It was typical of her motherly nature that the few moments when she was free of nursing because her husband was asleep, she would spend skipping rope with her daughter in an effort to relieve the horror and tedium of their circumstances. She went with her husband and one daughter to Italy, hoping that he might recover there, only to have him die in miserable quarantine at the docks of Livorno.

After her husband's death she was taken in by his Italian business friends, who were devout Catholics. They made such an impression on her that soon she was deeply torn between her Episcopalian faith and her great attraction to the Catholic church. When she returned to New York, she decided the Catholic church was where she was to belong. This meant she would have to relinquish the support of her

Episcopalian relatives and live in poverty with her little brood.

Eventually her piety and educational gifts came to the attention of Bishop Carroll in Maryland, who invited her to begin a teaching order for girls. She sent her sons to the local seminary high school and kept her daughters with her. They settled eventually in Emmitsburg, Maryland, where today there is a memorial shrine dedicated to her. Near the beautiful church, one can still see her former house, where she lived merry and hopeful in the Lord, in spite of the difficulties experienced with poverty, heat, and chill. The snow sometimes fell right through the makeshift roof onto their beds!

Her worst sufferings involved the early deaths of her daughters and other relatives and worry about the fate of her sons out in the world after their schooling. Happily, we have volumes of her letters which show us her marvelous homey and trustful spirit. These letters have great appeal to women of both motherly and religious vocations. She herself died in middle age, looking forward to eternity.

For Your Life

The life of Elizabeth Seton provides examples of courage in the face of adversity. The most poignant is her conversion and her willingness to put total trust in Providence not only for her own welfare but for that of five children. In this she is a model for single parents.

Prayer-Meditation

From a letter of St. Elizabeth Seton to a non-Catholic friend: "Peace, my dear…. We will jog up the hill as quietly as possible, and when the flies and mosquitos bite, wrap the cloak round and never mind them; they can only penetrate the surface. Darling Julia, how I wish you would have such a Catholic cloak also." And, as she was dying, "Eternity, eternity, when shall I come to you at last?"[49]

52 ✠

St. Joaquina
1783-1854[50]

As with so many other women saints, Joaquina was married against her deeper inclinations, which were to become a cloistered nun. At twelve this Spanish girl went to the convent and begged to be admitted. When the young aristocratic lawyer her parents had chosen for her, Don Teodore de Mas, noticed his young wife depressed and sad and was told of her earlier dreams, he confessed that he, too, had wanted to become a religious, but had agreed to his parents' wishes. Except for the fact that her in-laws did not like Joaquina, she had a wonderful life because her husband understood her so well. Every morning they went to Mass together and finished the day with the Rosary. They ultimately were blessed with nine children.

After military service, Teodore became gravely ill. At thirty-three years old Joaquina was left a widow with six children, three of the nine having died. She occupied herself with the Catholic upbringing of the children and her own penances. Two years after her husband's death, Joaquina entered the third order of St. Francis, wearing a brown sack instead of regular clothing, and devoting herself to nursing hospital patients.

A priest became convinced that Joaquina ought to found a group of nuns to combine Carmelite contemplative life with works of mercy for the poor. When her children were old enough, she founded the Carmelite Sisters of Charity. Here she was beloved as the "madre" to the sisters. During a time of civil strife, Mother Joaquina was arrested, dragged through the streets, and battered. This led to a flight to France, leaving her congregation and her family in the hands of God. When she returned, there was sufficient peace in Spain so that the community was able to make public vows. Twenty-five of her Sisters were martyred during the Spanish Civil War of our century.

Mother Joaquina was canonized in 1959.

For Your Life

Even when women are forced into vocations and lifestyles, God can bring great good out of this, as can be seen in the case of Joaquina. The practice of daily Mass of husband and wife together is a wonderful model for all Catholic couples. A great cross for women, that Joaquina bore heroically, was separation from her loved ones because of conditions of civil disorder. This cross has been borne by many older women whose sons left them for military service, by immigrant mothers, and also by those with adult children who live in distant parts of their own country or in other countries. St. Joaquina can teach us how to offer this painful suffering to God, always retaining confidence in divine Providence.

Prayer-Meditation

St. Joaquina, intercede for all religious Sisters who continue working, in spite of great difficulties within their congregations or with trials imposed by political conditions. Through Christ our Lord. Amen.

53 ✠

Cornelia Connelly
1809-1879[51]

O ne of the most dramatic paths to holiness was trod by the Catholic heroine, Cornelia Connelly, whose cause is about to conclude in beatification.

Cornelia might be considered as a patroness of divorced women, or even better, a patroness for those who began marriage with great joy and happiness and lived to endure tragic marital reverses. Cornelia was originally an American Lutheran girl who later became an Episcopalian and finally a Roman Catholic. Her entrance into the Episcopal church and then into the Roman fold came about by her attraction to Pierce Connelly who was an Episcopal clergyman in Philadelphia when she married him, but became a Catholic four years later. Both Cornelia and Pierce were charming people with wonderful minds. When they made a pilgrimage to Rome, they were received with open arms by the English and American Catholics who chose to dwell in the Eternal City.

By this time they had two small children. Due to financial difficulties, they returned from Rome to the United States where Pierce taught at a Catholic college in New Orleans. Although originally Cornelia had converted in order to follow the lead of her husband, at a retreat made with a Jesuit father in New Orleans her soul took wings, and her interior life began to grow by leaps and bounds. She now sought the will of God no matter how much suffering this might entail. This resolve did not cause Cornelia to long for the cloister, but rather to transform and supernaturalize her happy life as a wife and mother.

The sufferings she had asked for were not long in coming. First her youngest son fell into a cauldron of boiling sugar and died after forty-three hours of agony, during which she held him in her arms, helpless to relieve his misery. Next to be sacrificed was her husband, who announced he was sure that he was called to the priesthood. It would only be possible if she agreed to take a vow of chastity and perhaps later enter the convent. Shocked by this unusual request, Cornelia yet found it within her soul to accept it as the will of God. Their oldest son was sent to a school in England and the two little ones resided with her at the convent. Later she moved to Rome, keeping her little ones with her, and eventually founded in England the Society of the Holy Child Jesus, devoted to the education of Catholic girls.

Her trials culminated when Pierce, after becoming an ordained Roman Catholic priest, underwent a change of heart and mind and decided that his decision had been totally mistaken. He left the priesthood, returned to the Episcopal church, and demanded that his wife be restored to him, finally undertaking a legal suit in anti-Catholic England. Although Cornelia ultimately won the right to remain in her convent, Pierce managed to cause her great agony of soul, and was also able to alienate her children from her. Nonetheless she remained ever faithful to her vows and her trust in divine Providence. She died after many years, revered for her great persevering love and holiness.

For Your Life

Most Catholics will witness to crucial times in their lives when God seems to be taking away from them all chance of earthly happiness. It is said that God never takes something away without replacing it with something more beautiful, and what could be more beautiful than himself?

Prayer-Meditation

From the sayings of Cornelia Connelly: "We glorify God by accomplishing His will as He makes it known to us through those who represent Him, and by the events in our lives which He orders or permits.... Take the Cross He sends, as it is, and not as you imagine it ought to be."[52]

54 ✠

Blessed Paula Frassinetti
1809-1882[53]

*P*aula was the sister of a priest who was a fervent apostolic worker in Italy. She became a mother to poor children. A weak child, she was sent away from Genoa to the smaller town of Quinto for a change of air, there to live with her brother, the priest. When she began to teach poor children, it became evident that this was to be her life vocation. Soon other women began to take up the same work and in time founded the order of the Sisters of St. Dorothy, devoted to teaching of the young. This spread to Portugal and Brazil.

Founding an order then, as now, is no easy matter, especially as Blessed Paula had no financial resources. She spent the nights in prayer and the day in work. In this way, Paula triumphed over all obstacles. She also had great insight into character and could read hearts. She died in 1882 and was beatified in our century.

For Your Life

Among those with apostolic plans, sometimes agitation and protest consume energy better put into prayer for the success of the work. Only God can break down opposition that may be caused precisely because of our confrontational approach to some obstacle.

Prayer-Meditation

May all Christian girls around the world come to learn about their faith and to love it above all secular studies, through the intercession of Blessed Paula Frassinetti. Through Christ our Lord. Amen.

55 ✠

Blessed Marie Rose Durocher
1814-1849[54]

*E*ulalie, later to be called Sister Marie Rose, was the youngest of eleven children living in a well-to-do family in French Canada in the early nineteenth century. She became a spiritual mother to children in need of a Christian education. Although physically weak, her energy was always high when it came to studies and other activities. Eulalie's religious mother taught the children catechism and sent them to the St. Denis convent for a few years of formal teaching. After losing her mother in 1830, Eulalie, even though young, was so efficient that it fell to her to take over the whole household and act as helper in the rectory where her brother was a priest.

Becoming aware of the great need for Christian teachers in the countryside, Eulalie soon began to teach the children around the parish. Ultimately, after many difficulties, she was able to found a congregation in Quebec called the Sisters of the Holy Names of Jesus and Mary. This teaching order spread in Canada, and also in Africa, Japan, Brazil, Peru, the West Indies, and the United States. Blessed Marie Rose Durocher died in 1849 and was beatified in 1982.

For Your Life

There is a great shortage of teaching Sisters in some parts of the world today. This is a pity because with so many broken families many Catholic children are in great need of the loving support of holy women dedicated to their welfare. Perhaps someone reading the story of Marie Rose Durocher may be inspired to see if she is called to such a life.

The motto of the Sisters of the Holy Names of Jesus and Mary is "Jesus and Mary, my strength and my glory." Blessed Marie Rose also devised this prayer for teachers: "Give me the spirit you want them (the children) to have."[55]

56 ✠

Blessed Frances Scherviers
1819-1876[56]

*F*rances Scherviers was the daughter of a German father and a French mother. Her father was a high official in the government of Aachen in the Rhineland. Her childhood was darkened by the upheavals of the French Revolution and industrial developments, which led to a mass exodus from the farms to the cities where workers lived in dreadful slums. Frances' father was one of the few concerned industrialists of the day who paid good wages and treated the workers with dignity. Her mother wished fervently to help the poor. As a little girl, Frances used to secretly knit stockings for the poor in her bedroom and then distribute them to those in need. It had to be secret because her father disapproved of any actual contact with the poor, fearing contagious disease.

When Frances was only thirteen, her mother died. She was given the task of supervising the entire household. This position made it possible for her to give away to the poor all goods that were not needed. She also sold the silver plate meant for her dowry and gave the money to the needy. When an older sister returned from studies abroad, Frances was relieved of her household governance and devoted herself even more to caring for the sick and the poor.

In an effort to help the unfortunate, she swept floors, washed children, sat up at night with the sick, and even learned how to speak the dialects of the common people. Eventually with the help of some other similarly minded Third Order Franciscans, Frances formed a new order called the Sisters of the Poor of St. Francis. Into the poor house where they lived in Franciscan simplicity came a growing number of penitent women to find support after repenting of lives of adultery or prostitution. If there was not enough room, the Sisters slept on the floor and gave their bedding to the penitents. Once when one of the women guests returned to a house of prostitution, Frances disguised herself as a man. In this way she entered and was able to persuade the prostitute to return with her to the Sisters' house. This woman remained after that with the Sisters until her death.

The Sisters also played a large role in the nursing of the sick during a cholera epidemic in 1849. Soon vocations had increased to the point where there were sixteen houses in the Rhineland. All this work was accomplished by Frances, even though she suffered from asthma and sciatica, of which she was later healed at the Shrine of Lourdes. In 1858 the order sent five Sisters to America where there was need for ministry to the German-speaking Catholics of Ohio. Frances visited her American Sisters during the Civil War and nursed some of the wounded in Ohio.

After much exertion in nursing the wounded in battles throughout Europe, Frances died in 1876. She was beatified in 1974.

For Your Life

"Where there is a will, there's a way," might be the motto of the life of Blessed Frances. Do we love our poor enough to find ways to help them overcome their difficulties? Let us open our hearts to their cries for help, and open our lives to be willing to join in initiatives to alleviate their sufferings.

Prayer-Meditation

From the words of Blessed Frances: "Do not let your trust in the Lord waver. Put yourself in God's hands so that he can shape you like the blacksmith shapes iron on the anvil. Let yourself be put like gold into the furnace of inner and outer difficulties so that the impurities can be burned out."[57]

57 ✠

Mother Angela Truszkowska
1825-1899[58]

The cause of this Polish saint was opened by Cardinal Karol Wojtyla (now Pope John Paul II) in 1967. Zophia, later to be called Mother Angela, lived during the period of history when Poland was divided up between Russia, Austria, and Prussia.

Zophia was born in 1825 in Kalisz. She was the oldest of four children of a family of Catholic nobility. She was born prematurely and was not expected to live, but her mother devised an incubator for her and begged Our Lady of Czestochowa to save her little girl. These successful petitions led to a special love for Mary in the heart of the child.

From earliest childhood Zophia was intelligent, religious, and compassionate to the poor. She would give her candy money to the poor. When she was sixteen, Zophia became ill with tuberculosis. During her confinement in a sanatorium, she decided she wanted to be a nun. When she was cured, her parents absolutely refused to let her enter the convent of her choice, and soon they began to arrange a marriage for her. She was a shy girl and hated going to parties. At these balls she would flee to a corner to talk to a cousin who also had dreams of the cloister. In the interim, Zophia occupied her time in caring for the poor in the slums and taking care of orphans.

Soon Zophia and her cousin joined the Society of St. Vincent de Paul. Zophia also became a Third Order Franciscan, changing her name to Angela. Her father gave her money to start a shelter for orphans as well as homeless women. Gradually women joined her to help in the work. They grew into a congregation called the Felicians, after St. Felix. Within four years the Sisters were teaching in twenty-seven village schools.

During the Polish insurrection in 1863 in the Russian sector, the Felicians nursed Polish soldiers and hid refugees in their hospital. Even though the Felicians ministered to everyone without discrimination, when the Russians won the battle, the Sisters were ordered at gunpoint to disperse in secular dress. Finally Mother Angela was allowed to migrate with her Sisters to the Austrian part of Poland in Kracow. There she initiated a new ministry to add to their former works, that of feeding poor students at the University of Kracow. In 1874 some of the Sisters went to the United States to serve Polish immigrants. When after her death in 1899 many miraculous favors came from her intercession, the cause of Mother Angela Truszkowska was initiated 1949.

For Your Life

After reading about a Polish holy woman who was free from prejudice, even against the sworn enemies of her country, it is sad to think that some people consider it fun to indulge in off-color ethnic jokes deriding her culture, or any culture. In general, the example of Mother Angela could inspire us to refrain from all such ridicule, prejudice, and discrimination of those who are different from us.

Prayer-Meditation

From the words of Mother Angela: "Help all without discrimination, friend and foe alike.... Everyone is our neighbor."[59]

58 ✠

St. Soledad
1826-1887[60]

The mission of St. Soledad is of great relevance today since it involved caring for the sick in their homes. She became a mother to shut-ins who had no one else to turn to. Named Vibiana as a child, the future St. Soledad of Spain was aware even in childhood that there were poor, sick people in her neighborhood who could not pay the expenses of going to a hospital. Soon this lover of God and Our Lady began to visit the sick and do small penances for others.

When Fr. Michael Martinez suggested that there was need for a special order to visit the abandoned sick, Vibiana was very interested. The priest was unsure because Vibiana seemed very weak and small. As it turned out, of the original seven in the congregation of the Sisters, Servants of Mary, Vibiana was the only one to hold up under the strain of nursing. At the age of twenty-four, as Sister Maria Soledad, the young woman began visiting the homes of both the rich and the poor. At first she was revolted by some diseases and by the sight of corpses. She overcame her fears by trying to see Christ in each sick person.

At one point, during this earlier Spanish revolution, a decree went out that all Sisters must dress in ordinary garb. However, when the governor himself happened to contract cholera and experienced for himself the wonderful loving care of a Servant of Mary, he relented and overturned his previous law. Another cross the Sisters had to bear was the poverty of their conditions. Sometimes they had nothing to eat but bread. Even as mother general of the order, Soledad participated in all the ordinary chores of washing laundry at the river or gathering firewood and cooking. The congregation persevered through many trials of revolutions and sickness. In our times Servants of Mary minister to the sick in twenty-one countries around the world!

Mother Soledad was canonized in 1970.

For Your Life

Just as St. Francis had to kiss the leper on the road in order to overcome his horror of lepers, so did Mother Soledad need to serve the dying in their homes before God could heal her of her fears. It is wonderful to be liberated from fear. We need, sometimes, to plunge ourselves into the most frightening experience, so that we can truly say that we are ready to do God's will no matter what form it takes.

Prayer-Meditation

From the sayings of Mother Soledad: "Do not be so anxious about a house on earth when we have such a beautiful one in Heaven. We are poor, but charity compels us. We must share what God gives us among His poor."[61]

59 ☥

St. Maria Mazzarello
1837-1881[62]

Can an illiterate peasant woman found a large religious order? With God all things are possible! Maria Domenica Mazzarello was born in 1837 in Piedmont, Italy. She was the oldest of seven, and as a young girl loved competing with her elders at the job of working in the vineyards.

Several men were interested in marrying the very attractive Maria, but she wanted to help a circle of people larger than the family. Eventually, Maria became a mother to many girls, teaching them basic skills and their catechism.

Intelligent, able to read a little but not to write, and loving working with accounts, Maria also excelled in catechism. She was a Child of Mary, a pious group of girls just starting in her parish. When a typhoid epidemic hit her town, Maria helped tend all her sick cousins. Eventually she was stricken herself and never recovered her full strength.

The plan for an order began, as did so many others, with a supernatural vision. Maria was taking a walk when, in the open fields below a hill, she saw a vision of Sisters playing with the village girls. Happily, St. Don Bosco had a similar vision of a beautiful woman who said she would take care of the street girls just as he took care of the boys. Once when taking boys on a camping trip, he came upon the fifteen women that Maria had since formed into a group to help village girls learn elementary skills and catechism. Don Bosco formed them into the Congregation of the Daughters of Mary, Help of Christians. Maria Mazzarello became the acting superior, saying that "Our Lady is the superior of this house."[63] She called herself the vicar. Later an election was held. Hers was the only negative vote to the demand that she be superior even though illiterate.

At the age of thirty-five Maria did learn how to write for the first time. She used to joke with the older Sisters that if the younger, more educated ones knew how little their elders knew, they would throw them out! So many vocations came, soon they were off to South America as well. Within her own order Maria insisted, in her motherly affection, that all the Sisters were equal, and she demonstrated this by taking much time in listening to each person's problems.

Maria died at forty-four of pleurisy. After receiving the last sacraments she jokingly asked the priest, "Father, now that I've got my passport, have I permission to leave?" Maria Mazzarello was canonized in 1951.

For Your Life

The life of St. Maria reminds us that it is love that counts even more than knowledge. Let us imitate her by seeing educational goals as flowing out of love, so that we, ourselves, and our children may see our daily work not as a rung in a career ladder, but as a means of manifesting Christian love in the world.

Prayer-Meditation

From the sayings of St. Maria Mazzarello: "If we can do nothing more than save one soul for God we shall be more than repaid for any sacrifice that we make."[64]

60 ✠

Blessed Teresa Maria of the Cross (Bettina)
1846-1910[65]

*F*rom childhood, Bettina was a very religious, joyful girl living in the suburbs of Florence, Italy. As a teenager she was carefree, well-dressed, and loved to attract others to herself. Yet inwardly she had given her whole being to Jesus in constant prayer. In 1871 a young priest came to her town. He encouraged her and her young companions in their desire for a consecrated life with an apostolate of prayer and ministry to the needs of young girls and orphans of the area. They became Third Order Carmelites. They lived in a poor little cottage with Jesus in the Blessed Sacrament always among them. Eucharistic adoration was the center of the spirituality of the sisters in all the houses Blessed Teresa Maria founded. They devoted themselves to the young through motherly care, catechetics, teaching in the schools, and parish work.

Bettina's spirituality, so attractive to the followers who came to her foundations throughout Tuscany and in the Middle East, was marked by the image of motherliness. She insisted that her Sisters should not be overly concerned with their own sorrows and weaknesses, but instead avoid introspection and worldliness in order to pour themselves out in self-giving for children. Such generosity, Teresa Maria believed, can only come from embracing the cross. She, herself, identified her many trials as a founder with those of Jesus. To more subtle forms of persecution was added enemies who set dogs on her in the streets. Teresa Maria's spirituality was greatly tested toward the end of her life when she was suffering with painful cancer. She died in 1910, mourned by multitudes of the poor she and her Sisters had served. Her last words as she died in ecstasy were, "It is open!... Yes, I come."

The Sisters of her order continued to be mothers of all during the wars that followed after their founder's death, ministering to all without distinction of religion or national origin in Italy, Lebanon, Israel, and Brazil.

For Your Life

Bettina, Mother Teresa Maria of the Cross, teaches us that the font of all good works is the presence of Jesus. We ought never to place prayer second because of the activities of the day, but always instead turn to him in adoration and intimate prayer. Otherwise, we are in danger of finding our works becoming too burdensome to endure, and our beneficiaries coming to regard us as unhappy Christians whose faith gives no light and joy.

Prayer-Meditation

From the writings of Blessed Teresa of the Cross: "When I was in the world, it was enough for me to follow some fashion and the others would imitate me. Then I thought: if they all copy me in doing wrong, they will also follow me in doing good."[66]

61 ✠

Blessed Vincentia Lopez y Vicuna
1847-1890[67]

The founder of the Daughters of Mary Immaculate for the Protection of Working Girls of Spain was a woman who began her life in 1847 as the daughter of a lawyer in Navarre. When she went to Madrid to school, an aunt who had founded a home for orphans and servants began to influence Vincentia in the direction of religious life. Vincentia was concerned about what might happen to the orphans and servants when her aunt died. A Jesuit, Fr. Hidalgo, S.J., thought about founding a religious community with these needs in mind.

Vocations to the order kept coming in, largely due to the strong spirituality and practical bent of the founder. Through begging, they supported the many homes they initiated. Blessed Vincentia died in 1890. After her death the congregation spread to South Africa and other lands.

For Your Life

The problem that the order St. Vincentia founded to alleviate is certainly not solved in our times. How often do young working women, alone in apartments, having nowhere to go in the evening, get involved in singles bars and pursue similar activities to meet others? Every parish should have activities for young adults that can provide a wholesome social setting that draws them to love for the Lord.

Prayer-Meditation

From the motto of the Daughters of Mary Immaculate: "Steady employment is the safeguard of virtue."[68]

62 ✠

Mother Alphonsa Hawthorne
1851-1926[69]

Rose Hawthorne was the charming, delightful, dreamy daughter of Nathaniel Hawthorne, the great American writer of stories and novels. She was brought up together with her older brother and sister in an atmosphere of reverence and creativity in New England. Her parents had many Christian ideals. They were also drawn to the Catholic church, especially during the time they lived in Italy, but did not make any definite commitment. Rose became a mother to the sick and dying.

She was a merry, delightful child, yet she was perceptive and open to deeper thoughts as well. Rose was greatly impressed by her father's concern for the poor and homeless. She also felt drawn to the peace that could be found in Catholic churches in Rome.

At age twenty she married George Lathrop, a kindred soul, interested in art and literature. They lived in New York and at first seemed quite happy together, but for the nagging problem of George's drinking. After some years they had a little son, and Rose insisted he be baptized a Catholic, remembering her own feelings about the church in Italy. When their adored child died of a fever at five years old, Rose and George were devastated. By 1891 they decided to become Roman Catholics and were received at the church of the Paulist Fathers in New York City. Nonetheless Rose came to decide that she should leave her husband, largely because of his drinking, which her prayers were unable to overcome. For awhile she returned to him, but then left again for good.

This led, however, to a new vocation. It happened that a seamstress of hers had been sent away to Bellevue as a destitute cancer patient who could not be kept in a hospital, and then sent away from there to die in her own apartment. Filled with compassion for this woman, Rose, who had never considered nursing as a career, was moved by God's grace to want to do something for the poor who were dying of cancer. Her love for them led her eventually to get an apartment in a poor section of town and take in a few dying women to tend them and cheer them with her faith in God. When others joined her in this work, the order of Dominican Sisters for the Care of Incurable Cancer formed.

She used her writing skills now to raise money for buildings to house her cancerous poor. The emphasis was always on personal love for each patient. Rose Hawthorne (Mother Alphonsa) died in 1926 greatly beloved by her order, the patients, and many friends. The cause for her beatification is in progress.

For Your Life

Fear of cancer and contracting it are still dreaded today, in spite of much progress that has been made since the time of Mother Alphonsa. We ask Rose's intercession to be eager to minister to those with cancer and other terminal illnesses. If we are afflicted ourselves, we pray that we will be able to accept this cross with hope in Jesus, the final healer.

Prayer-Meditation

A poem by Rose Hawthorne Lathrop:

"Sorrow, my friend,
I owe my soul to you,
And if my life with any glory end
Of tenderness for others, and the words are true
Said, honoring, when I'm dead,
Sorrow, to you the mellow praise, the funeral wreath are due."[70]

63 ✠

Concepción Cabrera de Armida (Conchita)
1862-1937[71]

Concepción Cabrera de Armida, born in 1862 in San Luis Potosí, Mexico, is not only a holy mother but also a grandmother saint. Or so she will be, after her upcoming beatification.

Concepción, called Conchita, was a lovely, lively girl who spent her youth on the hacienda ranches of her family, horseback riding, laughing, playing the piano, and singing. One reason for the carefree youth of Conchita was that the Catholic schools were being closed as the Mexican persecution of the church, seen as part of the liberation from colonial influences, gained ascendency. Her family was very devout. She describes her mother, who bore twelve children, as a saint. Her father presided over the daily Rosary with the whole family and all the farm workers taking part.

So delightful was Conchita, she counted twenty-two suitors at the time that she finally decided on the one most dedicated to Christ. On her wedding day she asked but one promise of her spouse: no matter how many children they had, he would always arrange their life so that she could go to daily Mass.

Needless to say, such a request, which her husband kept faithfully even when they had nine children, did not come out of the childish fun and games that characterized Conchita's earlier outward life. Hidden within was a deep desire not only for prayer but for penance. These yearnings reached a climax when she was well-accustomed to her happy marriage and the challenges of child-raising. Always she longed for greater closeness to Christ. Mystical visions inflamed her with a great zeal for the salvation of souls and a particular attraction to the needs of the priests who were being jailed or exiled in alarming numbers due to the Mexican persecution of the church.

When Conchita's husband died unexpectedly, she was devastated but still prepared spiritually to take over the household and to grow in the mission to which she was called. With the help of a holy priest, foundations were laid for several apostolates. These were all dedicated to what Conchita called the works of the cross: ways to make known the interior sufferings of the heart of Christ and to unite one's pain to Christ for the sake of his church. Apostolates included the Missionaries of the Holy Spirit, an active order of priests. Then there is a contemplative order of nuns, an active order of catechetical sisters, and several lay apostolates. These vocations flowed from depths of prayer, even though Conchita was told that her place was to remain in her household, outwardly leading the same life as any middle-class Mexican widow.

It is touching to read that in the process of her beatification her children were not so much impressed by her holiness in prayer as by her perfection as a mother. Many women and men have been inspired by the published version of Conchita's spiritual diary and also by her letters to her children. Conchita died in 1937, a grandmother of more children than can be counted since more were always coming.

For Your Life

Many women think that if they want to be mothers they will have no time for an intense spiritual life. Conchita's example proves that the Holy Spirit has no limits. Some very spiritual women believe that meeting God in prayer is more important than taking care of the family. Conchita never made such a distinction, considering love of God and love of the family to be one thing. Many Catholics also spend much more time criticizing the deficiencies of priests than in praying for them. Conchita taught us to pray every day for all priests, especially those who minister to us.

Prayer-Meditation

From Conchita's diary: "To establish Himself in the innermost of souls, such is God's desire, God's need, granted the charity of His Being is avid to communicate what He is, infinite Love. He wants to possess souls, not only through His ordinary presence . . . but according to a wish of love on the part of the creature, in order to render him happy. Therein is the sole ambition of God: to transform us into His Unity."[72]

64 ✠

Blessed Maria Droste zu Vischering
1863-1899[73]

Maria was born in 1863 in Munster, Germany, to a family of counts. The family was noted for their great loyalty to the church. Maria, one of seven children, seemed to have inherited a will of iron which later, combined with her gentle charm, made her a wonderful leader and religious superior. She became a mother to girls with special needs and a mother who wanted to share with all humanity the heart of Jesus.

At the Sacred Heart Academy Maria learned to have a deep devotion to the Sacred Heart. She realized that love of the Sacred Heart was inseparable from the spirit of sacrifice. God drew her into the order of the Sisters of Charity of the Good Shepherd, devoted to the protection and rehabilitation of girls with special needs coming from social and family dysfunction. The Sisters bolstered the self-esteem and God-given dignity of these patients. When confronted with difficult cases, she always commended the girls she cared for to the Sacred Heart.

Later she transferred to Portugal where she would continue to spread devotion to the Sacred Heart. It was here, already afflicted with the spinal disease of which she would die, that Jesus made known his desire to see the whole world consecrated to the Sacred Heart. When Pope Leo XIII made the consecration, after receiving appeals from Blessed Maria, she was ready to die. She was beatified in 1975.

For Your Life

Devotion to the Sacred Heart is not a pious practice of the past, inapplicable to today's world. Many parents have found that consecration of their families to the Sacred Heart has brought tremendous spiritual blessings. Every diocese has priests and lay people eager to extend this apostolate. You may want to get in touch with them to find out about family consecration.

Prayer-Meditation

Most Sacred Heart of Jesus, through the intercession of Blessed Maria Droste zu Vischering, may all Christians come to know of the love in your heart and be brought by this knowledge out of sinful patterns and into a greater love for you and others. Through Christ our Lord. Amen.

65 ✠

Blessed Agostina Pietrantoni
1864-1894[74]

*B*orn in 1864 to a family of ten children in Italy, Livia Pietrantoni, later to be called Sister Agostina, was a poor child who helped with the children, worked on the farm, and made shoes. She was very motherly, always helping her brothers and sisters rather than beating them into submission. She was a lovely girl and received several proposals, but when asked, would offer the suitor a picture of Christ and say that he one day would be her bridegroom. She would become a patient and loving mother to the sick.

She entered the Sisters of Charity and was known for her joyfulness and obedience. Agostina worked in a hospital in Rome that was full of blasphemy and violence. Here some patients spat at her and even beat her. She confided these cases to Our Lady, doing penance for them. In 1894 a prisoner sent to the hospital decided wrongly that Agostina was responsible when he was made to leave because of his unruly behavior. Descending the steps in a narrow hallway, he accosted her and stabbed her to death. She died in great peace, saying she had forgiven him. Though given a life-sentence, the murderer was reconciled to Christ and received the last sacraments before his death a year later. Agostina was beatified in 1972.

For Your Life

Blessed Agostina thought that when her patients were cranky and even violent, it was because they had so much pain to endure. In ministering to the ill in our own families or in hospitals, let us think of them as generously as she did.

Prayer-Meditation

From the words of Blessed Agostina: "All is too little for the Lord. I am ready to do anything for Him.... We will lie down for such a long time after death that it is worthwhile to keep standing while we are alive. Let us work now; one day we will rest."[75]

66 ✠

Teresa Valse Pantellini
1864-1894[76]

*T*he life of Teresa Valse Pantellini is a study in contrasts. Brought up in a wealthy, cultured family in Milan, Italy, in whose home original paintings of Michelangelo and other great artists hung on the walls, Teresa chose to live in poverty. She was a beautiful pianist, yet would spend her days working in a laundry with poor girls. Educated to speak in many languages, she chose to speak the local language of the poor. She would become a mother to the poor.

As a little child, Teresa traveled in Europe with her family, staying at fine hotels and resorts. When both her father and mother died, she was left an heiress at twenty-one, living in Rome. Although charitable from her youth, Teresa was also imperious and domineering, and it took tremendous efforts of detachment to become the gentle, loving woman she was to become by God's grace.

When Teresa applied to enter the order of the Daughters of Mary, Help of Christians, the director could hardly believe that such a rich girl could make the sacrifices demanded of the life, such as living in a dormitory without even a small room for herself. She insisted that her calling was supernatural. Finally they let her in. When allowed to enter, the other Sisters expected her to be affected, but, on the contrary, she was the soul of humility. She taught catechism to the older girls of the streets of Trastevere, Rome. The children, though usually rude, loved to listen to her stories and teachings. As a result of her influence, a group of girls stopped loitering on the streets and instead worked with her in the laundry. She would always try to win over any girl who was unruly, even trying to shield from the police girls put up to insult her by anti-Christians. Everyone was astounded by the way she took criticism, never excusing herself. When dying of tuberculosis at the age of twenty-nine, Teresa's face lit up and she cried out, "Paradise. I am coming quickly." Many graces came from her intercession. Her cause was initiated in 1926.

For Your Life

Some Christians who lead exemplary lives in other respects are still quite proud, a trait that comes to the fore especially whenever they are criticized justly or unjustly. It takes much self-love and love of neighbor to realize that all of us have flaws which could be regarded humorously rather than catastrophically. It is the sin of pride to think that we are always above criticism. How much better to admit our failings and beg pardon for any appearance of wrong that leads someone to misjudge us.

Prayer-Meditation

From the sayings of Teresa: "God asks us to mortify ourselves in small things rather than in big ones because the big occasions are rare, whereas the small ones are continuous."[77]

67 ✠

Satoko Kitahara
1929-1958[78]

Could there really be a patron saint of homeless garbage-pickers? Read on. Satoko Kitahara, who would be called the Mary of Ant Town, a shanty town of the poor of Tokyo living on junk discarded by city people, was born to a wealthy family in a Tokyo suburb in 1929. Well educated, Satoko expected to live in the traditional way of a Japanese young woman of her class. This meant marrying the husband chosen by her parents, deferring to him to the point of refusing ever to give an opinion on anything, and not making any choices on her own, even in the smallest of matters. For instance, it would be considered impolite for a Japanese girl of ten to even look at a dish of ice cream until bidden to eat it.

Satoko's traditional way of life was altered during World War II when teenage girls had to enter the work force to help out with the war effort. This unexpected change in lifestyle was further accelerated after the war when American occupation brought the young people into contact with Western customs.

Satoko, now a young woman, decided to study pharmacy. It was during her university days that she happened to notice some Catholic nuns going into a church. Curious, she followed. Not herself religious, she was overwhelmed by the beauty of a statue of the Blessed Virgin. She decided to take instruction in the Catholic faith and was baptized in 1949. The nuns who influenced her served the poor. They collaborated with a certain Brother Zeno Zebrowski, a Franciscan of the order of St. Maximilian Kolbe, who begged in city squares in order to help the needy. He was particularly interested in helping the poor who lived in shanties in the Tokyo marshes in a slum called Ant Town. Rejecting either crime or state welfare as a means to alleviate their condition, these people chose to survive by collecting junk and selling whatever was retrievable.

Although the more prosperous Japanese wanted to get rid of this constant reminder of abject poverty, the slum was allowed to remain when Brother Zeno announced plans to build a church there. Hearing of these plans, Satoko visited Brother Zeno and became involved in the work among the poorest of the poor in Tokyo.

Her first concern was the evangelization of the children of Ant Town through Christmas celebrations. Gradually, she participated more fully in the life of the people of Ant Town by collecting junk with them. This she did part of the day, devoting the rest to teaching the children music, counseling them about family problems, and bathing them. Her love for Christ led to the conversion of some of the most hardened characters who ran the town. Satoko's deepest wish was to live herself in Ant Town and fully identify with these courageous, resourceful people. This desire was fulfilled when she became deathly ill and was brought to the town to die among her coworkers and fellow missionaries. Through her constant prayers and self-offering, God inspired city officials to cease their efforts to raze the slum and instead to help the poor who lived there.

For Your Life

At the time of the writing of this treasury of women saints, there has been little resolution of our nation's growing problem with homelessness. Diocesan offices, many orders of Sisters, lay ministries, and parish groups, however, do participate in social action on behalf of the homeless by providing legal advice, employment opportunities, and emergency help of all kinds. If our particular call from God leaves little time for such activities, let us at least offer financial and prayer support for those actively serving the homeless.

Prayer-Meditation

O Lord, we see that you can choose anyone, rich or poor, cultured or uneducated, to glorify you in love of God and neighbor. Help us to overcome any fear of not fitting in when the Holy Spirit calls us, as he did Satoko, in ways we would never have dreamed of. May we be especially open to your leadings in serving the poor and homeless in our own communities. Through Christ our Lord. Amen.

68 ✠

Praxides Fernandez
d. 1936[79]

Praxides Fernandez was a wife and mother living in twentieth-century Spain during the country's Civil War, which occurred just before World War II. In 1914 she became the spouse of an electrician who was killed six years later in a train accident, leaving her with four small boys. She worked hard outside and inside the house to provide for her family. Yet she found time to minister to the poor and sick, giving away to them her own food. Praxides also brought the sick into her house. She fasted and carried a crucifix with her on her rounds. In spite of her heavy schedule, this Third Order Dominican was able to meditate two hours a day. So fervently did she identify her own sufferings with those of Jesus and Mary that her body was found branded with a red-hot iron with the names of these beloved heavenly persons. She went to daily Mass whatever the weather or other conditions, even crossing Communist battle lines.

Two of her sons died: one in an accident, another in the Civil War. A third son was a Dominican seminarian. Praxides predicted that she would one day be a missionary. In 1936 the Communists had taken over her town from the royalists and rejected her request for a doctor to attend to her during an attack of appendicitis. When she died, unattended by medical help, the Communists threw her body into a common grave. After her death, the townspeople who had been the beneficiaries of her numerous acts of heroic charity, began to pray for her intercession. When help came in unexpected ways, the cause was opened for her beatification. At the celebration of this decision in 1953, the Mass at the

Cathedral Church of Oviedo was packed with two thousand people.

For Your Life

If our sister, Praxides Fernandez, with her many burdens as a single parent, could make such sacrifices to attend daily Mass, why should we not follow in her footsteps? Some mothers whose small children would disrupt the peace of the congregation and the priest if kept there too long make it a practice to come with them at least for part of the Mass, including the consecration and communion.

Prayer-Meditation

Lord Jesus, we intercede for the peoples of those countries still suffering under Communist domination or the effects of such oppression, that they may experience a new springtime in the Christian faith. Through Christ our Lord. Amen.

Part Three

Martyrs

69 ✠

St. Zoe
d. A.D. 135[1]

Z oe was the wife of Hesperus. They were both slaves of a man named Catalus, and lived during the reign of Emperor Hadrian of Pamphylia, Asia Minor. Brought up as Christians, they had become lax, yet they educated their sons as Christians. When under persecution, the example of their children, who were ready to die for the faith, inspired their parents to new fervor. When the whole family was arrested and Zoe and Hesperus saw their two sons tortured, the parents joined them. All four were put to death in a furnace. The relics of Zoe and Hesperus are honored in Constantinople where Justinian built a church dedicated to St. Zoe.

For Your Life

Most parents consider it their task to educate and inspire their children, but that these children have much to gain and little to give. What a mistake this can be. The example of St. Zoe shows us a mother humble enough to take the lead from her own sons in virtue and holiness.

Prayer-Meditation

May the intercession of St. Zoe bring about unity of faith in families, based not on doing the minimum required, but on heroic love of God and neighbor. Through Christ our Lord. Amen.

70 ✠

St. Glyceria
d. A.D. 177[2]

St. Glyceria was a Christian, martyred at Heraclea in the Propontis, around the end of the second century. She is thought to have been the daughter of a Roman senator living in Thrace. When it was demanded that she make a sacrifice to the pagan god, Jupiter, St. Glyceria threw the statue down to break it. In revenge her persecutors hung her by the hair and beat her, but miraculously, no harm came to her. Then they tried to starve her in prison, but an angel fed her. When put into a fire, the flames extinguished themselves. Next they pulled out her hair and brought her to be eaten by beasts. She died as a martyr to the faith.

For Your Life

Fear of different, horrible forms of death should never dominate a Christian, for we have no way of knowing in what manner God may console us in the midst of dreadful circumstances. We should live in the present, praising God, and leave the future to God.

Prayer-Meditation

Through the prayers of St. Glyceria, may we have courage to face persecution or even a martyr's death. Through Christ our Lord. Amen.

71 ✠

St. Agatha
early church[3]

*I*t is not known in what year St. Agatha was born, an early Sicilian martyr, who is mentioned in the canon of the Mass. Coming from a rich and noble family, Agatha consecrated herself to God in her youth and resisted many ignoble propositions to prostitute herself.

A consul who was enamored of Agatha decided to have a decree issued against the Christians in the hope that fear might lead her to relent. When she refused, the consul had Agatha sent to a house of prostitution. She refused to yield to the strategems of the proprietor and was sent to be tortured on the rack, her sides torn by iron rods and her body burned with torches. Observing how God preserved her in cheerfulness in the midst of such torment, the governor ordered her breasts to be crushed and cut off. Then he sent her to prison without food or medical attention. St. Peter is said to have come to her in a vision and healed her. Finally she died of further tortures. St. Agatha is invoked against fire because it is said that by her intercession, the lava erupting from Mount Etna can be arrested. She is also the patroness of nurses and of women with diseases of the breast.

For Your Life

Many women who do not endure martyrdom for the faith do have to suffer mutilation of their bodies in the course of medical treatment, as, for example, in the case of breast cancer. It is helpful to meditate on the wounds in the side of Christ or on any other parts of the body of the beloved Lord that underwent cruel torture during the passion, in order to unite oneself to him in one's own particular physical trial. For example, some with migraine headaches offer their pain in union with Christ's suffering from the crown of thorns.

Prayer-Meditation

From the accounts of St. Agatha's prayer when she found herself in the hands of her enemies: "Jesus Christ, Lord of all, thou seest my heart, thou knowest my desires. Do thou alone possess all that I am. I am thy sheep: make me worthy to overcome the Devil."[4]

72 ✠

St. Eugenia
early church[5]

*E*ugenia was the daughter of Philip of Alexandria. Eager to become a nun but unable to win her father's approval, St. Eugenia dressed herself as a man and fled with two holy servants to an abbey. No man ever knew she was a woman, and she was eventually elected abbot! This bizarre tale continues in a frightful manner, for a woman decided to accuse the maiden-monk of adultery when she refused this woman's seductions. This led to Eugenia being judged by her own unwitting father and put into prison.

Eugenia used this opportunity to try to convert her father. She drew away her cloak and proved to him that she was a woman and his daughter, and this convinced her father to become a Christian. The whole family was converted and moved to Rome where they brought about the conversion of many others. Eugenia was finally martyred in Rome.

Although the story is hard to believe, we can still learn from it. There are fathers who are non-believers whose daughters are Christians. There is a special bond between father and daughter which God can use to bring about openness to faith. May daughters never despair of fathers who are not believers, but do all in their power to witness to them.

Prayer-Meditation

St. Eugenia, pray for daughters whose fathers do not understand their faith commitment, that they may be witnesses of faith to the men who first gave them life. Through Christ our Lord. Amen.

73 ✠

St. Cecilia
second or third century[6]

St. Cecilia, patroness of music, is invoked in the canon of the Mass as a virgin martyr. According to tradition, she was a Roman girl of noble family and a Christian even as a child. She fasted and wore penitential garb beneath her conventional clothing. When her father arranged a wedding with a pagan, Valerian, Cecilia spent the time of the banquet after the wedding in prayer. Cecilia begged Valerian to be baptized. When Valerian returned from his baptism, he saw an angel with flaming wings next to his wife.

After this, Valerian and his convert brother expended their energies helping the church. When the brothers were sentenced to execution for refusing to make sacrifices to the pagan gods, the Holy Spirit descended upon their executioner who himself became a Christian and died a martyr. Before Cecilia was tortured to death, she gave all her worldly possessions to the poor and made over her house as a church. It is thought that her role as patroness of singers and of music comes from her listening to the voice of her angel.

For Your Life

St. Augustine wrote that he who sings prays twice. Even if our voices are not the best, we can praise God through church singing and support music ministries, which raise us above our humdrum concerns to joy in worship. Many people play classical or popular Christian audio-tapes in their homes and cars in order to elevate their everyday activities as well.

Prayer-Meditation

May St. Cecilia pray for inspiration for all Christian musicians, especially those in charge of our sacred liturgies. Through Christ our Lord. Amen.

74 ✠

Sts. Perpetua and Felicity
second or third century[7]

I n A.D. 203 in Carthage, Africa, five catechumens were arrested and martyred. Among these were Perpetua, the mother of a small baby, and Felicity, a slave who was an expectant mother. The record of their persecution has been preserved. Here are some excerpts from the letter of Perpetua:

"While... my father in his affection for me was trying to turn me from my purpose by argument... I replied 'I cannot call myself by any other name than what I am—a Christian.' Then my father... threw himself on me as if he would pluck out my eyes.... During those days we were baptized.... A few days later we were lodged in the prison.... I had never known such darkness,... terrible heat... rough treatment.... To crown all I was tormented with anxiety for my baby.... My baby was brought and I nursed him, for already he was faint for want of food.... I prayed and this was shown me. I saw a golden ladder of wonderful length reaching up to heaven, but so narrow that only one at a time could ascend.... At the foot of the ladder was a huge dragon which lay in wait for those going up and sought to frighten them from the ascent.... And I went up and saw a vast garden, and sitting in the midst a tall man in the dress of a shepherd... and round about were many thousands clad in white. He raised his head and looked at me and said: 'Thou art welcome, my child.'"[8]

Her father came to beg her to renounce the faith for the sake of the family, and especially for her little son who would die without her milk. At her trial she refused to give in. Her father tried to drag her away, but he was beaten off by the soldiers. Miraculously the infant no longer required milk.

The women were sentenced to be martyred during the gladiatorial sports in the arena. Felicity feared that she would not be sent forth because she was pregnant, but she went into labor in the prison and her daughter was adopted by another Christian. Their jailer himself converted as did many others who witnessed the supernatural joy of the prisoners. As she was being marched around the arena, Perpetua sang hymns. The two women were tossed on the horns of a heifer. Hurt but not yet dead, they were sent out and then called back to be killed by the gladiators. Perpetua had to guide the sword of the executioner, who could not bear to kill her. The names of these early martyrs appear in the canon of the Mass. St. Felicity is considered one of the patronesses of barren women.

For Your Life

It is not natural to wish to suffer, nor for a woman to leave her baby into the care of another forever. The story of these mother-martyrs should remind us that with God "all things are possible" (Lk 18:27). Only God can grant us such a vivid image of eternal life that we will fear nothing except betrayal of the faith. Women who have their babies and then give them up for adoption in loyalty to a pro-life ethic should always remember that those children are infinitely loved by God.

Prayer-Meditation

From the letter of Perpetua: "What takes place on that platform (at the trial) will be as God shall choose, for assuredly we are not in our own power but in the power of God."[9]

75 ✠

St. Restituta of Sora
d. A.D. 271[10]

This martyr was a Roman girl of noble rank who died for the faith at Sora, Italy. St. Restituta was asked by the Lord to go to Sora and was brought there by an angel. Many persons were converted to Christianity due to miracles attributed to Restituta. When the authorities became aware of her presence, she was cast into prison and scourged when she refused to recant. For seven days Restituta lived without food or drink, with heavy chains bound about her. These chains disappeared through an angel's ministrations. Several of her guards were converted by this miracle and later became martyrs themselves. Finally Restituta was beheaded.

For Your Life

Some readers might be tempted to automatically doubt the stories related about St. Restituta. Although some of what is told of early saints may be more legendary than historically true, it should be remembered similar miracles were attributed to the apostles when they were in prison.

Today pro-life witnesses are also arrested when they try to block the killing of the unborn in abortion clinics. They too are exercising an incredible apostolate in the jails to which they are consigned, converting many prisoners by their Bible studies, hymns, and Christian love.

Prayer-Meditation

May the prayers of St. Restituta come to the assistance of all those in prison for their faith and those to whom they may witness during their confinement. Through Christ our Lord. Amen.

76 ✠

St. Agnes
third century[n]

This famous martyr is referred to by many of the early Church writers, such as St. Ambrose, St. (Pope) Damasus, and Prudentius. Her name is mentioned in the canon of the Mass. Agnes lived during the reign of Emperor Diocletian in third-century Rome as the daughter of a rich nobleman. Her parents were Christian at a time when most of the upper classes were still pagan. They worshiped in secret because the emperors wanted the people to worship the pagan gods and even worship the emperors as if divine. It is still possible to visit the catacombs in Rome, dug out by night, with their hollowed out chapels where the dead were buried. Such must have been the places of worship of Agnes and her family.

Agnes was very beautiful, and being affluent, was considered to be highly marriageable at the age of twelve. She had many suitors, but she had made a promise to belong only to Christ.

At this time Emperor Diocletian was bent on the complete destruction of Christianity. Confiscating all Christian property and sacred books, he also destroyed all the churches, priests, and bishops he could find. The prisons were filled with Christians. His was to be the last of great persecutions that had taken place for two centuries.

One suitor insisted on winning Agnes for himself. He could not understand that she was pledged to another. In his history of this period, Pope Damasus alleges that Agnes was finally forced to acknowledge her Christianity publicly. At this point her resentful suitor arranged to have her cast into prison, hoping that she would chose him over torture. But

Agnes longed to die for her true love and witness with her blood. When dragged to do homage to the pagan gods, she made the sign of the cross.

Then she was forced into a house of prostitution to be tormented by lustful young men. They stripped her while she prayed but were frustrated when her long hair covered her body. The others left, but her suitor tried once more to approach her and was struck blind. She forgave him and asked Christ to restore his sight. For these sensational deeds, she was considered a Christian witch and set in a fire to die, but the fire reached for the onlookers, not for her. Finally they killed her with a sword in A.D. 304. She is a patroness of young girls.

For Your Life

In our times when rapes and threats of violence are so frequent, stories of girls and women of early Christian times who were forced to choose between purity and violent attack do not seem so legendary. It is important to seek healing if one has been sexually violated. Christian women should also avoid the company of those who do not share gospel values of chastity.

Prayer-Meditation

St. Agnes, intercede for us that we may be protected from rape and other forms of violence. Intercede for all those who do not know the Lord and seek pleasure instead in sexual sin. Through Christ our Lord. Amen.

77 ✠

St. Barbara
early church[12]

There was once a rich Greek man named Dioscorus, whose daughter, Barbara, was so beautiful that he feared for her safety and so locked her up in a high tower. Many princes sought her hand in marriage, but Barbara refused, saying she did not wish to marry anyone. Later, when Dioscorus went off on a trip, Barbara begged the workmen to make a window through which a holy man baptized her. After this she was gifted with many graces, leading her to disfigure all the idols in the tower.

When her father returned, he demanded an explanation for the window. Barbara witnessed to him about her new Christian faith. Furious, her father first tried to slay her with a sword. This failing, he sent her to prison where she was given a chance to recant, but refused. Beaten and tortured, she was comforted by visions of the Lord. Finally her father did kill her. According to the story, he was punished by a fire from heaven which left only ashes. Many miracles occurred in the town where she was buried.

For Your Life

In a fascinating book by spiritual psychologist Betsy Caprio,[13] the story of St. Barbara is used as an example of the journey many have to make from imprisonment by the image their parents have of them to their own future. Elements in the tale are used to help readers come into contact with the liberating spiritual forces and resources within themselves. Readers of this volume might trace their own journeys of faith in terms of the life of St. Barbara: What has been an imprisoning tower in your life? How has your Christian faith liberated you?

St. Barbara, intercede for all girls and women of your name, and for all Christians, that they may be so full of the Holy Spirit that they would die rather than renounce the faith. Through Christ our Lord. Amen.

78 ✠

St. Lucy
d. A.D. 304[14]

S t. Lucy was of Greek lineage, living in Sicily in the fourth century. Her parents thought she should be married to a pagan. When her mother was miraculously cured through the intercession of St. Agatha, she expressed gratitude to God for this healing by allowing Lucy to devote herself to Christ in the service of the poor.

When Lucy's suitor discovered that he would be deprived of the wife for whom he longed, he denounced her to the governor as a Christian. Ordered to a brothel as a punishment for her steadfast fidelity to Christ, Lucy was not able to be taken off by the soldiers since, by a miracle, she became immovable. Not even fire and burning oil could vanquish this courageous woman. Finally she was slain by the sword. She is invoked as patroness of the visually impaired, probably because the name Lucy means light.

For Your Life

Fear of assault, pain, or disfigurement render many women helplessly weak in confrontation with violent men. The short but valiant life of St. Lucy might help us to assert ourselves more powerfully, sure that Christ will ultimately be the victor.

St. Lucy, intercede for all those suffering from blindness or loss of sight. Also ask the Holy Spirit to fill our imaginations with pictures of victory in heaven, that we may not compromise ourselves for the sake of security on earth. Through Christ our Lord. Amen.

79 ✠

St. Anastasia
d. A.D. 304[15]

*A*nastasia came from a noble Roman family and married a pagan, even though she was a Christian herself. She hid Christians in her house during the persecution of Diocletian. Soon she was taken to prison. During her confinement, St. Theodota, who had died earlier, fed her miraculously. Next she was put on a ship that was to be abandoned at sea. Again Theodota miraculously came and piloted the ship to land, where the Christians on the boat succeeded in converting all the pagans. Finally she was taken to Palmaria and burned alive.

For Your Life

Stories of miracles, such as those experienced by St. Anastasia, fill some readers with skepticism. Even if a person has not seen a miracle himself or herself, there are so many accounts of them in Scripture that it would be foolish to consider such events as impossible. Although we are not obligated to believe them, should we not, in the case of saints, at least give the benefit of the doubt?

Prayer-Meditation

May St. Anastasia intercede for all those lost at sea literally and figuratively. Through Christ our Lord. Amen.

80 ✠

St. Eulalia
d. 304[16]

St. Eulalia of Merida is the most famous virgin martyr of Spain. When Eulalia was only twelve, the word came that all who did not offer sacrifice to pagan gods would be in danger of martyrdom. Apparently, Eulalia's mother, fearing the fervent piety of her daughter, decided to take her off to the country into hiding. But our saint fled by night and presented herself before the judge of Merida to witness to him about the faith.

When the judge tried to persuade her by telling her the offering was only a little salt and incense, Eulalia spat at him and trod on the offering. In response the judge had his torturers tear her body with hooks and put fire to the wounds. As she was dying, a white dove came from her mouth, which frightened the executioners into fleeing from the scene. St. Eulalia intercedes powerfully for those who come as pilgrims to Merida.

For Your Life

One cannot read about St. Eulalia without wondering how a twelve-year-old girl, with the grace of the Holy Spirit, would risk torture and death for the truths of the faith, while many of us find it difficult even to pray in public. May this account inspire us into a more visible public witness.

Prayer-Meditation

St. Eulalia, ask God to give us strength to overcome our fear of looking ridiculous by speaking the truth to those who stand against Christ and his church. Through Christ our Lord. Amen.

81 ✠

St. Ursula
fourth or fifth century[17]

Although the noted authority Butler considers the story of St. Ursula and her maiden martyrs to be legendary in its details, it seems important to tell the tale once more since the Ursuline order is so prominent in church history. What is sure is that some virgins were martyred in Cologne in the fourth or fifth century and that a church was built in their honor.

Ursula, a daughter of a British, Christian king, was to wed a pagan. Not desiring this marriage, Ursula arranged that the ship that was carrying her to her bridegroom should take the longest possible route to its destination. This same sea-going vessel was presumably accompanied by some eleven other ships, on which sailed thousands of other maidens. The real goal of their voyage was Rome. After their pilgrimage they made their way back on the Rhine, during which voyage the Huns, whose chieftain Ursula had scorned, killed them all.

For Your Life

What shall we think about such stories of the martyrs? Some scholars conclude that even if there is no factual evidence for the details, surely a church would not be built in honor of a saint and her companions if they had never existed at all. What also seems clear is that St. Ursula must have been granted many graces to have gathered such a huge following. We should never underestimate the drawing power, as of Mother Teresa of Calcutta in our day, of a woman inflamed by the Holy Spirit.

May the prayers of St. Ursula accompany all the Sisters of her order and their students. Through Christ our Lord. Amen.

82 ✠

Sts. Maura and Brigid
fifth century[18]

Maura and Brigid were princesses from Northumbria, England. On their way home from a pilgrimage to Rome, they were put to death by pagan outlaws. They were buried at Balagny-sur-Thérain in France. St. Bathildis, a British queen, once tried to bring their relics to her monastery, but divine intervention forced her to leave them in Oise, where they inspired many pilgrimages. It is said that a plague was averted due to the intercession of Sts. Maura and Brigid.

For Your Life

Some may have difficulty believing that saints can avert plagues, earthquakes, and other natural disasters. It is interesting to note that some intercessory prayer groups in our day are devoted to praying over earthquake faults, and many groups pray for healing of sickness with positive results. It is a fruit of living in a culture dominated by scientific skepticism that so many find it incredible to think that anything supernatural can be real.

Prayer-Meditation

St. Maura and St. Brigid, pray for those who have lost their faith due to the spirit of atheistic humanism. Through Christ our Lord. Amen.

83 ✠

Sts. Nunilo and Alodia

d. A.D. 851[19]

When we think of martyrs, we may overlook the period of Moorish persecution of Spanish Catholics in the ninth century. Nunilo and Alodia were two sisters who had a Christian mother and a Muslim father. When their father died, the mother of Nunilo and Alodia married another follower of Islam. The second husband persecuted the two girls for their faith. When teenagers, Nunilo and Alodia fled to the home of a Christian relative, not only to avoid ridicule but also because they wanted to remain virgins, and their parents were looking for husbands for them.

Nunilo and Alodia were among the first to be arrested when the persecutions began in their area of northeast Spain, for their great piety was known to all. It is said that they were full of joy when taken before the judge. As a punishment and inducement to renounce their faith, they were given into the custody of prostitutes, but they refused to relent. They were beheaded together in A.D. 851.

For Your Life

The very word "sister" suggests to many a solidarity that is a great comfort in the trials of life. Some girls and women, however, are at enmity with their blood sisters or treat them coldly. May the example of Nunilo and Alodia show how sisters in Christ can help each other to grow in the Lord.

Prayer-Meditation

Sts. Nunilo and Alodia, intercede for sisters who do not get along with each other, especially those where one is

strong in the faith and the other rebellious or negligent, that
these sisters may enjoy the same solidarity in life on earth as
you did, and be bonded forever in joy for eternity. Through
Christ our Lord. Amen.

84 ☩

St. Natalia
d. A.D. 852[20]

*A*nother martyr of ninth-century Spain is St. Natalia.
Aurelius, her husband, pretended to conform to the
Islamic faith, practicing Christian ways in secret. He converted his wife, who was half Moorish, to Christianity and
changed her name to Natalia. Seeing the example of brave,
open Christians, ready to die for their beliefs, Aurelius decided with his wife to make a public confession even though
the archbishop advised them that such a step would lead to
martyrdom. They made provisions for their two daughters
in case they would be orphaned, and both lived out their
faith publicly as well as in private prayer and penance. They
also opened their house for secret Masses. They were arrested and beheaded in A.D. 852.

For Your Life

It is wonderful when a married couple can be of one
mind, one heart, and one faith and live it out at any price,
even martyrdom. Couples should pray together that they
may never refuse the Lord any sign of love, even at the cost
of great sacrifice, for such public witness may be necessary
to advance his kingdom. They should pray that their children will take courage from their own examples of generos-

ity. Such prayers of surrender often have the side effect of making present crosses seem less terrible.

Prayer-Meditation

St. Natalia, pray for all interreligious marriages that the non-Christian partner may be led to the faith. Intercede for married couples also that they may be courageous in the defense of their faith in public situations. Through Christ our Lord. Amen.

85 ✠

Sts. Flora and Mary
d. A.D. 85[21]

During the time of the Moorish occupation of Spain in the ninth century, there was a young girl called Flora of Cordova whose father was a Muslim but who was secretly raised as a Christian by her mother. When her brother found out she had been baptized, he betrayed her to the judge, and she was beaten and her hair torn out. Then she was given into her brother's custody so he could persuade her to renounce the faith. Flora fled to the house of a sister of hers, but when it was decided that even those who sheltered Christians could be punished, she was asked to leave. When she arrived in Cordova, she went to the church to pray for guidance. There she was befriended by another Christian woman called Mary. Mary's brother had recently died as a martyr in defense of the faith. Soon Flora and Mary decided to make a public declaration of their beliefs. After this heroic act, they were thrown into a dungeon with prostitutes who were sent to win them over. St. Eulogious, also imprisoned, was able to visit them and encourage them. They were beheaded in A.D. 851. They had promised St. Eulogious that after their death they would, through their intercessory prayer in heaven, gain graces for his release. In fact, he was let go five days after their deaths!

For Your Life

The story of St. Flora, betrayed by her brother, reminds one of similar tales from behind the Iron Curtain. In our own country, right now, believers in the rights of unborn babies are being thrown into jail. They also must spend their time in jail many times surrounded by open practice of sexual sin. May God enable you and me to stand up publicly against the evils of our culture.

Prayer-Meditation

From the writings of St. Eulogious to Christian virgins about to be martyred: "They threaten to sell you into shameful slavery, but do not be afraid: no harm can come to your souls, whatever infamy they inflict on your bodies.... You cannot now draw back and renounce the faith you have confessed."[22]

86 ✠

St. Helen of Skovde
d. 1160[23]

Helen was a Swedish martyr, a noble lady of Vastergotland, devoted to piety and to the needs of the poor after the death of her husband. She had a son-in-law who was a tyrant. When Helen went on a pilgrimage to Rome, the relatives of this son-in-law decided to place the blame for his murder by his servants on St. Helen. They put her to death and brought the body to a church she had built at Skovde. So many miracles took place at this church due to her intercession that she was canonized in 1164 under Pope Alexander III. St. Helen of Skovde is honored not only in Sweden but also in Denmark.

For Your Life

Although most of us are not involved in murder cases, we certainly are familiar with the miseries of being blamed for something we did not do. If we consider that Christ himself was crucified unjustly, it may help us to endure false witness without the lifelong bitterness of those who do not know that final judgment rests with God. Usually, when others malign us, we can detect a trace of envy behind it. Thinking about the weakness of those who resort to such lies, we can more easily forgive them.

Prayer-Meditation

St. Helen of Skovde, intercede for those who are unjustly accused and convicted of serious crimes, especially those who are wrongfully convicted of murder and face life in prison or execution. Through Christ our Lord. Amen.

87 ✠

St. Margaret Clitherow
d. 1586 [24]

Margaret Clitherow was born in York, England, as Margaret Middleton. It was during the period of the terrible persecutions of Catholics by those who had made the monarch head of the English church instead of the pope.

The pretty, young innkeeper's daughter was married at age fifteen to a widower, John Clitherow, a butcher with two sons. She mothered his children and bore two of her own.

After becoming a Catholic, even though such a conversion was very dangerous, she was so joyful and fervent that she helped many others to retain the faith in the midst of persecution. Since her husband was a Protestant, Margaret did not want to risk his life by setting up secret Masses in their own home. However, when her friend's hiding hole for Catholic priests was discovered, she helped build a space on the top floor between her house and the neighbor's, with the principal entrance in the house next door.

In 1577 she was imprisoned. In those days many mothers were allowed to bring their children with them, but Margaret was denied. This was her greatest cross. Still she loved the fellowship of other imprisoned Catholics. After her release, she claimed that were it not for her love of family, she would gladly have stayed in prison with God forever. In jail she was taught how to read and write and studied the Gospels and Thomas à Kempis' *The Imitation of Christ*.

Her husband said of her, "Let them take all I have and save her, for she is the best wife in all England, and the best Catholic." What a tribute to the influence a wife can have on a husband!

In spite of the cruel executions of so many of her friends, Margaret continued to arrange hidden Masses. Finally she was arrested once more. Margaret refused a formal trial to spare her children the agony of being tortured to force them to give testimony against her. This meant that she would be subjected to the hideous torture of being stripped naked, laid on the ground, and pressed under a weight of some eight hundred pounds. Wishing to set her free, the judges begged her to renounce her faith and swear allegiance to the queen instead. Accusing her of cruelty to her husband and children, they tempted her to give in. Calmly she refused, commending all her persecutors to God.

The night before her execution she spent in fasting and

prayer. The next morning she walked barefoot to the place of torture. There she knelt and prayed and laid herself on the ground clothed only in the linen tunic made by herself, and covered her face with a handkerchief, her hands outstretched and bound as if on a cross. The weighted press crushed her, and she called out, "Jesu, Jesu, Jesu have mercy on me" and died within the hour.[25]

For Your Life

In what ways are you called upon to suffer for the faith? Do you refuse seeking remarriage after the termination of a first marriage that cannot be annulled, or refuse marriage to a divorced person you love deeply? Are you willing to suffer in support of the unborn or the homeless, or for other worthy causes? Are you willing to go through physical or mental suffering rather than end your life through suicide or euthanasia? Do you stand up for Catholic truth in social situations where it would be much easier to pretend to agree with those who dissent from the church's teachings? Sometimes Catholic mothers will think it necessary to play it safe on many public stances to avoid possible harm to the family income. What does the life of St. Margaret of Clitherow have to tell us about what is the most important legacy to provide for our children?

Prayer-Meditation

St. Margaret Clitherow, as we marvel at the graces you received in the midst of torture, we ask you to intercede for us so that we may be willing to suffer in whatever way the Lord asks and to offer this for the good of the church. Through Christ our Lord. Amen.

88 ✠

Blessed Margaret Ward
d. 1588 [26]

*B*lessed Margaret Ward was martyred with the group described in Butler's *Lives of the Saints* as the martyrs of London of 1588. Margaret was an upper-class woman born in Cheshire who lived with a companion in London. She was noted for her ingenuity in trying to effect the aid and eventual escape from prison of a secular priest, Richard Watson. It is said that once she disguised herself as a maid to bring him a basket of provisions. Having now established this identity, she returned with a rope hidden in the basket. Watson escaped from prison but was injured in the process and could not carry off the rope with him. When evidence of the rope was found hanging from his window, Margaret was apprehended as the only visitor on that day who could have been his accomplice. During Margaret's trial, she rejoiced "in having delivered an innocent lamb from the hands of those bloody wolves." She refused the pardon that would have been extended to her if she had been willing to renounce her faith. At the execution of Catholics in 1588, it is reported that neither she nor any of her fellow martyrs were allowed to address the crowds from the scaffold, so greatly was their eloquence feared.

For Your Life

At the time of Blessed Margaret, priests were greatly revered by Catholics because they were able to administer the sacraments in a time of intense persecution. In our times when many doubt the supernatural power of the sacraments, there is more of a tendency to evaluate priests in their roles as community builders and administrators who must know how to lead others, build consensus, and manage the life of a parish. Although such roles are certainly important we also need to be grateful to our priests for the graces that flow from their administration of the sacraments.

Prayer-Meditation

Blessed Margaret, may we always follow the example of your courageous and loving support of the priesthood. May we greatly value the way our priests administer the sacraments to us. Through Christ our Lord. Amen.

89 ✠

Blessed Lucy de Freitas
1542-1622[27]

*I*n 1614 the shogun Tokugawa of Japan decreed that Christianity planted in Japan by missionaries from Europe should be uprooted by means of persecution of the faithful. Many of the priests and their native followers were confined to wretched prisons where they were starved and tortured before being martyred. Among these was a Third Order Franciscan, Lucy de Freitas, a Japanese widow of noble birth who had been married to a Portuguese merchant. Because she had sheltered Franciscan priests, she was martyred at the age of eighty!

For Your Life

It is not uncommon for Christians nearing old age to imagine that the drama of life is over and that everything else until death is a slow, downhill road. The martyrdom at eighty of Blessed Lucy shows us that our greatest acts of witness to the faith can come at any time. With God there is no retirement!

Prayer-Meditation

May the prayers of Blessed Lucy insure new graces for her people and also enliven senior citizens with fresh zeal. Through Christ our Lord. Amen.

90 ✠

Sister Marina
d. 1634[28]

Sister Marina was a Third Order Dominican who lived on Omura, Japan, during the vicious persecution of Catholics that took place in the seventeenth century. Marina was a single woman with private vows, who lived at home and hid Christians. When called up for inquiry about her sheltering of foreign priests, Marina admitted that she gave them food, clothing, and ways to escape. The judges questioned her about the motives for her unusual lifestyle. When she tried to explain to them about vows of chastity, they decided that a fitting humiliation would be to shave her head and make her walk about barefoot and without a head covering, for this was the punishment for adulteresses.

Fear of dishonor plays a tremendous role in Japanese culture. This explains why some Japanese Christian women could endure torture without giving in, but would apostasize when threatened with the shame of appearing publicly to be unchaste.

Marina, however, decided to endure such misery for the sake of Christ. Her willingness to lose face in this manner greatly strengthened the other Christians who observed her on her long march. During this journey, a miracle was attributed to her when she found water for the thirsty prisoners in a place where there could be no water. When her judge realized that he had made a heroine out of Marina, he decided to burn her to death. Her ashes were dispersed in the sea, but all over Japan relics were kept of her clothing.

For Your Life

There are still many Christians who would balk at being humiliated by standing up for the faith in unfavorable circumstances. Opportunities to witness at the cost of possible ridicule could be: in the family, on social occasions where others are making fun of Christian truths, in the marketplace, and even at church liturgies where holy matters are sometimes mocked. Openly praying in public can be a first step. The story of Sister Marina may give us courage to be ready for any shame if by so doing we might even slightly influence a weak Christian or a non-Christian.

Prayer-Meditation

Lord, we ask for Sister Marina's intercession, that you would give us courage in the face of those who would make us feel like fools for our most cherished beliefs and practices. Through Christ our Lord. Amen.

91 ✠

Lugartha Lee Yu-Hye
d. 1801[29]

*L*ugartha Lee Yu-Hye was the daughter of a princely family of Korea. Her character was marked by strong will, great talent, and beauty. Strongly influenced by her mother's faith, when at fourteen she was to receive her First Holy Communion, she made a private retreat in her room for four days and vowed to live in perpetual virginity as a spouse of Christ. In Korean society of the eighteenth century, however, it was not possible for a woman to be single. Distressed that she could not fulfill her vow, she was later delighted to learn that the eldest son of a similar noble Catholic family had also made a private vow of celibacy. Their priest arranged for a special dispensation so that they could be married yet remain celibates, imitating the example of St. Joseph and the Blessed Virgin.

In spite of their great piety, Lugartha reports that keeping to her vow was quite a sacrifice, yet they persevered during the four years before their martyrdom and won great peace and joy in their celibate love. During the persecution, Lugartha's husband was taken off for execution. Three members of her family were sentenced to exile with Lugartha. So challenging to the judge were the words of defense by Lugartha, the judge had second thoughts after sending her to exile and recalled her for a death sentence.

In prison she was tortured by means of shattering the bones of her feet and thrashing her whole body. On the way to execution Lugartha encouraged her weaker relatives and was the first to offer her outstretched neck to the sword. Here are some words from Lugartha's famous letter to her relatives from prison:

"Here I am on the brink of death, and I cannot express myself, yet I dearly wish to say a few words to you about what has happened, and to make my farewell to this world forever.... No further desire to live remains with me, and I think only of giving my life to God when the time comes. I have firmly resolved to do this, and the more I think of it the more I try to become worthy of it."[30]

For Your Life

Often on the feast days of the early martyrs it is said "none of us will be martyrs, but it is for us to accept the sufferings of each day." Accounts of the Asian martyrs of more recent centuries, of tortured prisoners behind the Iron Curtain, and of Central American martyrs can inspire us to realize that at any time the clash between secular powers and the church can become violent.

Prayer-Meditation

Beautiful Lugartha, transfigured Korean flower of God, in our culture many women find it so hard to be kind, even in ordinary life. Pray for Christian women today to be loving to all they meet, realizing that courageous, prophetic strength need not be accompanied by rancor and rage. Through Christ our Lord. Amen.

92 ✠

Blessed Agatha Kim
d. 1839[31]

Korea was originally evangelized by a layman who had been baptized in China. When the first Chinese missionary priest came to Korea, he found four thousand Christians who had been catechized by this one layman. By the time other missionaries arrived, it was in secret because, in the meantime, Christianity had been outlawed. Nonetheless the faith spread to about nine thousand during two years of missionary work conducted in the middle of the night from house to house for fear of persecutors.

Blessed Agatha Kim was one of those executed during this terrible time for the Korean church. Taken with seventy-six other lay people and their three priests, she was asked to recant her faith. "I know Jesus and Mary, but I know nothing else," she replied to those who wanted to win her over. "If I have to die I will not renounce the faith." As a result of her courage, she was tormented and crucified on a wooden cross dragged by a cart. Then she was stripped naked and her head cut off. She was beatified with her companions in 1925.

For Your Life

It brings tears to one's eyes to read such accounts of bravery in the face of known torture and death. Yet we know that it is just as valuable in God's eyes when we accept, with sweet patience, the daily little crosses of our lives such as traffic congestion, irritating phone calls, and toothaches. Considering the price the martyrs had to pay, let us cease our complaining, looking forward, as they did, to a heaven where their will be no more tears of sorrow or vexation.

Prayer-Meditation

Blessed Agatha Kim, pray for your weaker sisters and brothers, falling under the same or lesser crosses that they may persevere with joy. Through Christ our Lord. Amen.

93 ✠

Blessed Mary Hermina Grivot and Companions
d. 1900[32]

During the Boxer Rebellion in China, many missionary priests and nuns were martyred. The period of evangelization of China began in the middle of the nineteenth century when China opened itself to international relationships, including tolerance of missionaries. But some factions resented imperialistic inroads from the West and took up arms against foreigners of all kinds. During this time some thirty thousand lay Catholics were persecuted as well as their European leaders and native seminarians.

Among these was a group of French, Belgian, and Dutch nuns, Franciscan Missionaries of Mary, ministering to Chinese orphans. When told by the vicar apostolic that they should dress in Chinese clothes in order to escape martyrdom, they insisted that God would give them the strength to witness to the faith just as the men were doing. The superior of the order was Sister Mary Hermina Grivot from France, who had been in China a scant fifteen months when the massacres began. It was her courage that gave strength to the other Sisters, all young, to face martyrdom rather than to hide. Instead they took their orphans off to place them in Christian households. This was unsuccessful, since they were turned back and the children taken away by the soldiers. Finally, with the bishop's absolution, they were taken off to be martyred. The Sisters knelt and sang the *Te Deum*, then their throats were cut. They were beatified in 1946.

In recent times missionary activity has been played down in many Catholic circles. Yet the gospel command to go and baptize all nations has surely not been completed. A Catholic who experiences a deep longing to see all peoples of the world know God's love, expressed in the person of his Son, Jesus Christ, might consider whether she or he is being called to be a missionary religious Sister, priest, brother, or lay missionary. Considering those who have been willing to live and die in far away lands out of love for Christ, we ought at least to support the missions generously.

Prayer-Meditation

Lord, your heart is wide open to embrace all the peoples of the world, created by your Father. May the martyrdom of your missionaries continue to bring down grace for all. Blessed Mary Hermina, pray for all missionaries. Through Christ our Lord. Amen.

94 ✠

Sister Susanna and Companions
d. 1914[33]

S ister Susanna was part of a Third Order Dominican community called the Catherinettes, who wore dark dresses and taught in Seert, Armenia, at the end of the nineteenth century and beginning of the twentieth. Susanna, born in 1854, was sixty years old at the time of the Turkish massacre during World War I.

In 1915 the Turks invaded the town of Seert. Turkey was an ally of Germany, and contributed to the war effort with the infamous holocaust of Armenians. They killed all the men and boys. The women and children fled into the school run by the Sisters. The Turks forced the women and children to march twelve hours a day in the hot desert sun, while the soldiers beat them if they could not keep up.

Sister Susanna collapsed while tending a group of orphan girls from their school. A soldier stripped her and shot her, while she was in prayer.

Others of the Sisters were killed in different circumstances. One Sister survived and lived to see their order formally joined to the Dominican Order. She was Sister Wareina, who, when being bribed to go to the harem of a Muslim in exchange for her life, cried out a Hail Mary and threw herself down a ravine. Later a good Muslim took her in and cared for her along with other Christians. The cause of these witnesses to the faith has been introduced in Rome.

For Your Life

At any time, even in our century, we may be called to heroic witness. We can prepare by meditating each day on the reality of eternity where God himself will reward us for all our sacrifices.

Prayer-Meditation

Through the intercession of the Armenian Christian martyrs, may God give graces of conversion to the Islamic peoples. Through the intercession of these martyrs, may God also protect Christians who face persecution in Islamic countries. Through Christ our Lord. Amen.

95 ✠

Sisters Carmen Moreno and Amparo Carbonell
d. 1936[34]

*T*wo sisters killed in the Spanish Civil War by the Communists have been declared "servants of God" as martyrs and are awaiting official confirmation for their canonization.

Carmen Moreno was born in Villamartin, Spain, in 1885. She made final vows in 1914 in the same order where she received her college education, Daughters of Mary, Help of Christians. Her gifts of intelligence, prudence, and loving kindness were so great, that after some years of teaching elsewhere, she was made superior of a house of the order near Barcelona.

Amparo Carbonell was born in 1893. When her parents refused to accept her vocation, she spent hours before the Blessed Sacrament offering herself to God. She was able to make her vows in 1923. When the revolution resulted in brutal massacres of priests and Sisters, it was decided that the Daughters of Mary, Help of Christians should flee to another country. But Sister Carmen did not want to abandon one of the Sisters who was in a hospital with a fatal illness. Sister Amparo decided to stay with her. They lived in an apartment near the hospital, in spite of the great danger they knew could overtake them. Soon afterwards both Sisters were arrested and executed. It is expected that they will be canonized as martyrs.

For Your Life

In our century countless Christians have been victims of wartime conditions entailing flight or death. Our instinct is to flee and to survive. This is legitimate self-defense. But it takes heroic grace to be willing to risk death in order to remain close to a helpless person who cannot flee. When it comes to a conflict, let us always choose love over survival.

Prayer-Meditation

May the intercession of the martyr-Sisters, Carmen and Amparo, give us courage to face hard choices in our own lives. Through Christ our Lord. Amen.

Part Four

Prophetic Saints

96 ✠

St. Prisca
first century[1]

From Scripture, we know of Prisca, sometimes called Priscilla, the wife of Aquila. Prisca and Aquila were disciples of St. Paul. They traveled fearlessly with him and proclaimed the Word by his side. Acts 18:1-3 tells of Prisca and Aquila coming from Italy to Corinth because all Jews had been exiled from Rome by Claudius. They were, like St. Paul, tentmakers by trade, so it was convenient for Paul to live with them. After following Paul to Ephesus, we see them functioning as evangelists and catechists, instrumental in the conversion of Apollo, from Alexandria. Their house became a church (1 Cor 16:19). Later, they came to Rome where their house was also a church. In his letter to the Romans (16:3) St. Paul salutes and thanks the couple for their great works. It is thought that they died in Asia Minor, though some scholars believe they were martyred in Rome. There is a church of St. Prisca still in Rome.

For Your Life

The prophetic lives of Prisca and Aquila provide us with an early account of couple-ministry, as it is called today. Although this is not possible for all couples due to differences of religion, different degrees of fervor, or simply unrelated callings in ministry, it is always a joy to see a couple with one mind and heart sharing the love of the Lord and, at the same time, their love for each other.

Prayer-Meditation

May the prayers of St. Prisca send graces down to couples who minister together and also to those whose marriages suffer from lack of agreement on matters of faith. Through Christ our Lord. Amen.

97 ✠

St. Helena
d. A.D. 328[2]

Although much of the life of St. Helena may be legendary, there are certain clear facts. Helena was the mother of Emperor Constantine of the third to fourth century. She was proclaimed empress by her son. She spent some time in Rome and then made a pilgrimage to Jerusalem with the plan of building churches at Bethlehem and Olivet. Most probably Helena undertook this at the request of her son who was anxious to venerate the holy places associated with his newly found Savior.

It is almost certain that she directed the excavations during which pieces of wood declared by all Christendom to be the cross of the Lord were found. The place was hard to find since the pagans had concealed these sites. Helena's discovery of the true cross is believed to be miraculous. Three crosses were found on Mount Calvary. To identify which was that of Christ, the bishop, Macarius, suggested applying each to a woman with an incurable disease. When the third one touched her, she arose, completely healed. Thereupon Empress Helena built a church on Mount Calvary for the relic, sending other sections of it to Rome and to Constantinople. After finding the true cross, Helena took some of these pieces away and left others in Jerusalem.

Relics of the true cross can be found in many churches today. Whereas some imagine that this is impossible, considering the tremendous number of accumulated relics, scholars can show that the true cross must have been many times this amount in its size.

Some scholars maintain that Helena was a British princess who embraced Christianity late in life. Her faith is said to have influenced her son, Constantine. In the midst of battle, the still-pagan Constantine thought of his mother's faith and prayed to her God, after which he saw a cross of fire in the sky and words saying, "Through this sign you shall conquer." After winning the battle, Constantine became the first Christian emperor of Rome. Helena is also said to have loved the divine office (now called the liturgy of the hours) and to have ministered to the poor.

For Your Life

In our times there are many who consider all interest in relics to be superstition. They prefer spiritualities where reason replaces claims of faith. Although love of God and neighbor is certainly considered more important than the possession of relics, still Christianity is a religion which respects God's own choice of using material objects as instruments of grace (Acts 19:12). Just as a husband might treasure the wedding ring of his deceased wife, so a Catholic will rejoice to venerate any relics of Jesus or of the saints that are considered by the church to be authentic.

Prayer-Meditation

By your cross, we have been saved. Dear Jesus, give us the zeal of St. Helena in our evangelization so that all men and women in the world may know of your saving work. Let us show our love for your sacrifice by displaying crucifixes and pictures of the cross in our homes and by wearing the cross around our necks as a sign that we belong to you. Through Christ our Lord. Amen.

98 ✠

St. Macrina
fourth century[3]

Macrina was born in Caesarea in Cappadocia, in the early fourth century. She was the daughter of two saints, St. Basil and St. Emmelia, and was the eldest of ten children. She was given a good education, especially in Scripture. When her fiancé died suddenly, she refused to marry and dedicated herself to the education of her younger siblings and to the spiritual inspiration of many of the most renowned theologians and saints of her time.

Her brothers, St. Gregory of Nyssa, Basil the Great, and St. Peter of Sebastea fell under her influence. These were the fathers of the church responsible for the great credal formulations of the faith. According to the account of St. Gregory in a dialogue concerning his holy sister, it was from Macrina that these leaders learned humility, prayer, and love of the Word of God. Later Macrina lived with her mother and other women in an ascetical community. When her mother died, Macrina gave all she had to the poor and lived on her own labors in poverty. Her brother found her eight years later on her deathbed, rejoicing in the prospect of eternal union with Christ. All she had was one garment.

For Your Life

It is sometimes falsely believed that women have little influence in the church. The life of St. Macrina indicates how a woman with prophetic gifts could work for the conversion of the great men of her age whose intellectual gifts might otherwise have led them down false, worldly paths.

St. Macrina, in our church today there are many theologians who lack the holiness of life and vision of the great fathers of the church whom you led to sanctity. Pray for us women that we ourselves may become so holy that the truths of the Holy Spirit may reach others through our ministry. Through Christ our Lord. Amen.

99 ✠

St. Paula
fourth century[4]

Born in A.D. 347 of noble Roman birth, St. Paula was married to a Christian husband and had four daughters and one son. They were a model Roman couple. When widowed at thirty-two, Paula realized she had a great deal of worldliness mixed into her Christian life. Her realization came when St. Marcella, another widow, helped her overcome her extreme grief at the loss of her husband and adopt an austere manner of living.

Impressed by the example of St. Marcella, Paula gave all her wealth to the poor, ate simply, avoided wine, slept on the floor, and renounced all social amusements. Through hospitality offered to holy persons passing through Rome, she became acquainted with St. Jerome, with whom she ministered for the rest of her life, first in Rome and Antioch, and then in Bethlehem. With her daughter, St. Eustochium, Paula built a hospice, a monastery, and a convent. Though living separately, both men and women met for the liturgy of the hours and for Mass.

In her convent, the Sisters lived in simplicity, making their own clothing. They were encouraged to avoid luxury in religious decoration and to give any extra money instead to the poor. They were exhorted to avoid talkativeness. During her time in the Holy Land, St. Paula worked with St. Jerome on his translations of the Bible, since she knew Greek and Hebrew. She is one of the patronesses of both widows and writers.

For Your Life

Grief at the loss of a beloved spouse and fear of widowhood often dominate the emotions of Christian women. Such unhappiness can witness to the beauty of a loving marriage, but can sometimes indicate over-dependency. Married women should pray with confidence that if one day widowed, God will find beautiful works of love for them of his own choosing.

Prayer-Meditation

St. Paula, we ask you to intercede for justice and peace in the war-torn Holy Land. Pray also for all widows and for women scholars, that collaborative ministries may abound for the good of the church and the greater glory of God. Through Christ our Lord. Amen.

100 ✠

St. Catherine of Alexandria
fourth century[5]

Although St. Catherine of Alexandria is usually numbered among early women martyrs, she has been placed here among the prophetic saints because of her role as philosophical defender of the faith. St. Catherine is the patroness of Christian philosophers.

According to tradition, Catherine was born of a noble

family of Alexandria and devoted herself from childhood to study. She was converted by a vision of Our Lady. When the persecution of the church began in Alexandria, Catherine went to rebuke the emperor for his cruelty. Since he could not answer the arguments she raised, he assembled fifty philosophers to refute her. When these sages admitted that she had won the debate, the emperor burned all of them to death. The wisdom of the Holy Spirit coursing prophetically through this woman was absolutely compelling if so many pagan thinkers gave her the victory at such a horrendous price!

When she was put in prison after refusing to become the consort of the same emperor, she managed to aid in the conversion of Faustina, his wife, and another high official, together with her prison guards. As a result, Catherine was sentenced to death by fastening her to a spiked wheel. When her bonds were miraculously broken, the spikes killing bystanders, she was beheaded. For this reason she is also the patroness of wheelwrights. It is said that her body was carried by angels to Mount Sinai where there is a church and monastery built in her honor.

For Your Life

It is commonplace to believe that men are more naturally gifted in thinking and women in feeling. Although this generalization may be accurate, it is also true that many women have keen analytical minds and know how to employ tactics characteristic of Christian apologetics. Women apologists should emulate St. Catherine of Alexandria by relying on the Holy Spirit as a helper in the defense of the faith.

Prayer-Meditation

St. Catherine of Alexandria, great apologist of the faith, intercede for all students, professors, and evangelists that they may find the words not only to defeat the enemies of truth, but also to become instruments of conversions. Through Christ our Lord. Amen.

101 ☒

St. Pulcheria
A.D. 399-454[6]

S t. Pulcheria was an empress of the Byzantine Roman empire at the age of fifteen! She was born in A.D. 399. Her grandfather was Emperor Theodosius the Great. She and her other siblings were orphans. Pulcheria reigned with her brother, but he was more interested in hunting, painting, and calligraphy than in the affairs of the state. So uninterested was he in his office that once Pulcheria teased him by handing him a decree ordering her own death which he signed as usual without reading it!

Pulcheria, on the other hand, was perfectly suited to her great governing task. She was intelligent, efficient, and very pleasant. She was able to read Greek and Latin and was knowledgeable in history, literature, science, and the arts. She founded the University of Constantinople and developed a code of law.

Pulcheria was very devout as well. She tried to teach her brother and sisters the Christian faith and beauty of devotion. As a result of divine grace and Pulcheria's teachings, two of her sisters took vows of virginity. Whenever there was a crisis of state, Pulcheria would pray for divine light and consult the wisest counselors. She was also a peacemaker.

When her brother married, his wife became jealous of Pulcheria's influence at court and exiled her. During this time Pulcheria dedicated herself to prayer and good works. Later Pulcheria was recalled to court when her sister-in-law was banished for sexual misconduct. Subsequently, when her brother died in a hunting accident, Pulcheria again took over, marrying a general called Marcian, on condition that their marriage not be sexually consummated, since she, too, had taken an earlier vow of virginity. The two dedicated themselves to the promotion of religion, notably through the building of Marian churches, and the promotion of the general welfare through low taxes and avoidance of warfare. They were also instrumental in the condemnation of heresies of the time.

For Your Life

Even though it is more usual for God to choose the weak and ignorant to advance his kingdom, he can use someone highly-placed to prove what benefits can come from a Christian, monarchical state. We should support good political initiatives with our time and funds when possible.

Prayer-Meditation

St. Pulcheria, intercede for all who govern our country and other countries throughout the world, that they may be wise and virtuous as you were, through the enlightenment of the Holy Spirit. Through Christ our Lord. Amen.

102 ✠

St. Melania the Younger
d. A.D. 439[7]

Melania was the granddaughter of Melania the Elder of the ruling classes of Rome. She was married against her will to Pinian when she was fourteen. She tried to convince her father that she belonged to Christ and wanted to live in a more austere manner, but her father insisted that, at least outwardly, she act like a married woman of her class. Finally on his deathbed her father repented of having impeded the vocation of his daughter. After that Melania's mother and her husband (Pinian) decided to follow her lead.

They left for the country, and Melania persuaded her husband to lay aside his luxurious garments and wear plain ones that she made herself. After a time about thirty families joined them in their life of piety and charity.

Melania wanted to sell all her property and give the proceeds to the poor. Relatives not part of her community were horrified. They connived in many ways to prevent her from carrying out her plan. Undaunted, Melania appealed to the emperor's mother-in-law, and Honorius took over the property in the name of the state. The moneys were given to the poor, the sick, those bankrupt, pilgrims, captives, churches, and monasteries. In the course of the sale, Melania was able to free eight thousand slaves!

Due to fear of the invading Goths, the family was forced to flee to various lands, including Numidia, where St. Augustine met them and lauded them for their sanctity. While visiting Africa, Melania formed double monasteries for former slaves who had been living on her land. She lived in the women's monastery, transcribing books in Greek and Latin. Finally she settled in Jerusalem to devote herself to contemplation, close to the group surrounding St. Jerome. There, after her husband's death, Melania presided over a convent of consecrated virgins. This astounding woman died at fifty-six in the Holy Land.

For Your Life

Although most readers will not have properties of the immensity of St. Melania to sell and give the proceeds to worthy causes, many of us do have some property and money that could be given to the poor in a regular manner during the prime of life, and in its entirety at retirement or death. It is a necessary matter of discernment to decide in what way the goods God allowed us to earn or accumulate should best be used on earth.

Prayer-Meditation

From the words of St. Ambrose: "The rich man who gives to the poor does not bestow alms but pays a debt."[8]

103 ✠

St. Bridget of Ireland
born c. A.D. 453[9]

One of the most delightful saints of all time is St. Bridget of Ireland, known mostly through tradition and knowledge of the history of the period in which she lived. In fifth century Ireland women were strictly bound to home and hearth. Yet they could own their own property and there were many possible grounds for separation from tyrannical husbands.

The life of women slaves, however, was abysmal. Bridget was the illegitimate child of a male chieftain and a female Christian slave. At an early age, Bridget had to witness her mother being sold. As a child of a free father, she herself was free, but was still made to spend most of her time as a slave girl would, grinding meal and tending the sheep.

Bridget was fearless in her prophetic role in the church and was very concerned about the plight of slave women. Bridget greatly annoyed her father and his wife by giving away whatever she found to poor beggars and lepers. Often the loss was made up by miraculous ways, missing food would be multiplied before Bridget could be punished. Her most spectacular deed involved giving away her father's favorite jeweled sword to a leper as alms, simply because she had nothing else to give! It is said that this act symbolized Bridget's desire to see the Sword of the Spirit replace the sword of war that was tearing apart the country during her times.

An independent lass, Bridget decided to go and visit her mother, still in slavery, in a faraway town. Once arrived, she begged to take the place of her poor, sick mother. Meanwhile her father was plotting to marry off his strong and beautiful daughter for the sake of a good alliance. But Bridget had chosen instead to live as a consecrated virgin. In those days there were no convents, but a girl might make such a vow and live at home, spending her time in prayer and charitable works. Bridget's chosen tasks included making vestments for priests and tapestries for the church. Soon Bridget founded communities for consecrated virgins who wished to leave the households of their parents. To build a convent was quite an enterprise. She needed the permission of the bishops. It appears, however, that unlike some less fortunate prophetic saints who were dismissed as misguided in their inspirations, Bridget always managed to win the bishops over quickly. Some of these convents became double monasteries for men and women. Some became little cities. They were always centers of art and literature.

Although playing a leadership role in her times, she was most humble and unassuming in her hospitality. No sooner did a guest arrive, than Bridget would leave her manual labors in the fields to come and wash their feet and serve them food. Food sometimes miraculously appeared in the larder. At the end of her life she was mostly found milking cows and tending sheep. Yet Bridget was ever merry, having become mother abbess of some thirteen thousand nuns!

For Your Life

There is nothing unusual in our times about children born to unmarried parents. What is wonderful is the way God helped Bridget to overcome this problem by interiorizing the virtues of both parents: taking on her father's boldness and her mother's Christian faith. Her life teaches us also how much good humor and joyfulness can overcome tensions that can exist when a gifted woman is involved in dealing with men in authority.

Prayer-Meditation

St. Bridget of Ireland, we beg you to intercede for your still battle-weary country of Ireland, especially Belfast, Northern Ireland, to help the Irish people come to the way of the Spirit instead of the way of the sword. Pray also, St. Bridget, for all children of unmarried parents that they may receive the nurturing and protection that they need. Through Christ our Lord. Amen.

From a poem of Phillis McGinley:[10]

The Giveaway

St. Bridget was
A problem child.
Although a lass
Demure and mild,
And one who strove
To please her dad,
Saint Bridget drove
the family mad
For here's the fault in Bridget lay:
She would give everything away.
To any soul
Whose luck was out
She'd give her bowl
of stirabout.
She'd give her shawl,
Divide her purse
With one or all,
And what was worse,
when she ran out of things to give
She'd borrow from a relative...
An easy touch
for poor and lowly,
She gave so much
And grew so holy
That when she died
of years and fame,
The countryside
Put on her name,
And still the Isles of Erin fidget
with generous girls named Bride
or Bridget.

104 ✠

St. Clotilda

A.D. 474-545[n]

S t. Clotilda of fifth to sixth century France altered the cen- ter of gravity of history by causing the sceptre of the West to pass into the hands of the church. Born in Lyons, Burgundy, France, Clotilda was the offspring of a pagan knight and a devout Christian princess. She was brought up among bishops and saints who surrounded the court. Her mother taught her to devote herself to prayer and works of mercy. Clotilda's sister became a cloistered nun, but Clotilda, renowned for her beauty, was sought after in marriage and wedded to Clovis, King of the Franks, when she was seven- teen.

Although reluctant to marry a heathen, she thought that this could be a way to exemplify the Scripture, "The unbe- lieving husband is sanctified by the believing wife," (1 Cor 7:14). She was determined to convert her husband. Another motive for the marriage was that a Christian could only marry a non-Christian if the future spouse agreed to baptism and a Christian upbringing for the children. In this way Clotilda might secure a Christian future for her realm.

In spite of such holy purposes, it was an ordeal to be mar- ried by proxy to a man she had never met and to set forth without her mother for the kingdom of Gaul in the ancient Roman city of Soissons. Fortunately, the marriage was a happy one. Clovis not only loved his charming wife but also respected her. Yet Clotilda's life was to be marked by sor- rows that resemble the worst horrors of Shakespeare's his- tory plays. It began with the death of her firstborn son, which the pagans of the court interpreted as a sure sign that her God was not as powerful as theirs. To this insult, Clotilda replied that it was a grace to have a child who would ascend immediately to heaven. It was Clotilda's heroic resignation to this death that was one reason for her husband's decision to become a Christian. More directly, Clovis was on the brink of losing a crucial battle. When his prayers to the heathen gods failed, he prayed to Jesus and vowed to be baptized should he win the victory. His forces won, and he decided to honor Jesus by being most merciful to his opponents. The baptism of Clovis and his followers led France to become the first European country to become wholly Christian.

After the death of Clovis, Clotilda suffered in an excruciating manner from the ferocious deeds of her sons. The realm of a dead king was divided among the sons. This led to intense rivalry. At one point two of the brothers decided to murder grandchildren who would become potential kings, tenderly raised by Clotilda. She was left to bury their bodies after their brutal murder.

In horror, Clotilda left court life and devoted herself to founding monasteries which would become counter-cultural centers for piety and good works. She continued, however, to pray for her sons who later tried to make up for their crimes by supporting Christian endeavors. She also lived to see her beloved, pious daughter be married off to an Arian heretic who eventually battered her daughter to death for her orthodox beliefs. Clotilda died at the age of seventy, much revered by all those whom she had helped during her sad life.

For Your Life

Clotilda's first child died in his crib. At that time such early deaths were expected, but in our time crib-death is unusual and received with terror and misery. Only a firm belief in the immortal destiny of a tiny child can reconcile parents to such a blow. Infant baptism can help parents to realize that their children belong to God first and to them only as trustees. Being in the hands of God is better than being in our own hands. In our times where ecumenical or even interreligious marriages are fast becoming more the rule than the exception, it is important for the Catholic spouse to earnestly, though respectfully and gently, strive for the conversion of his or her spouse. False ecumenism confuses respect for the beliefs of another with indifference to his or her embrace of the full truth. At the same time, one should never force the conversion of one's spouse, since it is ultimately a matter of the individual's personal conscience before God.

Finally, like Clotilda, mothers of violent children should always pray for their ultimate change of heart and repentance.

Prayer-Meditation

From the words of St. Clotilda: "I give thanks to Almighty God that He has not considered me unworthy to be the mother of a child admitted into the celestial kingdom. Having quitted the world in the white robe of his innocence, he will rejoice in the presence of God through all eternity."[12]

105 ✠

St. Bathildis
d. A.D. 680[13]

*B*athildis was an English girl sold as a slave to a mayor in France. When King Clovis II visited this mayor, he fell in love with Bathildis and married her. Their sons successively became kings. She was regent over these sons in their youth, after the death of her husband. Bathildis promoted religion and the release of captives who would otherwise become slaves. She also supported many monasteries, finally herself entering the monastery of Chelles. At her entrance she threw aside all pomp and chose to work at the lowliest of tasks. At the end of her life she suffered from terrible pain which she bore with holy resignation.

For Your Life

The practice of owning slaves, though tolerated by the church as an alternative to killing captives, was by no means the ideal. There are those who claim that because the church allowed slavery and now condemns it, this indicates that key moral teachings of the church can change. Facts reveal the church lauded the freeing of slaves and condemned the stealing of persons as potential slaves and selling them for profit. The lesson is that while the church's pastoral approach to moral and social problems may change with the times, its moral teaching about the dignity and worth of the human person remains the same. This is relevant whether the issue is slavery or abortion and euthanasia today.

Prayer-Meditation

St. Bathildis, we ask you to intercede for those whose dignity is demeaned in our day, especially the unborn, the disabled, and the terminally ill. Through Christ our Lord. Amen.

106 ✠

St. Ludmila
A.D. 860-921[14]

*L*udmila of Bohemia became a Christian when her husband was baptized in A.D. 871 by St. Methodius, the Apostle of the Slavs. They built the first church north of Prague near Borivoj, her husband's castle. An uprising by anti-Christians led to temporary exile in Moravia. When her husband died, Ludmila helped bring up her grandson, Wenceslas, who would himself become a saint, partly resulting from his grandmother's great learning and piety. But his mother Drahomira, who was sympathetic to the anti-Christians, became envious of her mother-in-law's influence over her son. Finally she had two henchmen visit Ludmila and strangle her with her own veil in A.D. 921. She is venerated throughout Czechoslovakia, the present name for Bohemia.

For Your Life

The story of St. Ludmila shows how a prophetic woman in a position of power can spread Christianity. It also shows how the spirit of holiness can be absorbed by grandchildren from grandparents. It is characteristic of all the saints that under pressure they do not give up. They try to evangelize whoever will receive the gospel message, even if it means laying down their own lives.

Prayer-Meditation

St. Ludmila, ask the Lord to help all grandparents whose ministry is challenging because the parents are either not Christians or are not faithful to Christ and his church. Especially pray for grandparents whose grandchildren are being raised in broken homes or dysfunctional families that God would grant them wisdom, discernment, and sensitivity as they minister. Through Christ our Lord. Amen.

107 ✠

St. Cunegunde
d. A.D. 1033[15]

St. Cunegunde was from the tiny country of Luxembourg. Her parents were very holy and she also married a saint, Henry, Duke of Bavaria. In 1013 Henry was made emperor, receiving the crown from Pope Benedict VIII. Cunegunde was also crowned.

Although virtuous, her husband doubted her when she was slandered by some enemies as an adulteress. To prove her purity, the empress walked through fire. Repentant, Henry lived after that in the closest bonds with his wife. Together they founded monasteries and cathedrals.

In one amusing incident, a niece who was placed as abbess of one of these monasteries became more and more lax, so that soon she was first to dinner and last to chapel. In righteous anger, Cunegunde once struck her on the face, and the marks of her fingers remained on the cheek of the unruly abbess for the rest of her life. Far from being angry in return, the niece reformed herself and the whole convent. Eventually Cunegunde herself became a nun, as did so many other empresses, giving up all claims to dignity and working like maids. After her death she was buried next to her husband.

For Your Life

The story of King Henry and Queen Cunegunde reminds us that political power should be subordinate to spiritual power in the way rulers conduct themselves, realizing that all authority is ultimately in God's hands. In our times this is expressed by the interest many world leaders have in obtaining the blessing of the Holy Father and listening to his advice. If a non-Catholic ruler wants to know what the pope thinks, should not all Catholics follow his teachings with avid interest?

Prayer-Meditation

Through the prayers of St. Cunegunde, may all rulers be used by God, knowingly or unknowingly, to advance his kingdom. Through Christ our Lord. Amen.

108 ✠

St. Margaret of Scotland
1045-1093 [16]

Margaret was an English girl who longed for the cloister but obeyed the wishes of her mother. She agreed to marry Malcolm, king of Scotland. After her wedding, her mother and sister entered convents, and Margaret was left alone with Malcolm, a rough, illiterate warrior. Because he loved Margaret so much, Malcolm allowed her to influence him in the direction of culture and virtue. Together the couple applied themselves to making their subjects happy, just, and educated. Margaret undertook, as well, the reform of the law courts so that cases for the poor would be processed quickly. She also forbade royal soldiers to loot Scottish homes and ransomed slaves Malcolm had won in battle. She insisted on a sabbath in the land, free from buying and selling.

Margaret also initiated grace after each meal and founded several churches. Indefatigable, Margaret organized synods to deal with laxity. She invited women of the court to spend their leisure embroidering vestments and altar linens. Margaret, though forceful, was joyful and never angry. She was given to prayer and penance and also devoted herself to alms for the poor, tending the sick and hospices for travelers. She had eight children whom she instructed in the faith. All of these children were later known for their virtues. Margaret died in 1093, four days after the death in battle of her beloved husband. She was canonized in 1250.

For Your Life

St. Margaret seems to exemplify the maxim, "Where there is a will, there is a way." Nothing seemed too difficult for her to tackle, from eight children, to revision of the laws of Scotland, to the running of synods. Not all women are called to such works; some are sanctified more by being loving presences in their own homes. Others, however, may have more energy for many good works if they place God first and dedicate more of their time to his service.

Prayer-Meditation

From an early life of St. Margaret: "The Queen united so much strictness with her sweetness of temper, so pleasant was she even in her severity, that all who waited upon her, men as well as women, loved her while they feared her, and in fearing loved her."[17]

109 ✠

St. Hildegarde
1098-1179[18]

St. Hildegarde was an outstanding woman, combining mystical gifts with scholarship, abilities in the fields of poetry, medicine (herbal), music, and politics. She wrote books of mysticism but also of natural history and medicine, including diagnosis of psychological disorders. She was also considered a prophetess.

Hildegarde was born in 1098 in Germany. At eight she was given over to the care of Blessed Jutta, a recluse. Hildegarde followed her mentor and other women as they founded a Benedictine convent. For many years, her life was outwardly uneventful, though she grew in mystical graces, especially prophecy of future events. When Blessed Jutta died, Hildegarde became the prioress. Weak of health, she was great of mind, with unquenchable energy. Eventually her visions came to the attention of papal commissions who approved them as genuine and said they should be published. In keeping with the details of a vision, she would build her own monastery at Rupertsberg. Hildegarde also wrote letters to popes, emperors, bishops, abbots, and kings, full of prophecy and revelation, usually warning of disasters to follow the laxity of the clergy. Of great beauty are her writings about God as light, the living Light. These are full of joy and refreshment for the soul. Hildegarde died in 1179, and many miracles were attributed to her intercession.

For Your Life

The gift of prophecy did not end with the Old Testament prophets nor with John the Baptist, nor with St. Hildegarde. Although all prophecies must be tested, we should not despise them as worthless, especially if they rebuke us for our failings.

Prayer-Meditation

From the writings of St. Hildegarde found in *Mystics of the Church*: "From my infancy until now, in the seventieth year of my age, my soul has always beheld this Light; and in it my soul soars to the summit of the firmament and into a different air.... The brightness which I see is not limited by space and is more brilliant than the radiance around the Sun.... Sometimes when I see it, all sadness and pain is lifted from me, and I seem a simple girl again, and an old woman no more."[19]

110 ✠

St. Elizabeth of Schönau
d. 1164[20]

Elizabeth entered the convent at twelve. Although suffering from illness, she practiced austerities and mortifications in order to feel the arrows of Christ in her own body. She was given to all kinds of beautiful, celestial visions, diabolical persecutions, and prophecies, especially in the form of a series of calamities that would come to the people unless they did penance. When some of these prophecies were seemingly not fulfilled, an angel told Elizabeth that her penances had averted the disasters predicted.

In her prayer life she often could visualize the scenes of the life of Christ as if enacted in front of her. Her brother later published the accounts of these visions. The most famous of these books is called *The Book of the Ways of God*. It is replete with threats against sinful clergy, lay people, and especially those who belong to false sects. In the last seven years of her life she became the superior under her brother who was abbot of the double community where they lived.

For Your Life

In can be a wonderful thing when a brother and sister collaborate together on writings and governance. As an analogy, many today in covenant communities, and some other lay apostolates, speak of their community members as brothers and sisters, trying to emulate that kind of closeness of mind, heart, and will.

Prayer-Meditation

By the prayers of St. Elizabeth of Schönau may more and more Christians be immersed in the scriptural accounts of

the life of the Lord and learn to love him passionately for redeeming us. Through Christ our Lord. Amen.

111 ✠

Blessed Agnes of Bohemia
1205-1282[21]

The story of Blessed Agnes reads like a sacred soap
opera! It begins with royal flourish. Agnes was the
daughter of Ottokar I, the king of Bohemia; her mother was
the sister of the king of Hungary. She also was the first
cousin of St. Elizabeth of Hungary.

At age three Agnes was sent under the care of a nurse to a
monastery near the home of her betrothed, Boleslaus, a future duke of Silesia, whose mother was St. Hedwig. Here
Agnes was taught by the abbess to love the faith. When the
child was only six, her fiancé died. She returned to Bohemia,
only to be betrothed to Henry, the son of Emperor Frederick
II, and was shipped off at the age of nine to the Austrian
court to learn German. Court life held no charms for Agnes
who wanted to be a virgin of Christ and spent her time in
fasting and mortification. Imagine her joy when a Duke of
Austria wanted the prince to marry his daughter and succeeded in his plot. Back home again, she had to face an offer
from Frederick II himself, the emperor, who had recently
been widowed. In horror Agnes increased her penances,
wearing a hair shirt under her royal robes. She got up before
dawn, dressing in plain clothing and going the rounds of the
churches. When she was twenty-eight, her father insisted
that she go to Germany and marry the emperor. Agnes
begged for time, during which she wrote to the pope begging him to let her follow her true vocation. Finally King

Wenceslaus decided to discuss the matter with the emperor himself who responded with these words: "If she had left me for a mortal man, I should have made my vengeance felt; but I cannot take offense if she prefers the King of Heaven to myself."[22]

On hearing this good news, Agnes started her religious life by first building a monastery for Franciscan friars, then endowing a hospital for the poor, and also the first convent in Hungary for Poor Clares. So great was the power of the Holy Spirit within her that the workmen building these edifices wanted to volunteer their services to the glory of God. To avoid Agnes' insistence on giving them their wages, they would leave work early in the evening before their pay was to be given to them!

In 1236 Agnes herself entered the Poor Clares and was joined by one hundred girls who wished to follow her, most of them of noble families. Once in an enclosed monastery, Agnes insisted on doing menial work herself. St. Clare herself the founder of the Poor Clares, was still alive during the time of Agnes and called Blessed Agnes her half-self. Agnes lived to the age of seventy-seven.

For Your Life

The drama of Blessed Agnes surely illustrates the merits of assertiveness when combined with inspiration by the Holy Spirit. In some cases, a woman is called upon to submit to legitimate authority even against her own inclinations, but sometimes God himself calls her to assert herself in the face of opposition.

Prayer-Meditation

May Blessed Agnes of Bohemia intercede for all those women whom the Holy Spirit is leading into bold initiatives for his glory, that they may overcome opposition and remain determined until his will is accomplished. Through Christ our Lord. Amen.

112 ✠

St. Birgitta of Sweden
1303-1373[23]

In 1303 there was born to a noble family in Finsta, Sweden, a seventh child, Birgitta. Both parents were devout and taught their children to pray and to love the Lord. One evening when Birgitta was eleven years old, she heard a sermon on the passion preached by a Dominican friar. That night while she was in prayer, the room was filled with light, and Christ appeared to Birgitta, pointing to his five wounds and claiming that these were made by all who forgot him and despised his love. Birgitta felt as if "the beak of a large bird plunged into my own heart."

The young girl was never to forget this vision as she grew in grace, beauty, and learning. She suggested that the Bible be translated into Swedish. Although she wanted to become a nun, she willingly obeyed her parents and married Prince Ulf of Nericia at the age of fourteen. She was very happily married and loved her husband dearly. They had eight children. She instructed the children in Christian life. She brought them to the hospital she had built and showed them that there was no shame or disgust in tending the wounds of the poor, feeding them, and washing their feet. Birgitta continually worked for justice. While outwardly living the courtly life in heavy brocade dresses and other fashionable clothing, underneath she wore a hair shirt.

Since the court become more and more corrupt, Birgitta exercised a prophetic ministry in constantly calling the other noblemen and women to task for their worldliness. During this time, Christ appeared to Birgitta and ordered her to found a double monastery of nuns and monks, headed by an abbess, at Vadstena. This was called the Order of the Holy

Savior. The nuns were ascetic and contemplative, and the priests had an active apostolic vocation.

On pilgrimages with her husband she felt a great yearning to devote herself to God alone, but God instructed her that even after her husband's death, her place was to return to the court and try to convert her relatives and friends. During this time there are more than two hundred miracles recorded of healing and of sending the devil away from sinners and converting them.

Birgitta prophesied in the name of Christ against the murder, looting, rape, and others sins of the Swedes. When the Black Death occurred, the king begged the people to repent, but they refused.

At this point Christ came to Birgitta and told her that she must journey to Rome to reconcile the pope in Avignon with the emperor. Living in Rome and constantly praying in the pilgrim churches, her prophetic revelations became quite well-known and greatly influenced history. She lived to see the emperor, Charles IV, accompany Pope Urban back to Rome from France.

Among the evils that greatly concerned St. Birgitta were slavery and abortion. About abortion she wrote (Revelations VII, 27): "Some women behave like harlots; when they feel the life of the child in their wombs, they induce herbs or other means to cause miscarriage, only to perpetuate their amusement and unchastity." Once the archbishop of Naples, where she was very influential, assembled all the leaders and doctors of theology to hear her proclaim God's Word.

On pilgrimage to the Holy Land, she received many revelations from the Virgin Mary such as the truth about the Immaculate Conception and the Assumption. Her visions of the mysteries of the faith have greatly influenced Catholic art, music, and literature. Followers of St. Birgitta often distribute popular devotions based on her revelations. They are also active in ecumenical concerns since they are impressed by a prophecy of St. Birgitta "that the time will come when there shall be one flock and one Shepherd, one faith and one clear knowledge of God" (Revelations VI, 77). Because of her founding of a university, Birgitta is also considered the patroness of scholars.

For Your Life

It is false to think that women have no influence in the church. In every century there are many women, including family women like St. Birgitta, with great prophetic gifts. They greatly inspire the laity, clergy, and religious women and men to fidelity to Christ, though they are not called to clerical ranks. Certainly Mother Teresa of Calcutta is one such woman in our own day, especially in her prophetic stance against the materialism and arrogance so indicative of Western society today.

Prayer-Meditation

From the writings of St. Birgitta: "The world would have peace if men of politics would only follow the Gospels."[24]

113 ✠

Blessed Jeanne Marie de Maillé
1332-1414[25]

Jeanne Marie was the daughter of a baron who lived in Touraine, France, in the fourteenth century. Her father died when she was still young and she married Robert, Baron of Sille, though she had wished to remain a virgin. Before their marriage they agreed to live together as brother and sister, an arrangement called a Josephite marriage. Their life together was blessed by great love for each other and for piety and virtue. There home was a hospice for the poor. They adopted three orphans. At one point Robert was taken prisoner in battle. When he returned, they extended their ministry to the ransom of captives.

When Robert died in 1362, his relatives were bitterly angry at Jeanne for depleting the family fortune in works of charity. They forced her out of her home. Eventually she went to live in a small house near the church of St. Martin at Tours. There she devoted herself to prayer and the care of the sick and poor as a Third Order Franciscan. She was insulted and mocked by those who thought she was eccentric, even to the point of being wounded by a stone thrown at her back, a wound that lasted all her life.

When her husband's family repented and gave her a château to live in, she turned it over to the Carthusians and renounced all. She lived in huts and dog kennels! Toward the end of her life, a Duke recognized her holiness and chose her to be godmother and teacher of his son. She also taught all the neighborhood children. Once at her request the king liberated all the prisoners at Tours. She died in 1414.

For Your Life

Many times Christians who are aiming for holiness are mocked by family and neighbors. This is part of the cross of those with a prophetic counter-cultural stance. However, later repentance by these scoffers indicates a secret admiration for the very saints they persecuted. We are called to bear up under such demeaning insults, calling to mind that "they know not what they do."

Prayer-Meditation

Blessed Jeanne Marie, help us to follow the Holy Spirit with true discernment regardless of the opinions of others. Through Christ our Lord. Amen.

114 ✠

St. Catherine of Siena
1347-1380[26]

Practically everything in the life of St. Catherine of Siena was incredible. Even her birth was remarkable since she was the twenty-fourth child, one of a twin birth where the other baby died immediately. Her mother, the wife of a local dyer, was so saddened by this loss that she hastened to insure a replacement!

As a little girl Catherine was lively, stubborn, and direct. Unlike many of the saints, she was never considered beautiful. Her adoring biographer and spiritual son, Blessed Raymond of Capua, remarks that she was never anything much to look at, and later, at the time when she ate nothing but the Eucharist, she was nothing more than "a bag of bones." Nonetheless she was so charming, everyone loved her. At age six she was gifted with a miraculous grace that would shape the rest of her life. She had been running an errand and paused for a moment to look across the valley. In the sky she suddenly saw a vision of heaven, of the Savior with Peter, Paul, and John the Evangelist. The Lord smiled on her with great love and made the sign of the cross over her head.

This vision and subsequent ones led her to want to devote herself to God as a virgin. When her parents tried to marry her off in a way beneficial to the family's financial needs, Catherine cut off her hair. Catherine's parents decided to punish her by putting her in charge of all the housework. This only inspired Catherine to make a cell of her own heart and to render menial service with such diligence that all were amazed. Finally her parents relented, surmising that it would be stupid of them to try to find a bridegroom more wonderful than Christ himself.

After a three-year period of solitude in her little room in the midst of the bustling household, she was told by Jesus that he wanted to send her out into the world to save souls. She was twenty-one. To facilitate his plan, he personally taught her how to read. At this time she was also less and less able to eat and lived mostly on the Eucharist. His union with her was sealed by what is called the mystical marriage.

In the beginning, Catherine's outside activities took the form mostly of ministry to the sick, to plague victims, and to criminals. In one dramatic instance she had persuaded a political prisoner to return to the sacraments before his death and promised that she would come right to the guillotine with him and comfort him as the ax was falling. She held his severed head in her hands afterwards and meditated long on the blood of the prisoner and the redeeming blood of the Savior. Afterwards in a vision she saw the soul of the young man entering the wounded side of Christ, full of mercy.

Gradually a family of priests and lay people began to surround her. She would read their hearts and bring them to confess their sins. After she became a Third Order Dominican and came under the direction of Raymond of Capua, her activities spread as she began to understand more about church politics. It was the time of disputes about the papacy, with the pope living in Avignon, and Catherine prophetically urged the pope to return to Rome. She also traveled to Avignon to plead with the pope further, in her conviction that the church could only be reformed by the Holy Father himself being in Rome. She also began to preach openly with great zeal.

Not everyone drank in every word of Catherine with loving obedience. Many mocked her openly. By the end of her life, she was filled with a sense of the failure of all her initiatives.

In 1377 she began to write and dictate the locutions of the Lord to her. This book, dictated to many priestly secretaries, is called *The Dialogue*, and is one of the reasons why

Catherine has been given the title of doctor of the church. The theme of many of these dialogues is the great mercy of God for all, even the most desperate of sinners. In 1378 Catherine went to Rome with an entourage of some twenty-four disciples to try to help Pope Urban overcome the Papal Schism, when there were two false popes opposing him and dividing all of Western Christiandom into rival camps. Sometimes Roman friends would take care of the group, but when there was no food, Catherine herself went out to beg. In Rome, Catherine spent her days at St. Peter's Church praying for unity and church reform and speaking to the pope and the cardinals. She died in 1380 and is one of the most popular of all prophetic women saints.

For Your Life

When Catherine objected to Jesus that as a woman she could not preach and mingle with men in the world, the Lord told her he was sovereign in his graces. As we see in the case of St. Catherine, men and women alike will listen to a woman if she teaches what the Holy Spirit wishes to be heard. Women of the Spirit, when they have genuine prophetic gifts, should not fear disapproval by men or by other women. When it comes to truth, only what the Holy Spirit says counts.

Prayer-Meditation

From Catherine's writings: "O lovely compassion... you are the balm that snuffs out rage and cruelty in the soul. This compassion, compassionate Father, I beg you to give to all."[27] "Not by... violence will she (the church) regain her beauty but through peace and through the constant and humble prayers and sweat and tears poured out by my servants with eager desire."[28]

115 ✠

St. Joan of Arc
1412-1431[29]

Joan of Arc, famous among all Christians and non-Christians for her unique place in European history, was brought up like any other peasant girl in Domrémy, France. She did not learn how to read or write, but was able to recite the Creed, the Our Father, and the Rosary, and to practice the feminine arts of sewing and spinning. All the village loved her for her gentleness and piety.

Joan was an obedient child and gave her parents no cause for alarm until the famous vision when she was thirteen. She was instructed to help restore the weak, hopeless, pleasure-loving Dauphin Charles VII to assume his rightful throne against the allied forces of the English and the Burgundians. Voices that she thought were those of St. Michael the Archangel, St. Catherine, and St. Margaret came to her insistently, demanding that she go to the dauphin and encourage him to enter the battle seriously.

It was during her first journey to the dauphin that she adopted male dress, not in order to look masculine, but to protect her virginity against the lusts of the soldiers she would encounter. She gained credence when she identified the dauphin who was disguised. By means of her supernatural knowledge, she was able to convince the dauphin that her mission was from God. She then asked to be equipped with soldiers to lead the battle, her standard bearing the words, "Jesus, Maria." Her first battle turned the tide of war in favor of France. Charles was afterwards solemnly crowned to the great joy of Joan and the people.

Later, however, she lost battles because of the lack of support of the king. Finally she was captured by the Burgundian allies of the English, who sold her to the English. Her enemies trumped up an ecclesial trial claiming that she was a sorceress and a heretic. She defended herself courageously, but the judgment of the court was that her revelations were from the devil, not from God. She was burned at the stake by the secular authorities, commending her soul to Jesus. One of the English dignitaries after witnessing her holy death, cried out, "We are lost: we have burned a saint!" Later her mother and brothers insisted on a review of the case and she was totally exonerated. She was canonized in 1920.

For Your Life

Are we willing to live and die for the unique inner voice of our conscience—when it has been properly formed by Christ and his church—or do we prefer to win in the world by silent complicity with evil?

Prayer-Meditation

From the records of St. Joan of Arc's words: "Alas that I should be treated so horribly and cruelly that my entire body, which has never known impurity, should today be consumed and reduced to ashes. I would rather be decapitated seven times over than be thus burned. Before God, the great judge, I appeal against the great wrongs and injustices done to me."[30]

116 ✠

St. Colette
d. 1447[31]

*T*he father of Colette was a carpenter in a monastery of France. Colette was a charming little girl, lovely, but so tiny there was fear for her survival. Seeing how religious she was, her parents left Colette free to occupy herself with prayer and housework. When Colette was seventeen, her parents died. She was put under the care of the abbot. She entered the third order of St. Francis and lived in a hermitage next to the church of Corbie. Many visitors were attracted to her because of her holiness. For three years she hid herself, longing for silence.

During this time she had a vision in which St. Francis told her to reform the Poor Clares who had fallen off their original strictness. By church authorities, Colette was given the power to reform already existing Poor Clare monasteries and also to found new ones.

When the saint began to make the rounds of convents in France and Belgium, she was opposed as a fanatic and a sorceress. She persevered with great patience and joy, and finally began to make headway in various monasteries with her reforms and to found some seventeen new houses of Poor Clare observance. Even royalty benefitted by meeting her. Animals and birds surrounded her as they had St. Francis.

Colette's many activities were sustained by a deep prayer life. Fridays from six in the morning to six in the evening she meditated on the passion. During Holy Week her whole body radiated supernatural light. She died at sixty-seven while praying for sinners to be converted. She was canonized in 1807.

For Your Life

Many Catholics, lay and religious, work for institutions that have fallen off from the original zeal of their founders. It takes much discernment in prayer to see what initiatives for reform can be implemented and which good ideas have to wait for more propitious circumstances. The example of the joy and patience of St. Colette can help us realize how important those two gifts are for success.

Prayer-Meditation

May the intercession of St. Colette result in an outpouring of grace for the whole Franciscan family. May she also pray for the renewal of other orders in the church, especially those that are in a state of confusion and uncertainty about their mission. Through Christ our Lord. Amen.

117 ✠

St. Teresa of Avila
1515-1582[32]

Along with St. Catherine of Siena, St. Teresa of Avila is the other of two holy women proclaimed as doctors of the church. The writings of this famous Carmelite nun are among the most seminal, in spite of the fact that she was not a highly educated woman, being taught more by the Holy Spirit than by the academy.

Teresa was the third daughter of a large upper class Spanish family. She had spurts of piety but was also rather wild. She was sent away to a convent school after the death of her mother, most likely because it was thought that her flirtateous tendencies could get her into trouble. In fact, this vivacious, charming, young woman was not at all inclined to religious life, but thought it to be at least better than being a wife and mother. The duties related to these latter vocations seemed burdensome to her, after watching the miseries of her own mother.

Once in the Carmelite convent, Teresa began a long double life. On the one hand, she was attracted to chatting with the guests in the parlor, and on the other, the Lord himself was leading her into deep, contemplative prayer. Twenty years of visions, locutions, and raptures were necessary before she was willing to break with her desire for constant human fellowship and seek greater seclusion. At one point she was thought to be dying. They had already sealed her eyes with wax when she suddenly recovered. Asked what it was like to die, she replied with the famous words: "Death is ecstasy."

Most of the convents and monasteries of her time suffered from worldliness, for many monastics joined them not because they were led so in prayer but because they didn't wish to live within their families or start their own. With the help of St. John of the Cross, Teresa was led through supernatural visions and locutions to found a large number of more contemplatively-oriented, reformed Carmelite convents and monasteries. This entailed all sorts of vexatious journeys and business transactions, all of which she accomplished by means of constant direction from the Lord himself, who appeared to her often. In the course of her life, she did not become a reclusive hermit but was able to minister to many nuns, priests, and lay people because they were attracted first by her lively personality.

We know best of the character of St. Teresa from her writings, especially her own autobiography, *The Interior Castle*, and *The Way of Perfection*. Her spiritual counsel is most helpful because of the utter naturalness and humor of her style, the open acknowledgment of her own difficulties, and the wisdom, not overladen with scholarship, which seemed to be spoken in her heart by the Holy Spirit.

Teresa died in 1582 after one of the longest and most fruitful lives in the history of spirituality. Because of the terrible headaches from which she suffered, Teresa is considered the patroness of sufferers from headaches.

For Your Life

Many women, like St. Teresa before her definitive conversion, enjoy chattering, gossiping, and being too much involved in the business of others. We admire women who seem more recollected and serious, but many of us easily find ourselves addicted to the emotional satisfactions of idle talk. The story of St. Teresa can make us realize that spending good parts of the day in silence and prayer will not destroy our natural vivaciousness, but only channel it so that our interest in others will be purified in the love of Christ.

Prayer-Meditation

From the writings of St. Teresa: "I had a serious fault, which led me into great trouble. It was that if I began to realize that a person liked me, and I took to him myself, I would grow so fond of him that my memory would feel compelled to revert to him and I would always be thinking of him, without intentionally giving any offense to God.... This was such a harmful thing that it was ruining my soul. But when once I had seen the great beauty of the Lord (in a vision) I saw no one who by comparison with Him seemed acceptable to me on whom my thoughts wished to dwell.... And, unless for my sins the Lord allows this memory to fade, I consider it impossible for me to be so deeply absorbed in anything that I do not regain my freedom when I turn once more in thought, even for a moment, to this Lord."[33]

118 ✠

Mary Ward
1585-1645[34]

Mary was the eldest daughter of devout Yorkshire English Catholics who sheltered priests in their homes during the persecution of Catholics at the height of the Protestant Reformation in England in the 1600s. They also paid heavy fines for not attending the Anglican Church services. Little Mary's first word was "Jesus." She was drawn to the secret Masses to which priests came at risk of their lives. How dramatic it was for her to be awakened in the night and told that the priest would come and hear confessions before Mass at five in the morning!

Mary longed to become a martyr as had so many of her relatives and friends, but finally she decided that she could express her single-minded love for God by entering a convent. Alas, convents did not exist in England since they had been outlawed. Mary reluctantly decided that she must leave her family and her beloved England and seek out a religious community on the Continent. She faced many difficulties from that time onward.

After some false starts, she was led to the idea of starting an institute of English women, like herself, privately vowed to poverty, chastity, and obedience. These women would start schools for English girls to transmit the Catholic faith, if possible, in England. However, the women of her proposed order were mocked as galloping girls and apostolic shrews. Detractors predicted they would give up when difficulties arose because of their perceived weakness as women. Mary responded by insisting that it is not because women are women that they fail to persevere, but because they are imperfect women who with God's grace could be as strong as Christian men and yet remain fully feminine.

Subsequently, the English women who joined Mary were of such excellent character and splendid educators that princes throughout Europe in Italy, Austria, and Germany begged them to come and set up schools for their girls as well. The story of how the enemies of Mary Ward managed to defame her character and eventually have the order temporarily banned is heart-rending. She herself was declared for some six months to be a heretic. However, this plucky, but always tender, English woman refused to show the slightest anger at her persecutors. It was said that it was better to be her enemy than her friend, so much time did she spend praying for her enemies.

There are some humorous touches revealing how creative an apostolic worker Mary was. Since in England it was not allowable to wear the widows' outfits members of the Institute wore in Europe, Mary took advantage of wearing secular clothing to mingle with the rich young people of London. Attracted by her beauty, several young men were brought back to the Catholic faith. This was reported by her enemies as a sign that she herself was worldly, frivolous, and a spendthrift. Another time, being told that a certain old dowager who had converted to Protestantism would never meet and speak to the famous Mary Ward, she dressed herself up as a serving girl and got a job as a maid in this same woman's house. She gradually engaged her in conversation until the woman finally came back to the Catholic faith.

In 1703, more than fifty years after her death, her pioneering Institute of the Blessed Virgin Mary for nonenclosed women to serve the church was approved by Rome. Her cause has been introduced in Rome for canonization.

For Your Life

Like Mary Ward, we should be eager to follow the leadings of the Holy Spirit, confident that even when we meet with failure, God's will can be victorious.

Prayer-Meditation

From the writings of Mary Ward: "If in your work anyone gives you trouble, meet him with friendly words. In this way you will soften both yourselves and him."[35]

119 ✠

Venerable Marguerite Bourgeoys
1620-1700[36]

M arguerite Bourgeoys, foundress of the Congregation of Notre Dame de Montreal, was born in Troyes, France, to the family of a tradesman with five children. As a child, she was exceptionally pious and good, as well as being extremely joyful. She soon became the teacher of other little girls who would sit in a sewing circle listening to Marguerite talk of the truths of the faith. Marguerite's mother died when she was but twelve years old. Her father entrusted to her the care and teaching of the younger children. Her only "sin" was a longing for fancy clothing, which was banished after a vision of Our Lady smiling at her tenderly. This experience confirmed little Marguerite in the desire to live a life of service to God.

As a young girl she entered an organization for youth devoted to Mary. She wanted to enter the Carmelites or the Poor Clares but was refused by both orders. Perhaps they sensed an active life was more suited to her gifts. Soon afterwards she would be chosen to collaborate in a heroic venture of a great layman, De Maisonneuve, who wanted to go to the wilds of Canada under the patronage of Our Lady to found a colony at Montreal for the sake of converting the Iroquois. Marguerite had a supernatural dream about De Maisonneuve as the one with whom she would pursue a work for God's glory. Seeing her great virtues of strength and courage, he asked her to come with the missionaries to open a school for children, mostly Indian converts.

Even though it would mean a journey that was perilous and required learning another language, as well as risking martyrdom at the hands of the Iroquois, Marguerite readily agreed, upon receiving her confessor's approval. He also advised her to overcome any fear of going off without women companions on the basis that God would protect her, since it was his will for her to go. This advice was confirmed by a vision of Our Lady.

Marguerite left on her journey after signing away her inheritance, with only a tiny bundle of clothing, thinking that course best suited to following Christ. Many were the trials that awaited her: the rejection of her relatives in France, a frightening sea voyage, death threats from Iroquois, poverty, fire, long journeys on foot in the snow, and rejection by the authorities to her idea of founding a nonenclosed teaching order. Yet she persevered and evangelized sailors, soldiers, and children everywhere she turned. Ultimately she founded an order called the Congregation of Notre Dame responsible for the teaching and evangelization of young women.

For Your Life

Venerable Marguerite Bourgeoys teaches us to live simply on Providence rather than weighing ourselves down with worldly possessions. She can show women of apostolic zeal not to fear working in situations where they are a minority among men, since she considered the company and imitation of Our Lady to be the greatest protection against all dangers.

Prayer-Meditation

From the words of her biographer, commenting on Marguerite's early longing to be a cloistered Carmelite: "The Holy Ghost often breathes such ineffectual yearnings in the souls of those whom he destines to a life of great activity, in order that they may be rooted and confirmed in prayerful union with Him and thus ever persevere, amid the cares and distractions of their busy lives, the deepest interior recollection."[37]

120 ✠

Catherine Jarrige
1754-1836[38]

We associate hiding of priests mostly with the persecution of the Roman Catholic church in England and in Asia. But the heroic tale of Catherine Jarrige occurred during the French Revolution.

Catherine was born near Mauriac, France, in 1754. She was the youngest of seven, and spent her time doing farm-work and dancing at festivals. At twenty-two she entered the third order of St. Dominic, and devoted the time free from her work at lace-making to ministry to the poor and the sick.

When the persecution of priests began during the Reign of Terror of the French Revolution, Catherine set up an underground for escaping priests. Gifted with superb cleverness, Catherine worked out successful plans for hiding priests in the most unusual ways. For example, one hide-out was in the forest in places used by robbers to conceal themselves. To these huts Catherine brought food, forged papers, and babies in need of baptism, as well as Catholics needing confession. In her region, there was not a single baby unbaptized or anyone who died without the sacraments. In another situation she decked out the priests as revolutionaries and got them drunk so that they could not talk. When confronted by a revolutionary leader on their path, Catherine cursed him out like a fishwife until he let them pass.

In one case Catherine went to the guillotine to comfort a captured priest. Afterwards a blind man and a blind baby were miraculously healed in the blood of this martyr. When the executioner saw these supernatural signs, he repented, screaming out, "I am lost, I have killed a saint, I am lost!"[39]

When the revolution ended, this plucky saint did not stop her work but entered into prison-ministry and hospital work. At eighty-two Catherine died, surrounded by her friends. Her cause was introduced in Rome in 1949.

For Your Life

The tale of Catherine Jarrige illustrates the way God can use natural ingenuity and cleverness for the sake of the kingdom. Sometimes those striving for holiness belittle their natural gifts, thinking only supernatural ones count. God wants to use our nature to the best advantage. After all, he created us the way we are. Instead of pining away for gifts given to others, we need to see how our own gifts can be transformed in Christ to work always for good instead of evil.

Prayer-Meditation

May Catherine Jarrige be present at the executions of all modern martyrs, to sustain them on their holy journey home. Through Christ our Lord. Amen.

121 ✠

Blessed Anna Maria Taigi
1769-1837[40]

When six years old, Anna Maria Taigi moved with her parents to Rome where they worked as domestics. This was a fall from her father's previous occupation as a pharmacist. He took out his bitterness over their poverty on little Anna Maria. When she was old enough, Anna Maria joined her parents as a servant at the palace. Here she was flattered for her beauty and came to spend more and more time before the mirror. She was considered to have all the wiles of a budding coquette.

Anna Maria was married to a porter, Domenico Taigi, at age twenty. Although he was a rough, ill-tempered, and sometimes violent man, Anna Maria loved him dearly and was happy that she had married him. For awhile after her marriage, she indulged in jewelry and pretty clothing, but after her conversion she wore the plainest clothes with her husband's permission.[41]

Once, while taking care of one of her seven children, Anna Maria had a vision which remained all her life. She saw a luminous circle above her and before her, in which she could see present and future events all over the world. She saw the spiritual states of people she met as well as the destiny of those who died. She also saw scenes from the life of Christ and answers to theological dilemmas. She also was gifted with miracles of healing and reading of hearts.

In spite of these spectacular visions and gifts, Anna Maria was always faithful to her duties as wife and mother. Her parents lived with them, and her mother picked quarrels with Anna Maria's irascible husband. The saint, however, was always patient and peaceful in the midst of this tumult.

This porter's wife became so famous for prophecy, she was consulted by Pope Leo XII, Pope Gregory XVI, Napoleon's mother, and St. Vincent Pallotti, to mention just a few.[42] When her husband would arrive, if the house was full of such people, she would leave them and tend to his needs first.

Holy Mass and prayer were at the center of her life. She made sure the family prayed in the mornings and said the Rosary after dinner, as well as singing hymns and reading the lives of the saints. She stayed up all night making clothing for sale, then went to early Mass. Anna Maria Taigi died surrounded by her large family in 1837. Her husband was able at age ninety-two to testify to her virtues, crowned by miracles after her death. She was beatified in 1920 and is a protectress of mothers.

The life of Anna Maria Taigi illustrates the way God can make a prophet out of anyone, for her early youth gave no indication of the splendid graces to come. This blessed one did not use her gifts as a reason to neglect her family but instead beautifully integrated her home life with her public witness.

Prayer-Meditation

Blessed Anna Maria Taigi, intercede for all mothers who have spiritual gifts that they may, like you, be able to balance home duties with special calls of the Holy Spirit in ministry to the church and the world. Also help Christian adults who live with their parents to be as patient and gentle as you were. Through Christ our Lord. Amen.

122 ✠

Venerable Pauline-Marie Jaricot
1799-1862[43]

*P*auline-Marie was a very happy child, the youngest of seven children of a family of silk manufacturers in Lyons, France. She was a pretty girl and became a popular figure in society. At fifteen Pauline fell and had a paralyzing accident. It took her a year to recover, but afterwards she returned to the balls, always in the latest fashion. It was a sermon by a priest about the vanity of women's dress that began to change Pauline-Marie. She sought out the same priest as a spiritual director and soon spent her mornings not dressing herself but dressing the wounds of the incurably sick. She prayed to love "without reluctance... without measure... without end."

The avenue for the expression of her fervor for Christ began with a Society of Reparation to the Sacred Heart she formed with girls of the lower classes. Soon this group began collecting pennies and prayers for the missions. The pooled offerings of factory workers and parish members were sent to the missions for abandoned children in China. This mission-aid society grew in its first year to five hundred members. Gradually aid spread to missions in Africa, the Middle East, the Pacific Islands, Australia, and the United States. The founder did not fare so well. Giving away everything, she spent her last years in great poverty, her leadership rejected.

For Your Life

The Second Vatican Council stressed the evangelization of the world as a prime duty of every Catholic, not just of those formally called to be full-time missionaries. The Society for the Propagation of the Faith is the church's central means of aid to missions today. We should try to spread the faith that gives us so much joy and hope and also give generous support to missionary activities in our own country and abroad.

Prayer-Meditation

From the prayer of Pauline-Marie Jaricot: "If only I could love without reluctance... without measure... without end."

123 ✠

Blessed Anne-Marie Javouhey
1779-1851[44]

A s a young girl, Anne-Marie Javouhey was active in French revolutionary times in helping rescue fugitive priests and in teaching catechism to children bereft of religious education. In 1798 she took private vows, intending to spend her life teaching the faith to the townspeople during this time of a priestless France. During this period of her life, Anne-Marie had a vision that she should found an order of Sisters that would provide for people of all races, many whom she had never even seen or heard of.

For six years she attempted to convince her father that she had a vocation and that he should help her find a suitable house for the new order she was meant to start. Finally he agreed and bought a large house in Cluny for the women she had assembled and the children they were teaching. Three of Anne-Marie's younger sisters joined her, and the new congregation was called Sisters of St. Joseph of Cluny. This teaching order spread to the Island of Reunion in the Indian Ocean and French Guinea in South America. She personally trained many native peoples in these foreign lands and fought for their emancipation. Since then her congregation has opened schools and hospitals in many other countries as well. Anne-Marie was so admired for her bravery that King Louis-Philippe called her a "great man," and during the 1848 uprisings against the French monarchy, the soldiers let her pass under the title of General Javouhey! She died in 1851.

For Your Life

The desire of most young women to be feminine should not be misconstrued as passivity and a lack of leadership. With the help of the Holy Spirit, Christian women should be ready for daring endeavors, always mingling courage and conviction with gentle goodness and compassion.

Prayer-Meditation

Blessed Anne-Marie Javouhey, intercede for an end to the terrible battles between races and the oppression of native peoples going on in our time, especially in South Africa. May Christ and we, his emissaries, become true peacemakers and genuine liberators. Through Christ our Lord. Amen.

124 ✠

St. Madeleine Sophie Barat
1799-1865[45]

Madeleine Sophie was born in Burgundy, France, in 1779. Her brother was a priest. By the time Madeleine was age ten her brother discerned that she was destined for great works of God. He formed her the same way a seminarian would be educated, in both secular and sacred subjects and in virtue. She learned Latin, Greek, history, physics, mathematics, Scripture, the church fathers, and doctrine.

All this education was going on during the worst horrors of the French Revolution. When it was over, there was need for building new Christian schools to replace all those that had been destroyed. Under the direction of her brother and of the Jesuits, she was ordered to relinquish her own desire to be a Carmelite and to help found a new order which would be called the Society for the Sacred Heart, devoted to the education of girls. Madeleine Sophie was appointed as superior when only twenty-three, the youngest of the Sisters, because so many discerned her great abilities. She remained superior for sixty-three years.

Soon St. Madeleine Sophie was founding schools all over France, Belgium, England, Austria, and even in America. By the end of her life she had founded one hundred five houses, some for girls of well-to-do parents and some for the poor. Among Madeleine Sophie's fine leadership abilities was her understanding that curriculum and methods must be flexible to meet changing needs. This she secured by arranging for a general council to meet every six years. All these foundations required much travel under very difficult conditions. St. Madeleine Sophie died in 1865 and was canonized in 1925.

Sometimes others may discern talents in us which we ourselves can hardly see or know how to evaluate. The influence of St. Madeleine Sophie's brother and of others directing her may help us to take seriously the opportunities offered to us because of another person's inspiration from the Holy Spirit.

Prayer-Meditation

From the words of St. Madeleine Sophie Barat: "Too much work is a danger for an imperfect soul.... For one who loves our Lord... it is an abundant harvest."[46]

125 ✠

Henriette Delille
1813-1862[47]

*B*eing considered for canonization is Henriette Delille, a most brave and fascinating woman of New Orleans, the daughter of a family of freed slaves married to white men. Henriette was raised as a French Catholic, learning the rudiments of religion, literature, and music. By fourteen she had become a lay catechist. She also loved to help poor black slaves and the sick and aged of her race.

In spite of many legal barriers, Henriette was able to establish an order for black nuns to help in arranging marriages among slaves, to take care of black orphans, the poor, and the sick, and to help educate the children. They were called the Sisters of the Holy Family. Such choices were particularly heroic since most free blacks from mixed racial marriages were eager to pass as whites and avoid the stigma of identification with the slaves. Henriette died in 1862 and is considered a servant of the slaves.

For Your Life

Like Mother Teresa of Calcutta, Henriette identified with those who were neglected and abandoned in the society of her day. The result was opposition and undoubtedly persecution as she sought to found an order to care for the poor, sick, and orphaned among her people.

Perhaps the choice is not so stark for many of us today. But the opportunity may be just as real and pressing. What do we do when we encounter the homeless on our city streets? If we know someone with AIDS or someone in jail, do we take the time to visit him or her? What is our reaction when a teenage girl is pregnant with nowhere to go?

Prayer-Meditation

Lord Jesus, inspired by the example of Henriette Delille, help us to recognize the needs of those who have been neglected and abandoned by our society today. Give us the courage and strength to offer our help and encouragement to them—no matter how meager our resources. Through Christ our Lord. Amen.

126 ✠

Blessed Eugénie Smet
1825-1871[48]

The Catholic faith holds that those in purgatory can no longer do anything to further their salvation, and they depend on our prayers for their release into a full experience of heavenly joy. Eugénie Smet was inspired by the Holy

Spirit to found an order dedicated to prayer for the souls in purgatory. Born in 1825 to a family of six in Lille, France, Eugénie loved to decorate the walls of the nursery rooms with religious pictures. She was also full of fun and a leader in the games the children used to play. One day in the fields, Eugénie said, "Suppose someone we loved was shut up in a prison, could we go on playing and catching butterflies outside the locked door if we had the key to open it? That is exactly how the souls in purgatory suffer when we forget them."

This image was to influence the entire life of Eugénie and many others. As a young girl, Eugénie began her ministry to the souls in purgatory by offering up for them her small sufferings. She wanted to enter a convent but many obstacles stood in the way. While waiting to found her own order dedicated to the holy souls in purgatory and to works of mercy for the poor, she devoted herself to charitable works in her own city. She formed a small association of other women with the same goals. They would make themselves available for any need, including the nursing of soldiers. It was only when she reached the age of thirty in 1856, with the encouragement of the Curé d'Ars, that Eugénie was able to realize her dream of founding the Helpers of the Holy Souls. With their beautiful mother house in Paris, the Sisters of this order can now be found all over the world. Eugénie herself died of cancer with intense pain at forty-five. She was beatified in 1957.

For Your Life

In the past, many Catholics included the souls in purgatory in their daily prayers. They would offer up many sufferings of ordinary life for the release of the souls in purgatory, both of those they had known and believed to be in purgatory or unknown souls. Among many today, it is considered almost ludicrous to imagine that people do not go straight to heaven, and so prayers for the souls in purgatory have been neglected. But this is not the teaching of the church, which declares the doctrine of purgatory to be true. Many saints prayed for the souls in purgatory until such time as they had a vision or a spiritual sense that their help was no longer needed. We might try doing the same. Thus, we will be prophetic in our modern, materialistic age in which many have lost a sense of guilt and sin and the reality of the supernatural.

Prayer-Meditation

From the motto of the Helpers of the Holy Souls: "Pray, Suffer, and Labor for the Souls in Purgatory."[49]

127 ✠

Mother Margaret Hallahan
1803-1868[50]

*I*n 1963 the cause was introduced for a popular English holy woman, Mother Margaret Hallahan. Born in London in 1803 of Irish parents, orphaned early, Margaret learned how to turn to God and Mary for the love denied her by her French caretakers. At the age of twenty Margaret became a nanny in a family who moved to Belgium. She loved the Catholic atmosphere of Belgium and began to long for the restoration of public Catholic devotion in England which still banned such demonstrations.

Margaret considered a religious vocation in an English community in Bruges but soon realized that this was not for her. Instead she became a Third Order Dominican, having to overcome by a pilgrimage to Our Lady the opposition of her director. She spent her time working for the family as a nanny, begging for the Poor Clares and for poor seminarians, and visiting the poor of the city. She could do all this by rising at four in the morning! In the evening she prayed the Rosary with her friends and made other private devotions.

Finally her vocation in England began to unfold when she was asked to teach in a school in Coventry. Soon she had two hundred poor girls under her tutelage. A group of similar women became the first group of Dominican Third Order Sisters in England with Margaret as mother superior. She was also responsible for relighting the sanctuary lamps in the neglected churches of England as well as organizing public processions in honor of Mary. These were the first processions since the sixteenth century. Mother Mary Hallahan died in 1868 in excruciating pain, beloved by all she had served.

For Your Life

Recently there has been a revival of participation in traditional devotions like the Rosary and other outward manifestations of the faith. Some Catholics wear crosses and medals or bring holy pictures to the office, for example. In a time of so much loss of faith, such a visible sign can begin dialogue and be a witness to many lapsed or indifferent Catholics who haven't thought about God as a central part of their lives for a long time.

Prayer-Meditation

May the prayers of Mother Mary Hallahan lead to a powerful profession of faith among Catholics and all Christians the world over. Through Christ our Lord. Amen.

128 ✠

Sister Mary MacKillop
1842-1909[51]

Mary MacKillop, founder of the Sisters of St. Joseph, was born in 1842 in Australia, of Scottish immigrant parents. Noticing how intelligent Mary was, her father spent many hours teaching her about God. Later she would dream of becoming a teaching Sister.

Throughout her life Mary was to suffer crosses that would have discouraged a less hardy soul. Her parents were very poor at practical matters, and they and the other children became dependent on Mary. It was her spiritual director who helped Mary to keep in mind the goal of consecrated life.

Catholic life in Australia in the 1860s was in ferment. There was little money, the number of priests was small. The flock of the bishop was scattered over hundreds of thousands of square miles. When the bishop refused to cooperate with the government system of national schools because he believed that it would undermine the faith of the Catholic children, he met with opposition from parents who didn't want to pay fees for Catholic education.

Although the bishop was excited about having an Australian religious order of teaching Sisters, the plan was revolutionary to him. Mary MacKillop thought it natural that in the vast territory of her country her Sisters should be free to ride about on horseback to wherever there was the greatest need rather than being subject to a local bishop. Meanwhile, more women were attracted to Mary's teaching methods and her work was flourishing. In 1867 Mary made her vows as a religious. Eventually her order would accomplish many works for the poor in Australia, New Zealand, Ireland, and Peru.

It might be tempting to imagine Mary as leading a peaceful life compared to that of some more dramatic women saints, but that would be to ignore the vast and sometimes terrible accounts of her trials. She was continually victimized by church politics of her day. At one point she was excommunicated for following a rule the bishop had originally affirmed. On his deathbed, however, the bishop regretted this rash act, to which he had been urged by Mary's enemies, and reinstated the Sisters. Mary died in old age surrounded by the love of her Sisters and beneficiaries. Her cause for beatification and canonization is now being advanced.

For Your Life

Like Mary, many Christians find that their relationship to the families of their birth is both a blessing and a difficulty. It is a great help to seek guidance through spiritual direction or to join a support group of those with similar goals when seeking God's will in such circumstances. Many times, also, we are tempted to give up an apostolic effort when we meet with failure or misunderstanding from those in authority. Mary's life shows us that humble obedience is not opposite to assertiveness in clinging to one's own sense of God's will. The key is patience and faithfulness to one's call.

Prayer-Meditation

We pray for Catholic schools in our own country today. May they provide a genuinely Catholic education for our children. And may they prosper and grow through the generous support of the parishes they serve. Through Christ our Lord. Amen.

129 ✠

Blessed Teresa de Gesu, Jornet y Ibars
1843-1897[52]

A wonderful role model for women taking care of elderly relatives is Blessed Teresa de Gesu, founder of the Little Sisters of the Aged Poor. Born in Lerida, Catalonia, Spain, in 1843, she became first a Third Order Carmelite. Aiming for a more intense spiritual life, she tried to become a Poor Clare but had to leave because of ill health. Later she was asked by the bishop to form a congregation of nuns dedicated to the spiritual and material help of the aged poor. She was able to open some forty-seven houses for the aged poor in Spain, then in Cuba, and then in almost all the countries of Latin America. By the time of her death her order had one thousand two hundred members and one hundred three houses for the poor. She was beatified in 1957.

For Your Life

Some women have a natural desire to help others in need, regardless of their age or circumstances. Some others, however, can only tend to those in need as a heroic sacrifice, being repelled by certain requirements of such care. Whether we fit into one category or the other, we will always want to bring Jesus with us when we minister so that our physical help will be matched by even more needed spiritual graces.

Prayer-Meditation

May the intercession of Blessed Teresa de Gesu bring the blessing of strength and compassion to all those who work in health care facilities for the aged poor and also to those who serve them in their homes. Through Christ our Lord. Amen.

130 ✠

St. Frances Xavier Cabrini
1850-1917[53]

Frances Cabrini was born in 1850 in Lombardy, Italy. Longing to become a nun near her own birthplace, but turned down twice because she was not considered sufficiently healthy, God used her instead as an extraordinary missionary sister. Frances' first step was to start her own novitiate in Italy for women serving in corporal and spiritual works of mercy. Part of her strategy was to take as novices women who, like herself, had been rejected by other orders.

Pope Leo XIII was so impressed by her zeal and her organizational abilities that he decided she might be the solution for a gnawing problem. Italians were immigrating in droves to the United States. Once arrived, not speaking any English, they were not able to understand the German or Irish priests in their parishes, and their children were starved for religious instruction. He decided to send Frances with seven of her nuns to a parish in New York City to minister to this need.

Although terrified of the ocean, Frances agreed. Imagine her surprise when she arrived in New York City only to learn that the priest who had asked for them had no means for their support. He wanted them to return on the next ship! Undaunted, as ever, Frances simply went begging in the streets in the Italian quarter until she could open a house for her Sisters, called the Missionary Sisters of the Sacred Heart. The number of apostolic projects she undertook in the

United States and around the world mounted up to sixty-seven by the time of her death.

There is space here to share only a few examples of Mother Cabrini's daring initiatives. Once, in Louisiana, she heard that there were Italian immigrants working far from the city with no access to catechetical instruction. There was no transportation in those days save horse-driven carts full of fruit and vegetables. Without hesitation, Mother Cabrini and her Sisters got up before dawn, hitched rides on the carts, and were off to their apostolate. Often when there were no funds, or no food, the money or the makings for meals would appear miraculously. Hearing of Italian miners working deep underground for months with no access to news of their families in Italy, Mother Cabrini gathered up the letters and went down into the mines herself to deliver them. She also walked through heavy snow in the Andes Mountains to cross barriers considered impossible in order to minister.

Mother Cabrini became a naturalized citizen of the United States in 1909. After her death in 1917, reports of some 150,000 miracles flooded the Vatican. She was canonized in 1946. She is the patroness of immigrants.

For Your Life

There are innumerable problems facing us in society and the church which require bold solutions. If St. Frances Cabrini were living today, she would not rest until she had decided how to arrange shelter for the homeless, just to mention one pressing need. All Christians should support such projects and also think of ways and means on their own for helping those with no resources.

Prayer-Meditation

St. Frances Cabrini, intercede for Christians all over the world not to be daunted by difficulties, but instead, as you did, to start worthy initiatives, confident that the ways and means will be given in answer to prayers and requests for assistance. Through Christ our Lord. Amen.

131 ✠

Blessed Katherine Drexel
1858-1955[54]

The tale of the American saint, Katherine Drexel, is a Cinderella story in reverse. Born in 1858 to a rich banking family in Philadelphia, her mother died when she was but a year old. However, unlike the Cinderella story, her stepmother loved her tenderly as well as the two other daughters of the family. She was also particularly close to her father, a man who came home from the bank only to shut himself in his study to pray in secret. Both parents were devoted to the poor, even to the point of hiring one servant whose only job was to take care of the needs of whoever came to the door, and there were plenty.

Katherine went to an academy of the Ladies of the Sacred Heart from whom she received a rich heritage of love for Jesus. When she was old enough, her stepmother let Katherine and her other daughters run a Sunday school for the children of her father's employees. Although Katherine dreamed of entering a convent, there was a margin of uncertainty that plagued her until after the death of her father in 1891. During her late teens and twenties, however, she spent both her time and her money doing good in obedience to a vision she had of the Virgin Mary telling her, "Freely you have received, freely give." The cause that most interested Katherine was the plight of the Native and African Americans. She dreamed of setting up schools for them, and before starting her own order, gave vast sums of money to those who could found schools.

Once on a trip to Europe, the family had a private audience with the Holy Father. Katherine took the opportunity to describe in graphic terms the plight of the poor Native and African Americans. So impressed was the pope, he told Katherine that she was the one to found an order of missionaries specifically designed to minister to these needs. This ended Katherine's doubts about her vocation. Using the vast sums of money at her disposal, with the full consent of the family who were all devout and generous, Katherine founded a motherhouse for the young women eager for the same mission she had around her. She also founded countless schools, orphanages, and hospitals for the poor. Her order was called Sisters of the Blessed Sacrament for Indians and Colored People. At a time when she herself was often living in abject poverty among those to whom she was ministering, she was dubbed "the richest nun in the world," for the fortune she had at her disposal to give away.

Blessed Katherine Drexel died at the age of ninety-seven! Native and African Americans came from all over the United States to Philadelphia to honor her memory. She left behind six hundred Sisters to carry on her work and sixty-one schools for Native and African Americans. Katherine Drexel was beatified in 1988.

For Your Life

The life of Katherine Drexel and her exemplary family show us how much good can be done by a wealthy family, and how parents can inspire their children to even more heroic lives of charity.

Prayer-Meditation

From anecdotes about Blessed Katherine Drexel: "Whenever a polite reference was made to the vast wealth Mother Katherine had renounced, she was quick to remind her listeners that she had given up only what every Sister of the Blessed Sacrament gave up—everything she had!"[55]

132 ✠

Blessed Sister Teresia Benedicta (Edith Stein)
1891-1942[56]

O ne of the most unique of recently beatified saints was born as Edith Stein in Breslau, Germany, in 1891, part of a large family of devout Jewish business people. When her father died suddenly, Edith was only three, but her mother, a woman of amazing efficiency, took over the lumber business while also raising the whole family.

Strongly intellectual and considering herself to be an atheist, at the university Edith Stein gradually became interested in the philosophy of Edmund Husserl. A turn toward the Catholic faith came about when she was helping the widow of a professor sort out the papers of her late husband. Edith was profoundly moved by the way this Catholic widow accepted the death of her beloved husband as her way of participation in the cross of Jesus. Later, at the house of another friend, Edith picked up by chance the autobiography of St. Teresa of Avila. She read it in one sitting and at the end proclaimed, "This is the truth." Immediately she bought a Catholic catechism and missal, read these through, and then went to Mass and asked the priest to baptize her on the spot! The astonished priest wanted to know what kind of instructions she had received, ready to recommend a long course of study. The fervent young woman however politely asked him to test her himself. He was so surprised by her comprehensive knowledge of the faith that she was soon baptized.

Although drawn to deep silent prayer, she was directed by her priest to become a teacher. Many sections from her pioneering philosophical work on the Christian education of women reflect her own observations as the beloved mentor of young girls. During this time she also participated, through writing and lecturing, in the revival of Thomistic philosophy. The abbot of the Benedictine Abbey of Beuron wrote of her as "one of the greatest women of our time. She was simplicity and naturalness personified. She was completely a woman, gentle and even maternal.... Gifted with mystical graces.... She never gave any sign of affectation or a sense of superiority."[57]

When, because of the persecution of the Jews, Edith was no longer permitted to teach, she was finally allowed to follow her deepest desire: to become a Carmelite. As Sister Teresia Benedicta, Edith grew continually in Carmel in radiant joy right in the midst of the interior sufferings she bore, in union with Christ, for the Jewish people suffering the Holocaust.

The prophetic side of Edith's gifts expressed itself with vehemence when it came to complying with the edicts of Hitler. "Time and time again she urged the Sisters not to (vote) for Hitler no matter what the consequences to individuals or to the community. He was an enemy of God and would bring Germany into the dust along with himself.... It is the shadow of the Cross that is falling on my people. If only they would see this! Woe also to this city and this country when God's wrath descends upon them for what they are now doing to the Jews."[58]

Eventually, she was sent to the concentration camp. Here she spent the brief time left to her in prayer and in helping the abandoned children of Jewish parents. Pope John Paul II, who was a great admirer of her philosophical work as well as of her holy Carmelite vocation, beatified her in 1987.

For Your Life

Some Christians think that fostering good interreligious relations means having nothing to do with efforts for the conversion of the Jewish people. Although forced conversions are to be deplored, every heart should long for the re-union of the Jewish Messiah with members of his own peo-ple. The life of Edith Stein can stimulate us to pray for the conversion of the Jewish people and to witness to them with diplomacy and charity, always bearing in mind the historic wounds they have suffered at Christian hands.

Prayer-Meditation

From the writings of Edith Stein: "The clear and irrevoca-ble word of Scripture declares what daily experience teaches from the beginning of the world: woman is destined to be wife and mother. In three different ways, woman can fulfill the mission (of motherliness) accorded to her by nature and grace and suitable to her individual disposition: in marriage; in the practice of a profession which values human develop-ment as the noblest professional activity; and under the veil as the Spouse of Christ."[59]

133 ✠

Edel Quinn
1907-1944[60]

*A*mong the most charming and delicate of the prophetic women saints is Edel Quinn, a missionary of the Legion of Mary, whose cause was introduced very shortly after her death since there were so many living persons who could testify to her holiness.

Edel was born in Ireland, in County Cork, to a family who eventually lived in Dublin. It was while working as a typist in 1927 that she was introduced to the now famous Legion of

Mary, the international lay organization for door-to-door evangelization and other spiritual works of mercy. Soon her dedication and efficiency were noted, and she was asked to head a branch of the Legion that ministered to lower-class women in miserable lodging houses of Dublin. Visits to these women were made after long, regular working hours as a secretary.

Edel's dream, however, was not to work for the Legion of Mary but rather to become a Poor Clare nun, but she was unable to enter when she was diagnosed as having a grave case of tuberculosis. She was forced to spend a year and a half at a sanatorium. There she impressed all by her beautiful kindness as well as her spiritual presence. On partial recovery, Edel resumed her secretarial work and her Legion missions, begging to be one of a team going to England to try to bolster the faith. Then came an urgent appeal from the bishops of Zanzibar and Nairobi, Africa, for a missionary envoy to start up Legion groups of lay people to evangelize Africa. Edel felt greatly called to this possibility, but most of the Legion members in Ireland thought it a crime to send a weak, sick, young woman to so difficult an area.

Upon unexpected, unanimous approval of the council of the Legion, Edel was sent to Africa. Arrival in Nairobi began an amazing adventure of grace. This slight woman began trips of incredible difficulty through jungle territory from one mission station to another, forming lay leaders to carry on the evangelization of their own people under the aegis of Jesus and Mary.

What charmed those who came into contact with Edel was her great cheerfulness. Always smiling, happy, and eager for fun, no difficulties of travel could disconcert her. Besides, she was absolutely faithful to her tasks. Insisting the Legion members come to all the meetings regardless of distance or other obstacles, she herself would keep her appointments no matter what the problems. Sometimes storms made driving impossible, and the only means to arrive at a distant village would be to wade through the mud. Yet, she would arrive. The model of dedication she gave would lead to similar efforts in those she was training for leadership. When her old car broke down, she would hitch rides on trucks, getting up at five or six in the morning to jump into a vehicle full of African men. Fearless, she was never molested by anyone, for all saw the great love she had for the people she met.

Finally her health gave out and she died in 1944. She has been eulogized by many biographers, including Cardinal Suenens, and her beatification is expected soon.

For Your Life

How far out of our way do most of us go in order to bring the good news to others? The description of Edel Quinn's missionary work might interest us in looking into the Legion of Mary, or some other evangelistic endeavor, as a means of reaching out to our neighbors.

Prayer-Meditation

Written by Frank Duff, founder of the Legion of Mary: "Was she grim or insensitive like many hard men who have no sense of fear, but who have no other sort of feeling in them either? Do not think that about her.... She was ultra-sensitive... she loved her family intensely, especially her mother, but she never intended to go back to them again.... Now the best explanation I am able to give is this one: that to an extent which is very seldom met with, spiritual motives were in possession of the center of her being.... The Lord and His Mother were living there in a way they are not in most of us.... The ordinary weaknesses and temptations which afflict us and toss us about like hay did not affect her. It was as if her defenses kept the enemy out, whereas with us the enemy gets in and is only dislodged after a struggle."[61]

134 ✠

Mother Thecla Merlo
1894-1963[62]

Thecla Merlo was born to a poor family in a small town near Alba, Italy. Even as a young girl she was appointed as a catechist to younger children. Because of ill health, anemia in particular, her vocation to become a nun was not accepted. Instead, she helped out the family as a seamstress.

Her new life for the apostolate began with her association with Fr. Alberione, founder in Italy of the Society of St. Paul (best known in America as the order that founded Alba House Press). Fr. Alberione, a seminary professor of theology, had a great dream. He thought it would be important to use modern media for the conversion of anticlerical Italians. Having gathered about him some young men apt for running the printing side of his ventures, he wanted a group of consecrated women to work actively in a modern apostolate. This idea was revolutionary and met with much opposition from those who thought women belonged only in their homes. Fr. Alberione singled out Teresa Merlo as an ideal woman to begin a ministry to the Italian girls of his region, starting out with sewing, but leading into help with publishing and distribution of the popular tracts he was writing. In fact one of the first entries of the women into the Christian book distribution work started with the sewing of bindings onto booklets.

Eventually Teresa would become Mother Thecla, the name taken from St. Thecla, the first disciple of St. Paul. She also was cofounder with Fr. Alberione of the Daughters of St. Paul, devoted to prayer and the establishment of publishing houses and book and media centers all over the world. Branches of the Daughters of St. Paul can be found in twenty-five countries on all continents. The cause for her canonization was started shortly after her death in 1963.

For Your Life

Sometimes Catholics bemoan the evil effects of technology, dreaming of how good it must have been to live in the Middle Ages or the time of Christ. Although industrialization has become a blight in many ways, the life of Thecla Merlo demonstrates how modern inventions can be used for evangelization. The flourishing centers of the Daughters of St. Paul are in the vanguard of books and media suitable for a renewal of the church. We should turn energy that could be lost in bitter regret for the evils of society into creative ways to meet the challenge of evangelization in the spirit of St. Paul.

Prayer-Meditation

From the writings of Thecla Merlo: "One cannot have recollection during the day if she does not make her meditation. Have you ever experienced this? One becomes nervous; she sees everything distorted; she succeeds in nothing.... We need God. We must be united to Him or else we will do no good."[63]

135 ✠

Dorothy Day
1897-1980[64]

Some Catholics were surprised when, after the death in 1980 of Dorothy Day, the famous founder of the Catholic Worker Movement, Cardinal O'Connor of New York immediately told the press that he would begin to advance the cause for her canonization.

Why the surprise? Even though she was probably the most prophetic Catholic woman in the twentieth century, second only to Mother Teresa of Calcutta, her past and the views of her movement were highly controversial. She was a divorced convert, a single parent, who had previously been a radical and who had gone to jail protesting against the defense of the country.

She also was a Benedictine Oblate whose favorite prayers included the Rosary and the stations of the cross. A closer look at her life bears out her holiness.

Born in 1897 in Brooklyn, New York, she was of Scotch-Irish, Presbyterian ancestry. Her father was a journalist who concentrated on horse-racing news. He was a tough atheist hailing from Tennessee. Her mother was from New York. Unlike her daughter, Dorothy (who did not wear make-up, wore her hair in a braid, and dressed in whatever was left over from Catholic Worker bins for the poor), Mrs. Day liked to dress like a queen.[65] Her mother was an Episcopalian but never went to church. However, at eight years old Dorothy liked to go to church with her friends. These visits, however, left her with a feeling more of fear of God than of joy.

In Chicago, for a time the family lived in poverty when her father could not find work. One Catholic friend used to talk to her about her faith, and Dorothy was enchanted by the idea of angels, saints, and Mary. For awhile her father permitted the children to go to Episcopal services where Dorothy learned to love singing and the Psalms. She was baptized and confirmed, and in her teen years loved reading about the saints. She also began writing down her thoughts.

By sixteen, Dorothy's religious mood waned and she began to get more interested in studies. When she went to college, she picked up the idea that religion was for the weak. She became more and more influenced by the idea of social justice and improving the world so that the poor could be helped. By the time she began her journalistic work, she was heavily involved in socialist ideals and protest movements against the draft.

Ultimately, although resisting for quite a time, Dorothy was sucked into an uncommitted love affair so characteristic of her radical lifestyle. During one unhappy episode, when she was twenty-one, she was so miserable she thought of suicide and even made a weak attempt. Discovering that she was pregnant and that the father of the child did not want her if she kept the baby, she went through a traumatic abortion. This terrible episode led Dorothy to think that marriage was a much better way of life. A hastily-conceived marriage ended after a year, because the man she married was unstable and would go on to marry eight women in sequence, never staying with any one!

During these years described in her own autobiography, *The Long Loneliness*, Dorothy tried to find solace in political activism. She also entered into a common-law marriage with an anarchist and bought a little house in Staten Island with the intent to do serious writing. By 1925 she was pregnant again and very happy to think she would keep this child, for she had feared that her abortion might have prevented her ever being a mother. She took the birth of her baby girl as a sign of God's forgiveness.

During this time, Dorothy started praying the Rosary to thank God and also began visiting the Catholic chapel. Her common-law husband did not want to be a father and also resented Dorothy's new piety. The baby was a girl whom she named Tamara. She had a great longing to baptize the baby and save her from the problems of her own life. Tamara could not be baptized unless there was someone to raise her in the faith, and so Dorothy started reading Catholic catechisms. When the baby was baptized, her common-law husband seemed to realize that it was only a matter of time before Dorothy would follow Tamara into the church and he eventually left her. He did not want to be married in the church, considering marriage to be a hypocritical ceremony.

In 1927 Dorothy was received into the Catholic church. Dorothy found her Catholic calling, with the prophetic figure of Peter Maurin, a noted Socialist Catholic thinker, as her guide, in the attempt to find a way to transfigure the Communist ideals of a just society into a radical personal faith within the Catholic church. This took the form of the Catholic Worker Movement. She combined life with the poor in the slums, and corporal works of mercy in the form of soup kitchens and hospitality with her own traditional Catholic spirituality. A newspaper selling for one cent peddled by movement people on the street corners and protest marches against war led to imprisonment of herself and many followers all over the country.

The influence of the Catholic Worker Movement has gone way beyond the membership, for it is still energizing Catholic social justice concerns today.

For Your Life

Because of their political connotations, some Christians think that it is better to avoid social justice causes in favor of personal charity. The life of Dorothy Day shows that it is possible to combine personal works of mercy, as in the Catholic Worker soup kitchens, with protest against unjust conditions. As the present-day pro-life and anti-war protest movements show, there is room for nonviolent activism, no matter what one's political persuasion.

Dorothy Day's life shows in a most beautiful way how a rocky past of sin can be transformed by Christ into a future of heroic virtue. If every parish worked as hard as the Catholic Worker for the needs of the poor, no one would dream of Marxism or any other political system as a solution to the ills of the world.

Prayer-Meditation

The favorite passage of Dorothy Day from Dostoyevsky's *Brothers Karamazov:* "Love in practice is a harsh and dreadful thing compared to love in dreams."[66]

Part Five

Interior Women
of the Spirit

136 ✠

St. Syncletia
d. A.D. 400[1]

S t. Syncletia was born in Alexandria, Egypt, to a wealthy family. She refused marriage, wanting to be a virgin for Christ instead. At the death of her parents, Syncletia was left with a fortune and also the care of a blind sister. She gave everything away to the poor and lived with her sister in the house of a relative. She devoted herself to prayer and penance. Many women came to ask her counsel. This led to attacks from Satan who did not like having so many saved through the intercession of St. Syncletia. At eighty years of age, Syncletia was afflicted with terrible fever and cancer of the larynx so that she could no longer speak. At the hour of her death a heavenly light glowed on her, and she received many joyful visions.

For Your Life

Some women dream of being contemplatives, imagining that this would put an end to their earthly trials. It is true that contemplative prayer brings great joy and union with Christ, but it is always accompanied by great sufferings, interior as well as exterior. This mental and physical pain renders the joyful contemplative visions all the more authentic. We are to love God more than the gifts of God, and that can only be demonstrated by accepting the painful natural and supernatural happenings as sources of union with the beloved Lord who lived and died for us in great pain.

Prayer-Meditation

From the words of St. Syncletia: "O, how happy should we be, did we but take as much pains to gain heaven and please God as worldlings do to heap up riches and perishable goods!... They (the worldlings) venture among thieves and robbers; at sea they expose themselves to the fury of winds and waves; they suffer shipwrecks and all perils; they attempt all, dare all, hazard all; but we, in serving so great a Master for so immense a good, are afraid of every contradiction."[2]

137 ☩

St. Scholastica
d. A.D. 543[3]

St. Scholastica was the twin of St. Benedict, the famous founder of the Benedictine Order. It is said that she was, herself, consecrated to God from early childhood. As an adult she became abbess of a Benedictine monastery some five miles from Monte Cassino where St. Benedict lived. Once a year St. Benedict would visit her monastery to give direction. On his last visit, St. Scholastica begged him to stay longer, foreseeing that she might die during the next year. She wished him to talk with her concerning the joys of heaven. When St. Benedict protested that his rule forbade him to be away from his monastery in the night, Scholastica implored God to intercede, immediately after which a terrible storm descended on the region. St. Benedict was unable to leave, and they spent the whole night in holy conversation. Three days later St. Scholastica died. Her brother, back in his cell, saw her soul ascending to heaven in the form of a dove.

For Your Life

Benedictine spirituality emphasizes love of liturgical praise of God in the Mass and the liturgy of the hours. Some Catholics are called to be Benedictine Sisters or Brothers. Others, called to lay vocations, can join a particular monastery as an Oblate and participate in their graces and receive means for spiritual growth through retreats and days of recollection. All Catholics can make use of the book of the liturgy of the hours, available in many Christian bookstores, as a way to consecrate their days and nights to God.

Prayer-Meditation

St. Scholastica, intercede for all women that we may find in our brothers, priests, and other male Christians, the complementary wisdom that we need for our growth. May we recognize our need for each other as brothers and sisters in Christ. Through Christ our Lord. Amen.

138 ✠

St. Romula and Companions
sixth century[4]

St. Gregory the Great chronicled the lives of St. Romula and her companions, Redempta and Herundo. They lived in a hermitage near the Church of Santa Maria Maggiore around the year A.D. 575. St. Gregory knew them and said that they lived in perfect silence, except to open their mouths to pray. Struck with paralysis during the last years of her life, Romula saw this as a boon, enabling her to be even more quiet and recollected so as to receive the graces of God, free from any distraction. Once, during this time, her companions heard a loud noise from the cell of Romula. Rushing in, they saw a wonderful light and realized that the sounds were of a heavenly choir. This lasted until her death three nights later, after which the music gradually faded away.

For Your Life

Special gifts of the Holy Spirit and supernatural visitations from God should be viewed as blessings and should not be despised and ridiculed because we do not understand them. Such gifts of the Spirit—as prophecy and miracles and supernatural visitations—characterized the lives of many of the saints and were used by them to the greater glory of God and the building up of the church. We, too, should be open to receiving gifts from God. After all, there are many things in heaven and earth that we do not understand, but that is no reason to reject them outright. As God, through the psalmist, tells us, "My ways are not your ways."

Prayer-Meditation

Through the intercession of St. Romula and her companions, may we come to love contemplation and silence, and when we speak, do so in a manner pleasing to God. And may we be open to whatever gift or consolation God chooses to bestow upon us. Through Christ our Lord. Amen.

139 ✠

St. Radegunde

d. A.D. 587 [5]

Radegunde, the daughter of a pagan king, was born around A.D. 518 in Thuringia. When her father was assassinated in a political plot, she was carried off to the castle of King Clotaire, who brought her up as a Christian. At eighteen she married Clotaire I, the first Christian king of what is now France. Although a baptized Christian, he was considered by priests to be a brutish, sensual man, who married five times!

Radegunde devoted herself to piety, and care of the poor, sick, and captives. She also founded a hospital and tended lepers. When discovered once kissing a leper, a friend remarked that he would not want to kiss her himself from fear of infection. She responded pertly, "If you don't want to kiss me, I really do not mind at all."[6] Gradually the king felt unhappy about the character of his wife. He used to say that he had married a nun rather than a queen and that she had converted his court into a convent.

Although always trying to please this difficult husband, she lost patience and hope when the king had her beloved brother murdered. At this point Radegunde asked to leave the court for a convent. The bishop was afraid to consecrate her, thinking the king might take revenge in a bloody manner. To overcome his doubts, Radegunde dressed herself like a nun and demanded that he bless her, otherwise proving that he feared man more than God.

She left for a remote estate of the king and spent all her money in charity. Later she built a monastery in Poitiers. The king thought to drag her back, but finally repented and begged her forgiveness. This good turn did not last long, for he lived on to burn alive one of his sons and his grandchildren. Again he repented and gave financial support to Radegunde's double monastery, which became a center of learning and peacemaking. During the last years of her life, Radegunde lived in total solitude. After her death her face was replendent with light. At her funeral a blind man received the gift of sight.

For Your Life

The relationship of St. Radegunde to her husband shows that holiness can influence an evil disposition but that finally goodness is a matter of each person's free will. Sometimes those who pray in depth for others imagine that grace can overwhelm human nature. That is not God's plan. He wants the free gift of love from each of us. Our prayers help open the door, but only the individual can invite Christ in.

Prayer-Meditation

May St. Radegunde join in the prayers of all Catholic women unhappily married to sinful men, that these spouses may repent and find reconciliation in the Sacrament of Penance. Through Christ our Lord. Amen.

140 ✠

St. Hilda of Whitby
A.D. 614–680[7]

St. Hilda was related to the first Christian king of Northumberland. She was baptized at thirteen. Wanting to become a nun, she was sent to a monastery in Paris where her sister, St. Hereswitha, was living as a nun. After a novitiate in France, the bishop of Lindisfarne, England, St. Aidan, sent for Hilda and made her abbess of Hartlepool. It is said that all the religious men who knew Hilda loved her for her wisdom and joy in the Lord.

Eventually Hilda founded a monastery in Whitby, three hundred feet above the sea. It was a double monastery, with the women taking precedence under the abbess. Hilda was always called mother because she was so helpful to all. Bishops and kings sought her advice, and soon Whitby became a center of learning. A synod of bishops was held at St. Hilda's monastery. St. Hilda died in A.D. 680. A nun thirteen miles away saw her soul carried to heaven by angels.

For Your Life

The story of St. Hilda shows that there is precedence in church history for female leadership not only in prophecy, but even in governance. This does not contradict the usual complement of having men in leadership roles, but shows that such role differentiation need not be rigid. In the case of a saint, many patterns can be broken. Evidently, St. Hilda used her power to inspire men rather than to domineer, as can sometimes happen to women in leadership, just as it often occurs when men are at the helm.

Prayer-Meditation

St. Hilda, the wise and gentle, help women in leadership in our time to avoid a domineering attitude in favor of Christian persuasion. Through Christ our Lord. Amen.

141 ✠

St. Winifred of Wales
c. A.D. 650[8]

Of Welsh saints, Winifred is the one most honored in the world. According to the available accounts, she was the daughter of a sister of St. Beuno. This uncle was her teacher of the faith.

Caradog of Hawarden fell in love with Winifred. When she refused to give into his lusts and fled to St. Beuno's Church, Caradog ran after her and cut off her head. It is said that this villainous man was immediately swallowed up on the spot where he had killed Winifred. Her head fell into a stream which is now the miraculous Holywell, the site of innumerable miracles. St. Beuno is said to have found Winifred's head and set it back on Winifred's shoulders and miraculously raised the girl back to life.

After this amazing incident, Winifred entered a convent at Gwytherin in Denbighshire. This was a double monastery with two houses of both sexes under one abbot. After the death of the male abbot and his female successor, Winifred was made the abbess. Although some doubt the details of Winifred's remarkable story, it is hard to make light of the many healings of Catholics and Protestants that have made Holywell a famous shrine.

For Your Life

It is remarkable how many converts declare that it is love for Our Lady and, sometimes, interest in the saints, that has brought them into the church. Many converts-to-be visit famous shrines dedicated to Mary or a saint first out of curiosity, but then are drawn by the grace-filled atmosphere into a deeper interest in Catholicism. A Catholic with friends of other faiths, or of no faith, might suggest to these friends that when they travel about the world they make a stop at a shrine such as Holywell and see firsthand for themselves evidence of the miraculous power of God.

Prayer-Meditation

May visitors to Holywell and other shrines find, through the intercession of St. Winifred, not only physical healing but spiritual hope. Through Christ our Lord. Amen.

142 ✠

St. Etheldreda or Audrey
d. A.D. 679[9]

St. Etheldreda was a widow and founder of a double abbey. The alternate name of Audrey came about in a comical manner. The word tawdry was used to describe the cheap junk that was sold at the monastery fairs in times after the death of the founder. This "tawdry" became Audrey!

Nonetheless, Etheldreda was one of the most popular saints of England. She came from a whole family of saints in Suffolk. After the death of her husband, with whom she lived like a sister rather than a wife, Etheldreda lived in prayer on the island of Ely. Her relatives insisted she remarry Egfrid, king of Northumbria. As he was a boy at the time he readily consented to a continent marriage, which was Etheldreda's wish. When he grew older and wanted a real wife, church authorities decided that since St. Etheldreda had vowed her virginity to God, it would be better to let her become a nun. Soon she founded a double monastery at Ely. She ate once a day only and wore rough clothing. Every night after the last prayers of the divine office, she remained in church praying until dawn. St. Etheldreda died in A.D. 679, buried in a simple grave, as she had instructed her nuns.

For Your Life

Unconsummated marriages are hardly the rule. The story of St. Etheldreda indicates once more that the church has jurisdiction over the sacraments and can, in rare cases, make exceptions for the common good. This example should not lead readers into thinking that they can live out their own marriage vows in such an interior way or easily dissolve their marriages in such circumstances. Such a possibility can only apply under the most unusual circumstances. In any case, these matters require the judgment of church courts since otherwise marriage would be in danger of becoming a charade of uncommitted or unconsummated partnerships instead of a sacrament, which reflects the unity of love between Christ and his church.

Prayer-Meditation

Through the prayers of St. Etheldreda may all those in unusual marriage situations have their cases resolved with the discernment of the church. May their first priority always be love of God and love of their spouse. Through Christ our Lord. Amen.

143 ✠

St. Gudula
d. A.D. 712[10]

Gudula was the daughter of St. Amalberga and was educated at Nivelles, Belgium, by St. Gertrude, her godmother and her cousin. After the death of St. Gertrude,
Gudula returned to the house of her father and led a life consecrated to prayer, fasting, and almsgiving.

Every morning while carrying a lantern, she walked two
miles to the church to attend Mass. She died around A.D. 712
and many miracles have been attributed to her in the different churches in which her relics were deposited. She is much
venerated in Belgium.

For Your Life

Daily liturgy is available to most Catholics without having
to walk two miles in the dark. Nonetheless many Catholics
prefer spending the time they might be communing with
God in church reading the newspaper, watching the TV
news, or jogging. While there is nothing wrong with this in
and of itself, it is sad because the great problems that weigh
us down can only find an ultimate solution in trust in God
and his grace. The practice of daily Communion is the closest we can get on earth to the presence of the Lord Jesus who
loves us so much and longs for our company.

Prayer-Meditation

May the prayers of St. Gudula shower graces on her country and help us to appreciate the gift of Holy Communion.
Through Christ our Lord. Amen.

144 ✠

St. Ulphia
d. A.D. 750[11]

When we think of hermits our minds usually travel to the deserts of Egypt, but St. Ulphia was a hermit of Amiens, France. She was not totally isolated from all human company, for Ulphia was directed by St. Domitus, another hermit. Each day Domitus would awaken Ulphia in her cell by knocking on her door with a stick so she could follow him to Mass. Apparently this was necessary because she would sleep late, since her rest was always interrupted by the croaking of frogs in the night. Finally she spoke to the frogs and told them to cease their noise. It is said that frogs in her region of France are silent at night even to this day! After the death of her director, Ulphia was joined by other women in a community, but eventually left them to return to solitude. St. Ulphia is revered in the Cathedral of Amiens.

For Your Life

Even if most women of the church are not called to be hermits, it is good to have a solitary cell in the soul to which one can return from time to time during the day to commune with the Lord Jesus. Otherwise, we become so busy that we easily lose sight of the very meaning of our lives: to grow in love of God and neighbor in preparation for an eternal life of love.

Prayer-Meditation

St. Ulphia, intercede for all contemplative women, especially hermits and those living in cloisters that they may find Jesus drawing close in their prayers, and as a result enjoy closeness to nature and to all in the mystical body of Christ. Through Christ our Lord. Amen.

145 ✠

St. Walburga
d. A.D. 779 [12]

S t. Walburga was English and the sister of two male
saints. She went to school at the monastery of Wimborne
and afterwards entered as a nun. When her brothers joined
St. Boniface in evangelizing the German peoples, they
begged for some nuns to come to the new Christian towns.
St. Walburga volunteered. After two years, her brother
founded a double monastery at Heidenheim, and she was
abbess first over the nuns and then over both houses after
the death of her brother. She is also said to have converted
some women from the practice of witchcraft.

She was a doctor as well. When she died, her body was
transferred to Eichstatt to rest with her brother who was
buried there. Apparently a miraculous medicinal oil flows
through the crevasse of a rock where her relics are buried.
Even today this place is a pilgrimage for the sick who are often cured there.

For Your Life

Before the 1970s, when one read of witch covens, it was
assumed, by most educated people, that so-called witches
were just eccentrics, persecuted by the narrow-minded.
Nowadays, with the widespread revival of witchcraft, we
can look back and understand somewhat better that earlier
time of persecution. There may well have been some genuine cause for concern. The newspapers today report bizarre
occult rituals by covens that include physical and sexual
abuse of victims, sometimes even grisly ritual murders. An

interesting part of the story of St. Walburga is that she didn't vanquish witchcraft by persecution but by real miracles from God. Winning over persons who have come under the influence of occult practices can sometimes succeed by opening to them the riches of our Christian faith. The protection of good angels, miraculous healings at shrines, and the intercession of the saints are all spiritual weapons we can use in drawing those in satanism and witchcraft into God's kingdom.

Prayer-Meditation

Through the intercession of St. Walburga may we attract to the church all those straying into the realms of evil spiritual forces. Through Christ our Lord. Amen.

146 ✠

St. Lioba
d. A.D. 780[13]

A companion of St. Walburga, St. Lioba was a missionary nun to Germany. When appointed abbess of Bischofsheim, she was so effective that many of her nuns were sent out to found other monasteries. She was so beautiful and kind that she seemed like an angel. She never spoke evil of anyone. Aside from prayer and manual labor, the nuns also studied theology and copied manuscripts. Not a severely penitential woman, Lioba insisted on mid-day rest. Men important in government of church and state often sought her advice. St. Boniface himself loved her so much that he asked that when she died she be buried with him, "that their bodies might wait the resurrection and be raised together in glory to meet the Lord and be forever united in the kingdom of His love."[14] This request was not honored by St. Boniface's monks who did not want to see his relics disturbed by the bones of another.

For Your Life

There used to be many double monasteries for women and men. Perhaps some of the reasons were practical, involving mutual use of resources, but primarily these double monasteries were designed to provide benefit from the complementary gifts of men and women, while yet separating the two sexes into different spaces for all but spiritual needs. There are still a few double monasteries which seem to attract those with a monastic vocation who find seclusion from the other sex in most monasteries to be too rigid.

Prayer-Meditation

St. Lioba, pray especially for those in double monasteries that their unique charism may be protected and grow in our times. Also pray for all those who do not understand the complementarity of men and women that they would come to a healthy appreciation of how this great gift is meant to build up the mystical body of Christ and give glory to God. Through Christ our Lord. Amen.

147 ✠

St. Susanna
A.D. 840-918 [15]

St. Susanna lived for fifty years in total solitude! Born to a rich family in Constantinople, she lost her father early in life. Her mother wanted her to marry. When she refused, she was badly treated and finally had to flee to Leucadia. There she went to a mountain cliff and spent the rest of her life alone in prayer. After her death, many miraculous cures took place at her tomb. Those possessed by demons were healed. Her body was found incorrupt when her grave was opened. St. Susanna is also venerated under the name of St. Anne.

For Your Life

Although very few would like to imitate St. Susanna as hermits, the tale of her life is awesome. It indicates how far God can go to sustain a person, without the company of other human beings, by his own love. Meditating on such a life, one can wonder if a little less dependency on humans and more on God might not help us all to arrive at greater peace.

Prayer-Meditation

St. Susanna, pray for all those who find solitude frightening, to rejoice in knowing that Christ can give his beloved ones everything they need. An hour of his company is better than that of anyone else. Through Christ our Lord. Amen.

148 ✠

St. Humbeline
1092-1141[16]

St. Humbeline provides us with a perplexing story. She was the beautiful, charming daughter of a family of saints. Her mother was extremely holy, but died when Humbeline was still fairly young. Her brother was the fiery and apostolic St. Bernard who founded an order of severe Cistercian contemplative monasticism at Citeaux. Soon all her five brothers had joined St. Bernard as monks. They all became saints. Her father also eventually joined this order and is himself a saint![17]

There was Humbeline, odd girl out, indeed. A great lover of pleasure, amusement, fancy dress, and court life, Humbeline was married to a nobleman exactly suited to her. They loved each other dearly.

One day, Humbeline, in a spirit of bravado, went to visit the monastery of her brothers, decked out in her usual finery. One brother, Andrew, horrified at her worldliness, bluntly accused her of being "a dressed up dunghill." Stung to the quick, Humbeline insisted on seeing Bernard, her favorite brother and the abbot of the monastery, crying out, "Let my brother despise my body, but let the Servant of God not despise a soul for whom Christ died." St. Bernard came out to his beloved sister and admonished her to give up all her vanity. After this famous scene, Humbeline went home and tried to live like a Cistercian ascetic in her own home. Finally her husband agreed to let her leave him and become a Cistercian nun, following the same rule of St. Bernard, adapted to the life of the women. She eventually became an abbess.

For Your Life

It is extremely rare that the church gives permission for a spouse to leave the married state for a religious vocation. In St. Humbeline's days this was not as infrequent. So much was the celibate state admired, the devout would not be scandalized by Humbeline's decision. Since the consent of her husband was necessary, it can be assumed that he, too, was a very pious man, considering that eternal joys would make up for the loss of earthly ones.

What lesson can we derive from this story? Perhaps the most important perennial truth is that saintly siblings can deeply affect each other's conversions. May we strive to be such holy sisters and brothers within our families.

May the intercession of St. Humbeline bring forth more vocations of women to the contemplative life. May the example of her life also inspire blood brothers and sisters to seek to lead their siblings to Christ. Through Christ our Lord. Amen.

149 ✠

St. Euphrosyne of Polotsk
d. 1173 [18]

St. Euphrosyne was the daughter of Prince Svyatoslav of Polotsk. She entered a monastery at the age of twelve, and later became a solitary in a cell at the Church of Santa Sophia. Although called to a contemplative life, St. Euphrosyne still cared deeply about the needy. To satisfy this compassion, she copied books and sold them, using the proceeds to aid the poor. Although basically reclusive, she made pilgrimages and founded a monastery for women. Here she was given the icon of our Lady of Korsun. In her last years she went on pilgrimage to Jerusalem to see the monastery of Mar Saba in the desert between Jerusalem and the Dead Sea. She died in the Holy Land but was buried in Kiev. She is venerated by the Russians, the Ruthenians, and the Lithuanians.

For Your Life

There is a caricature in some people's minds of contemplative women as eccentric people who can't stand ordinary life and who could care less about the needs of others. The life of St. Euphrosyne is actually typical of the way most interior women loved to give of themselves to others, without sacrificing their precious time with the Lord.

Prayer-Meditation

Through the intercession of St. Euphrosyne may the churches in the West come into greater contact with contemplative spirituality of their brothers and sisters in the East and so be enriched in their own spiritual life. Through Christ our Lord. Amen.

150 ✠

St. Clare
1193-1253[19]

*B*efore the birth of St. Clare, her mother was praying in church when she head a voice saying, "Do not be afraid, for you will joyful bring forth a clear light which will illumine the world."[20] Accordingly, the baby girl who came after this prayer was named Chiara, Italian for "clear one."

Even before meeting St. Francis, Clare was considered to be a holy young girl because of her obedience, generosity, love for the poor, and devout prayer life. When her parents wanted her to marry, she sought the advice of St. Francis and shortly after consecrated herself to pursue the way of perfection he was teaching. At first Francis advised her to live in various convents, but finally moved her to San Damiano, a church the Franciscans had rebuilt. She lived in great poverty and penance in an enclosure for forty-two years. Soon she was joined by others. Nowadays, Poor Clares, as they are called, live a similar life in many countries around the world, following the rule she devised. They live in great simplicity, devoting themselves to contemplation.

Clare experienced quite a bit of difficulty getting her rule approved, for some prelates thought it should be more like the Benedictine rule and independent of the Franciscan friars. Clare wanted to emphasize poverty and closeness to the Franciscan rule. During her juridical struggles, she was continually ill. But she courageously fought for the original ideals of St. Francis in a time when many friars were relaxing his rule. St. Clare is the patroness of television, presumably because her name means clear light.

For Your Life

In every age some women want God to be their only possession, joyfully giving up all material goods in order to live in the greatest simplicity. Their charism brings graces to the whole mystical body of Christ. No one can visit a Poor Clare monastery without sensing a remarkable happiness in the faces of the Sisters. The sight of such joy in the Lord can lead women to discern carefully about their own possessions and inspire them to divest themselves of any unnecessary items.

Prayer-Meditation

St. Clare, intercede for good Christian television programming that can shed the clear light of the gospel and bring others to Christ. May Christian families have the discernment and resolve to reject the glamour, violence, and wanton sex that typifies secular network programming today, opting instead for a simpler life focused on the gospel. Through Christ our Lord. Amen.

151 ✠

Blessed Alpais
d. 1211[21]

A peasant born in Orléans, France, Alpais worked in the
fields by her father's side until she was stricken with an
illness of which she was cured by a vision of the Virgin Mary.
Later Alpais was paralyzed and confined to her bed. She
lived entirely on the Eucharist, as was confirmed by a commission appointed by the archbishop.

When the archbishop had confirmed the miracle of
Alpais' nurturing by Holy Communion alone, he had a
church built next to her room so that the invalid could watch
the Mass. All kinds of important people came to Alpais for
advice, even Queen Adela, wife of Louis VII. Alpais was
beatified in 1874.

For Your Life

It is beautiful to see how even royalty, if they are discern-
ing of the Holy Spirit, will hasten to seek aid from those with
a supernatural gift of counsel. No one who is poor, uneducated, or in other lowly circumstances should consider
herself to be inferior. The only real superiority is that of
grace, and this is free, limited only by our lack of interest in
receiving it.

Prayer-Meditation

Blessed Alpais, pray for the poor that they may understand that their true dignity comes from God who freely
bestows his graces. Through Christ our Lord. Amen.

152 ✠

Blessed Diana
thirteenth century[22]

*L*ittle is known of the childhood of Diana except that she was from a noble family of Bologna. It is known that as a young woman she was beautiful, eloquent, learned, charming, and courageous. Converted by the preaching of a Dominican, she continued to lead a luxurious court life outwardly but inwardly wore a hair shirt, iron chains, and rose early in the morning for prayer. In 1219 she made a vow of virginity to St. Dominic himself, in hopes of becoming a Dominican nun.

St. Dominic approved the founding of a convent of contemplative nuns, viewing such enclaves as a necessary source of grace for the more active male Dominicans. Blessed Diana is most well known because of the famous letters written to her by Blessed Jordan of Saxony, master general of the Dominican Order after the death of St. Dominic. This holy priest wrote Diana beautiful letters comforting her in the midst of the many trials the new convent had to endure from poverty, war, and interior sufferings. A master of spiritual friendship, often far away in lands distant from Italy, he would reassure her that Jesus can speak to her heart even better than he could. Yet the image of Diana was ever in his heart. It was to her that he confided his joys and disappointments in his apostolic ventures. Brought by grace to a high level of spiritual union with Jordan in this life, Diana was consoled for her anxiety about his health and welfare by his hopes for eternity where they could be united forever in Christ.

The life of Diana was formed by the Dominican ideal of liturgical prayer, joy in the Lord, silence, penance, unity of heart and soul with the other Sisters, and intercession for the Dominican missionaries. Blessed Jordan once wrote to Diana: "You, who have the kingdom of heaven, are not a poor little woman but a queen."[23] Diana left for the church a model of how a woman's love can help a priest to combine fidelity to Christ with Christ's own deep love for the women to whom he ministered.

For Your Life

Spiritual friendship is a difficult ideal to attain. The love of Christ burns more intensely than any human love, and purifies friends to be able to love others with a genuine non-possessive warmth of the heart.

Prayer-Meditation

From the Letters of Blessed Jordan to Blessed Diana and her Sisters: "If anyone of you be for a time cast down with weariness of spirit or afflicted with aridity of heart so that the torrent of devoted love seem to be dried up... (realize the Lord's way) for a time He will draw away from you that you may seek Him with greater ardour, and having sought may find Him with greater joy, and having found may hold Him with greater love, and having held may never let Him go."[24]

153 ✠

St. Mechtild of Magdeburg
1207-1282[25]

B orn in Saxony of the noble classes, well-educated, Mechtild was first touched by the Holy Spirit when she was twelve. By twenty she had left her family and joined the Beguines, a group of widows and single holy women living together without vows, devoted to prayer and works of mercy.

By order of her confessor, Mechtild began to write down her mystical experiences which came to be called *The Overflowing Light of the Godhead.* This book is full of wonderful revelations written with a tone of joyful exaltation that is characteristic of the writings of the women mystics who followed Mechtild's way. In 1270, Mechtild went to the Cistercian convent of Helfta, in flight from the enemies she had made by criticizing the laxity of the church of her time.

Mechtild once wrote that God had become so real to her as a young girl that she could never have given way to any sort of sin, so great was the love of God in her heart[26]. She lived a long, fruitful life, eventually becoming weak and totally blind.

For Your Life

Only deeply felt love of God can initially bring people out of sin or tepidity. The sense of his great personal love for each of us can come in many different ways: Marian devotion, love of the Sacred Heart, opening to the charismatic gifts of the Holy Spirit, and many more. Fear of being too emotional should not stop us from begging God for the grace we need to draw closer to him.

Prayer-Meditation

From the writings of St. Mechtild: "His divinity is never foreign to me. For always and without any fetters I feel it in every one of my limbs.... The soul ran out originally from God's heart and must needs return there."[27]

154 ✠

Blessed Isabella of France
1225-1270 [28]

A daughter of King Louis VIII of France and Blanche of Castile, Isabella was born in 1225. Not only was she extremely devout but also a fine student of biology, medicine, logic, Latin, and Eastern languages. She studied languages in order to be able to read the liturgy and the writings of the church fathers.

Isabella chose for herself a life of seclusion and prayer and refused all offers of marriage. She began her prayer early in the morning and continued until noon each day. At dinner she would serve meals to the poor and then go out to the sick. All this time she herself was very ill. She never received Holy Communion without first begging pardon of her servants for any fault she might have committed. Blessed Isabella also founded a convent for Poor Clares near her home, supporting them with income from her properties. She did not enter herself because she was too sick to keep the rule, yet she kept silence as much as possible. Isabella died at forty-five, often going into ecstasies in her prayer as she approached her heavenly fulfillment.

For Your Life

Having periods of silence during the day and making retreats where silence is encouraged can be very important if we are to hear the voice of God speaking of his love and his promises in our hearts.

Blessed Isabella's practice of asking pardon of her servants can be a model for anyone in a position of authority over others, where so often the absence of an encouraging smile or some curtly expressed directive can cause discouragement or anger in employees. Whenever the Holy Spirit reveals that there is some friction between ourselves and others, it is good to open dialogue by asking pardon.

Prayer-Meditation

We ask you, Blessed Isabella, to pray for us as we try to find quiet time for God in our busy days. Through Christ our Lord. Amen.

155 ✠

St. Lutgardis
d. 1246[29]

A Dutch saint, born in the twelfth century, Lutgardis went to the convent for a strange reason. Her dowry had been lost in a business matter, and it was thought she would not find a good suitor without one. At first Lutgardis lived at the convent like a boarder, for she was very attractive and loved amusement. However, God brings about his will in strange ways. One day our Lord appeared to her right in the middle of a frivolous visit and asked her to love him, especially in his sacred wounds.

After this vision, Lutgardis changed completely. She talked to Jesus all day and experienced him constantly present. She also had visions of Our Lady and other saints. Others could observe her levitating from the ground with a halo around her head. At times the blood from the crown of thorns of Jesus could be seen on her own forehead. Often she would plead for souls in danger.

After a time Lutgardis felt drawn to a stricter type of convent and went to live with the Cistercians. There she was given special gifts of healing and prophecy and an infused knowledge of the meaning of passages from Scriptures. A decade before her death, St. Lutgardis became blind. She understood this affliction as a way to become even more detached from the visible world.

For Your Life

What seems most impressive to some about the life of St. Lutgardis is the way God could take a totally unmotivated person and woo her with his love to make her a saint. This story might give courage to parents bewailing the light-mindedness or frivolity of some of their children.

Prayer-Meditation

St. Lutgardis, please pray for all girls and young women who lead superficial lives that they may find the deeper value of being loved by the Lord. Through Christ our Lord. Amen.

156 ✠

St. Gertrud the Great of Helfta
1256-1301[30]

At the time of St. Gertrud of Thuringia, it was not uncommon for upper-class families to entrust their children to the care of Sisters and Brothers of the great abbeys. Indeed, the abbey at Helfta was to become one of the most renowned centers of culture and piety of Germany. Gertrud, who was nurtured at this monastery, wrote books that were to make her the most famous of German Benedictine mystics.

At the abbey Gertrud studied Latin and philosophy. Always a visionary, she was especially devoted to the passion and to the Sacred Heart of Jesus. Not only was she a beautiful, gentle, poetic soul, she also was filled with the gifts of prudence that made her, in her own turn, a beloved abbess for forty years. The most well-known of her writings is *The Messenger of Divine Loving-Kindness*. Recently a volume has been published called *Spiritual Exercises* consisting of her direction to her Sisters.

As is characteristic of all Benedictine spirituality, Gertrud's writings are replete with reference to Scripture and liturgical praise. The translators note as well that whereas most biblical writing is in masculine terms, Gertrud adapts this for herself and her nuns by speaking of "the prodigal daughter," "adopted daughter," and so on. Gertrud's writings also fall squarely within the category called "bridal mysticism," so much popularized by the meditations of St. Bernard of Clairvaux. She is most joyful to identify herself with the bride of the Song of Songs and also to consider herself, by virtue of her consecrated virginity, to be the wife of Christ. Gertrud died in 1301 surrounded by her loving community of nuns.

For Your Life

It is characteristic of women to live primarily for love. How sad, then, if a woman does not find a way to adore God and to experience his love in return. Many women are afraid either of sentimentality or loss of control and therefore avoid reading the beautiful, sweet writings of women mystics. However, if we release ourselves, getting in touch with our own yearning for love and letting our souls be carried by the music of St. Gertrud, we will allow our hearts to soften and our lips to sing a new song unto the Lord.

Prayer-Meditation

From the writings of St. Gertrud: "Ah! Cement me to you, O true love. I offer you my chastity because you are altogether dulcet and pleasant, my spouse full of delight. I vow obedience to you because your fatherly charity allures me, your loving kindness and gentleness attract me. In observing your will, I tie myself to you because clinging to you is lovable above everything."[31]

157 ✠

St. Jutta
d. 1260[32]

S t. Jutta, patroness of Prussia, was much inspired by the example of St. Elizabeth of Hungary, the princess who became a pauper out of love for Christ and the poor. Jutta was married at fifteen to a nobleman. Like St. Elizabeth, she was happily married yet spent most of her time ministering to the poor. She had quite a time convincing her husband that plain dress was better, but finally she won him over. He died on a pilgrimage to the Holy Land, which was a terrible grief to his wife.

When all Jutta's children entered religious orders, she gave away everything and begged in the streets, wandering around the countryside, barefoot in the summer, giving whatever she had to the poor she met on the road. Finally she settled in Prussia, living alone in a broken-down building. From this hermitage she taught that one comes closer to God through illness, exile, and poverty, loved for Christ's sake. Often the villagers saw St. Jutta levitated in the air, as if held by angels.

For Your Life

These beautiful accounts of the lives of interior women of the Spirit sound thrilling from a distance. What would you think if your children started going about barefoot, without a cent in their pockets, talking to street people about God? Would you even consider that they might be inspired to do so by the Holy Spirit, or would you quickly draw the conclusion that their acts were escapes from the "real world"?

May the prayers of St. Jutta loosen us all from our overly-secure grip on the things of this world. Through Christ our Lord. Amen.

158 ✠

St. Julia Falconieri
1270-1341[33]

St. Julia Falconieri might well be described under the heading of motherly saints for her works of charity. However, the description of her mystical experiences tags her primarily as an interior contemplative woman whose fiery love for the Lord led her to expend all her spare energies on works of charity.

From a noble family of Florence, Julia was born when her parents were quite advanced in years, in answer to a prayer. From earliest childhood Julia liked to pray in church. She was so neglectful of ordinary feminine tasks of sewing and spinning that her mother teased her by saying she would not be a fit wife and mother when she grew up. This did not dismay Julia who, at fifteen, insisted that she wanted to belong to God and not to any husband.

St. Philip Benizi invested Julia with the Servite habit as a tertiary. She lived at home, but as soon as her mother died when Julia was thirty-four, she founded a house of similarly-minded women which eventually became an order of Servite nuns. Devoted to prayer and penance, she also extended a helping hand to everyone. The most famous of her contemplative graces occurred when she was dying. Her stomach had become dysfunctional, due to her many fasts. Because she was no longer able to digest food, it was not thought prudent to bring her Holy Communion, even as part of her last anointing. Much distressed that she could not receive her divine Lord, she begged a priest to bring the Eucharist near to her. When he came, her heart so burned with love for Jesus in the Eucharist that she implored the priest to lay a veil over her heart and lay the host upon it. When he did so, her face became full of light, as an angel, and the host disappeared, as testified by the members of her convent. She died in ecstasy at seventy years old.

For Your Life

Burning love of Christ as experienced by St. Julia is uncommon. However, such an account has power to move less fervent believers to yearn for the grace of knowing his love. The purpose of praying for contemplative graces is not self-glorification or spiritual gluttony. Rather it is the humble knowledge that without a greater personal love for Christ we are not able to live as he wishes us to, putting his love before all and loving our neighbor to a heroic degree.

Prayer-Meditation

May the prayers of St. Julia for us increase our love for God and neighbor that we may also fulfill God's will in all things. Through Christ our Lord. Amen.

159 ✠

Blessed Sibyllina Biscossi
1287-1367[34]

Sibyllina of Pavia, Italy, was orphaned early and by age nine was already working as a servant. As a result of illness, Sibyllina became blind and was taken to live with some Third Order Dominicans. She prayed to St. Dominic to bring about a healing. Instead of this grace she was sent a vision of the light of heaven and realized that she would be rewarded in eternity for her resignation in this life.

As a result of the mystical graces she began to receive, by fifteen years old Sibyllina chose the life of a recluse, living in a room under the Dominican church. For sixty-five years she gave counsel to others from the window of her cell. She was especially devoted to the Holy Spirit and her words led many to repent of their sins. Sibyllina died at eighty and was beatified in 1853. Her body is incorrupt.

For Your Life

The witness of recluses in the church is of great value. They prove to us that it is possible to live solely on the love of Christ. Many of us, instead, clutch frantically at human friends as if we would shrivel up and die without them. We need to grow in appreciation of solitude and closer communion with Jesus, who will always be our greatest friend.

Prayer-Meditation

Blessed Sibyllina, pray for all blind people that they also may glimpse the light of heaven and take heart in the struggle to cope with their infirmity and with uncharitable attitudes of others toward their visual impairment. Through Christ our Lord. Amen.

160 ✠

Dame Julian of Norwich
1343-1423 [35]

*A*lthough there is no formal cult of Julian of Norwich, she
takes her place in *Butler's Lives of the Saints* with the
notation that the title "Blessed" is one of affection. Since she
is one of the most beloved and popular mystics of all church
history, it seems fitting to include her here under holy interior women.

Little is known of her family except that it is surmised that
she must have come from the upper-class, since her famous
writing, *Revelations of Divine Love,* is written in an educated
style. She was born in the fourteenth century in Norfolk,
England. As a child she was unhappy. She prayed for an
early death. In the midst of an illness, however, she received
such clear visions of the passion that she decided to become
an anchoress and spend her time in prayer and in the reading of theological and spiritual works. Julian's writings are
characterized by a mixture of feminine, homey imagery, and
high philosophy. Their delicacy and beauty have made them
an essential part of any study of English mysticism. She lived
a long life and was consulted by many seeking spiritual
growth.

For Your Life

Although doctors of the church and male contemplative
writers have written masterpieces in the realm of spirituality
which all Catholics should read, there is often a direct emotional appeal to women and men that comes from the writings of women mystics such as Julian of Norwich. Those
who appreciate a poetic style would do well to read Julian of
Norwich's *Revelations of Divine Love.*

From Julian's writings: "Our Lord showed me a ghostly (spiritual) sight of his homely loving. I saw that He is to us everything that is good and comfortable for us; He is our clothing that for love wrappeth us, claspeth us and all be-closeth us for tender love, that He can never leave us; being in us all-thing that is good, as to mine understanding."[36]

161 ✠

Blessed Dorothy of Montau
1347-1394[37]

D orothy was a poor girl of Montau, Germany, who married a swordsmith of Danzig. She had nine children, but only the youngest one survived. This girl eventually became a nun. Dorothy's husband was an angry, domineering man who caused gentle Dorothy much anguish. However, he gradually improved because of her good character, and after twenty-five years of married life, agreed to go with her on a pilgrimage. This was followed by many other such journeys. At forty-three Dorothy was left a widow. She chose to live as a recluse in a cell near the church at Marienwerder. Although Dorothy only lived one more year, she gained such fame for holiness that many visitors came to her cell for counsel and healing. In a book of her visions and revelations written by her confessor, there is stress on devotion to the Blessed Sacrament. She is venerated as a patroness of Prussia, and is revered also in Poland, Lithuania, and Czechoslovakia.

For Your Life

Many women saints spend the first part of their lives in a manner common to all wives and mothers. Later, often after the death of their husbands, they are opened by grace to want to lead a contemplative life in relative solitude. In our times where, also, there is often a gap of many years between the death of a husband and of his wife, God can use that circumstance to draw a woman close to himself in deep prayer of union. The words he speaks into the heart of such women are greatly edifying to active members of the church. Opportunities should be provided in prayer groups for such sharing.

Prayer-Meditation

May Blessed Dorothy intercede for all women who have lost their children and ask the Holy Spirit to send them special graces so that they may find these children in his loving embrace. May she also intercede for all widows that they would find their consolation in God. Through Christ our Lord. Amen.

162 ✠

St. Rita of Cascia
1381-1457[38]

Rita was the long-desired child of previously infertile shepherding parents who lived in the hills of Umbria in Italy. Born in 1381, Rita's specialness was signified by the appearance of a singular type of large bee with no sting and a unique hum. The bees first came to her house at the day of her birth and still come throughout the centuries during Holy Week and on St. Rita's feast day. This unusual sign has been documented and was part of the process of Rita's canonization.[39]

Rita was brought up to love Christ and to give generously to the poor. She longed to become a Sister someday, but her parents begged her to marry that she might be among them in their old age and be protected by a husband. Receiving divine inspiration to obey their request, she gave up the call of her heart to serve God in an undivided manner. So Rita Mancini was married to Paolo Ferdinano, a leader of the town who was both quick-tempered and brutally quarrelsome. Soon this bad side to his character manifested itself by constant anger and brutality to his wife. Rita offered her suffering to God for the sake of Paolo's conversion. Their two sons, John and Paul, were unfortunately also of their father's temper. Rita tried by her joyful love of God and her many other virtues to cover over the faults of her family members. She often went out to visit the sick and to encourage any straying Catholics to come back to the sacraments.

Shortly before his death Paolo did convert and try to make up for all his wrong-doings. When he became the victim of an assassin's knife, his young sons pledged themselves to vengeance. Rita prayed constantly for a spirit of forgiveness and tried hard to teach her sons to avoid the same violent path their father had adopted. She wished that they would think about the mercy Jesus showed his assailants and take him for their model instead of falling into the feuding mentality of the times. In despair of converting her sons to a Christian way of thinking, Rita finally prayed that her sons should rather die still innocent than live to commit sins of murder. Within a year her two sons died.

Rita was now free to spend all of her time in prayer, penance, and good works, but she longed for the cloistered life of an Augustinian nun. Rita used to pray to St. John the Baptist, St. Augustine, and St. Nicholas of Tolentino as intercessors. One night she heard her name called, and the three saints were at her door. They led her into the locked convent to the chapel where the nuns found her in prayer the next morning. Since there was no way she could have entered through the locked door, they believed her story and decided it was God's will she should remain among them.

Especially devoted to contemplation of Christ crucified, God chose to give her the stigmata in the form of a thorn that wounded her head permanently, accompanied by a horrid stench and by an infestation of worms. This supernatural occurrence led Rita to remain in her cell. However, the miraculous graces coming from her presence made the disagreeable aspects of the wound quite bearable to visitors. Innumerable healing miracles also are attributed now to contact with the remains of St. Rita after her death at seventy-six. She is one of the patrons of impossible and desperate cases.

For Your Life

How many parents try to urge marriages on their children with spouses lacking in solid virtue because of a promise of career contacts or because they want to insure that their children remain near them geographically. We should pray our children will consider solid virtue and commitment to Christ in a future husband or wife as more important than other superficial qualities.

In some cases a wife married to a man of anger and brutality should seek separation and annulment, but some wives may choose as Rita did to accept unhappiness as a cross to offer for their husband's ultimate salvation.

Prayer-Meditation

St. Rita, intercede for all women who suffer in difficult marriages that they may discover the best response to their cross. May we, like you, someday find our highest longing for holiness fulfilled. Through Christ our Lord. Amen.

163 ✠

St. Lydwine of Schiedam
1380-1433 [40]

Lydwine was born in 1380 in the Netherlands, into a family of nine children. Both of Lydwine's parents were very faithful Catholics. Her father was a watchman. Lydwine spent her youth helping her mother with the housework. She took a vow of chastity before her fifteenth birthday.

Once Lydwine was skating with her friends when she had an accident that broke one of her ribs. This led to an abscess which became incurable and so painful that Lydwine could hardly lie or sit or stand without great discomfort. After awhile she could only go about on her knees and finally had to stay in bed all day. Her condition worsened to include gangrene, ulcers, neuritis, pounding noises in the head, toothache, and gradual blindness. It would seem that the girl would die under these conditions, but instead God sustained her life and let her become a victim-soul. She offered all these sufferings in penance for the sins of others and the benefit of the church. Instead of praying for healing, she was led by the Holy Spirit to accept her sufferings willingly. She lived in pain for thirty-eight years from the time of her accident until her death in 1433. She is invoked as patroness of skaters.

During the last years of her life Lydwine lived without any food except Holy Communion. She also could live without sleep. Her family loved her deeply and always helped her in every way. They often testified to a smell of sweet perfume emanating from her diseased body. Right after her death, her body was transfigured so that she looked at burial like a girl of seventeen. During her life, many visitors came to see her, first out of curiosity but later to benefit from her many supernatural gifts, which included miraculous healing of others, prophetic visions, bilocation, reading of hearts, and ecstatic visions of angels, Mary, the infant Jesus, and the passion. She was also given the stigmata.

For Your Life

The sad and incredible tale of St. Lydwine illustrates the way union with our suffering Savior can come about through uniting our own physical pain with his. Saints given this burden often bemoan the way most squander, as it were, the graces that could flow into the church if they would only offer their sufferings by uniting them with those of Christ and praying for the salvation of souls.

Prayer-Meditation

Words from St. Alphonsus Liguori about St. Lydwine: "Let it, then, be your endeavor, during the remainder of your life, to love and have confidence in him; and do not become sad when you find yourself in affliction and tribulations; for this is a sign, not of his hatred, but of the love God bears toward you."[41]

164 ✠

Blessed Helen dei Cavalcanti
1396-1458[42]

B lessed Helen, an Italian, was married at fifteen to Antonio dei Cavalcanti, a knight. She became the mother of a large family. Her husband died suddenly when Helen was forty years old. She cut off her hair and laid it with her jewelry on her husband's bier, saying, "For love of you alone have I worn these. Take them down into the earth with you."[43] Helen then joined a third order attached to the Hermits of St. Augustine. She made over her dresses into vestments and gave all her other goods in alms for the poor. Soon she also gave up meat, eggs, and milk and lived on bread, water, and roots. She lived in silence except when absolutely necessary in her care of her household.

Like all who are led into higher prayer, Helen had much interior suffering. The devil liked to batter her and tempt her with thoughts of suicide and even tried to throw her into the river. Helen's prayer was often drawn up into ecstasy. She was also given the gift of healing. She died in 1458 and was beatified in 1848.

For Your Life

Blessed Helen's bouts with Satan are mirrored, usually less spectacularly in our own lives. Any serious Christian will find her or himself deluged with temptations, at least at certain times. We know that the good angels and God himself have more power than the devil, so while we are praying our way through such sieges, we should always know that even if he chooses to leave us with certain "thorns in the flesh" (2 Cor 12:7) for quite a long time, God will have the victory in the end.

Prayer-Meditation

Through the prayers of Blessed Helen, may we be strengthened in time of trial. When the devil's attacks begin, may we never allow ourselves to be cast into discouragement, but, instead, call upon the all powerful Lord and our guardian angels. Through Christ our Lord. Amen.

165 ✠

St. Catherine of Bologna
d. 1463[44]

Catherine was the daughter of a prominent diplomat attached to Marquis d'Este of Farrara, Italy. At the age of eleven she was sent to be maid-of-honor to the daughter of the Marquis. They became close friends and studied together. After the death of her father, Catherine became part of a Third Order Franciscan monastery.

Once within the community the prayer life of Catherine was graced with remarkable visions, both from Christ and from the devil. Her method of discernment was to notice that before visions coming from Christ she felt great humility, first from within and then forcing her to bow her head. With Jesus came peace. From the devil came terrible doubts, especially concerning the real presence of Christ in the Blessed Sacrament. In a locution from God, the truth about the Eucharist was explained to her, along with the caution that doubt, on the part of the communicant, unless purposely cultivated, does not diminish the effects of Holy Communion.

Once, alone in the chapel at Christmas, after having said one thousand Hail Marys, she was given a vision of Our Lady who gave the baby Jesus into her arms. She held the infant and kissed him. After this she wrote many verses in honor of Jesus and Mary, as well as a work on spiritual warfare circulated after her death. She also spent much time illuminating her breviary. This beautiful, colorful book is still preserved. This and paintings made by her which hang in Italian museums, have made her the patroness of artists. The death of Catherine in 1463 was so peaceful that no one knew she had left the world until they smelled a sweet fragrance.

Many miracles have been attributed to her intercession, and her body is incorrupt.

For Your Life

The spiritual meaning of art is not always valued highly enough in the modern church. Since we are sensory creatures, and God has decked the world out in beauty, it is important to be lifted up to a sense of the heavenly by beautiful Christian art. It would increase the spirituality of every Catholic to have works depicting Jesus, Mary, and the saints in prominent places on the walls of our homes, so that the mind could be subtly lifted to God throughout the day.

Prayer-Meditation

Through the intercession of St. Catherine of Bologna, may all Christians come in contact with great art that can help us visualize the joys to come. Through Christ our Lord. Amen.

166 ✠

Blessed Beatrice da Silva
1424-1490[45]

*B*lessed Beatrice is a Portuguese saint of the fifteenth century. Raised in the court of Princess Isabel, she was married to John II of Castile. Beatrice was charming and beautiful, and apparently this led to false gossip for which she was imprisoned for three days. This traumatic experience led Beatrice to quit court life.

Happily she was allowed to leave for a Cistercian convent. The saint had her own plan to found a new order of women which was called the Congregation of the Immaculate Conception of the Blessed Virgin Mary. The first house was a castle given to them by Queen Isabella. The rule of the order was similar to that of the Cistercians, but they wore a white habit with a blue mantle since this was the dress of Our Lady in a vision Blessed Beatrice was given. Her order still thrives in Spain and elsewhere. Beatrice died in 1490 and she was beatified in 1926.

For Your Life

Those who have not been much acquainted with contemplative women's orders may wonder why there are so many different foundations. Why shouldn't every interior woman be either a Carmelite, Poor Clare, Dominican, or Benedictine? It seems that the Holy Spirit loves variety. When one visits convents of contemplative women, it becomes very clear how different are the charisms of each order. Most cloistered convents have retreat houses where lay women can stay for a day or a week and participate in the graces of silence and solitude. Sometimes busy mothers will take turns baby-sitting so that each one can have such a time with Christ.

Prayer-Meditation

Through the intercession of Blessed Beatrice, may many women hear the call to spend more time in prayer for the greater glory of Christ and the good of his church. Through Christ our Lord. Amen.

167 ✠

Blessed Eustochium of Padua
d. 1469[46]

O ne of the strangest tales of the life of a saint, indicating
how marvelously God can work through terrifying
circumstances, is the story of Blessed Eustochium of Padua.
The first strike against this saint was that she was the daughter of a nun who had been seduced. She was born within the
convent. Baptized with the name Lucrezia, very early on she
was considered to be possessed by devils. She was sent to
the convent school, where she was a very good girl. She
wanted to become a nun of the same group, but most of the
community were put off by the scandal of her birth. Nonetheless the bishop approved of her entrance. She was to be
called Eustochium.

Her novitiate was most dramatic, for she seemed to have
two different personalities. Generally she was gentle, kind,
fervent, and obedient. Suddenly she would change into a
violent, rude person, sometimes harming herself, a transfor-
mation attributed to diabolical influences. During the most
violent of her outbursts she was treated as a mad woman
and tied to a pillar for several days. When the abbess fell ill,
many thought that Eustochium must have poisoned her or
hurt her through magic. The townspeople once decided to
burn her, thinking her to be a witch. Again the bishop inter-
vened and, instead, had her kept in a cell by herself on bread
and water. Even though her confessor declared her to be
innocent, she was maltreated by those in the community
who thought her to be evil. They even went so far as to offer
her a good marriage if only she would leave the novitiate for
good. In her good periods, however, Eustochium extended
the greatest charity to her enemies.

At the end of four years, this poor nun was allowed to

take final vows. In the end she gained the love of all the Sisters. She died at twenty-six in 1469. When she was being buried, it was noted that the name Jesus was found imprinted upon her breast. A beautiful fragrance came from her grave, and many miracles followed. Such was the happy ending of this seemingly terrible life.

For Your Life

It is sometimes thought that anyone who indicates signs of neurosis or psychosis could not possibly be holy. The story of Eustochium contradicts this belief. Whether her maladies came from diabolical possession or mental illness is not clear. What is evident is that her holiness transcended the conditions of her birth and her strangeness. The ministry called deliverance prayer, long associated with missionary work in countries given to pagan rites, has now become much more prevalent in formerly Christian countries where satanism now abounds. Anyone suffering from afflictions like those of Eustochium should apply to their parish priests or the bishop for such healing ministry.

Prayer-Meditation

Through the intercession of Blessed Eustochium, may all those suffering from diabolic influences or mental illness be healed. Through Christ our Lord. Amen.

168 ✠

Blessed Paola Gambera-Costa
1473-1515[47]

*B*orn in Brescia, Italy, in 1473, Paola was married against her will at twelve to a nobleman, Lodovicantonio Costa. She accepted this marriage when her saintly Franciscan director told her that it was God's will. This did not deter Paola from following a path of holiness within the duties of marriage and family. Early in her married life, Paola wrote herself a rule of life: to rise every morning early for prayer, Rosary, and Mass; later in the day to recite the Office of Our Lady; at night to pray Compline and another Rosary. She also bound herself to obey her spouse and not to talk about his faults.

Paola and Lodovicantonio had several children, but continued to take care of the poor as well. When, during a lean year, her husband objected to her bounty to strangers, the food was miraculously increased. Unfortunately, Lodovicantonio at this point became unfaithful to his wife, bringing his mistresses right into the house, one of whom he allowed to take over the household. Paola showed her forgiving spirit by nursing this same woman when she was ill, thus leading to the woman's conversion. Gossips, however, claimed that she only nursed the woman in order to poison her. In time Paola proved that she had acted solely out of goodness. Her husband was converted and the rest of their lives were led in marital peace, her husband approving of all his wife's good works. Blessed Paola died at forty-two and was beatified in 1845.

For Your Life

When Paola vowed never to speak of her spouse's failings she probably had no idea how terrible these might become. This interior vow and her practices of prayer and Communion at Mass made it possible for her to endure the trials to come. What a spirit of forgiveness must have dwelled in the heart of a woman ready to minister compassionately to a rival. In addition, she had much forgiveness to receive her husband back with love after his conversion.

Prayer-Meditation

Blessed Paola, pray for all those women whose husbands are unfaithful and also for their lovers, that all may find the answer to their restless cravings in the peace of God. Through Christ our Lord. Amen.

169 ✠

Blessed Maria Bagnesi
1514-1577[48]

As a child, Maria, born into a rich family of Florence, was given over to a foster mother who starved her in such a way that she could never eat properly for the rest of her life! Returned to the family home, Maria took over the household after the death of her mother, all the while longing to be a Carmelite. Her father wanted her to marry. When he insisted, she became so ill that she was reduced to the state of a permanent invalid. Eight times she received Extreme Unction, now called the Sacrament of the Sick, so terrible were her illnesses. During this time of pain she never complained and many came to her for spiritual counsel. She was able to heal the sick, read hearts, effect reconciliation of enemies, and convert hardened sinners. To add to her miseries, a servant abused her for over twenty years. The direction of Dominican priests who ministered to her as a Third Order Dominican led her to great holiness. Maria died at sixty-three in 1577. Her body was discovered incorrupt when her coffin was transferred to the Carmelite convent. It is still incorrupt in this century. She was beatified in 1804.

For Your Life

Although we do not have details as to how Blessed Maria Bagnesi was able to reconcile enemies, it is instructive to reflect how God could use an invalid who was helpless physically to bring about peace. Psychologists think that behind anger lies fear—fear of being a victim instead of a lordly person. Perhaps the sight of a person full of peace who is yet a physical victim, such as Blessed Maria, gave angry persons pause to rethink their premises and to be ashamed.

Blessed Maria, intercede for all those who are trapped in anger and bitterness, unable to forgive, especially those in our own circle of family members and friends. Through Christ our Lord. Amen.

170 ✠

St. Catherine dei Ricci
1522-1590[49]

A Florentine saint, Catherine dei Ricci is one of the most spectacular. At thirteen she entered the Dominican convent. There she suffered great pain from illness and learned how to offer her sufferings to Christ in imitation of the passion. So gifted was Catherine by nature and grace that she was made prioress for life by the age of thirty. She became a close friend of St. Philip Neri in Rome by means of bilocation, as confirmed by five witnesses. Every week from Thursday to Friday for twelve years, Catherine enacted the passion in her own body while she, herself, was in a state of trance. During these experiences, watched by many, she would speak to the onlookers in words inexplicable for an uneducated woman. She also was given the stigmata. It is also attested that Jesus gave her a ring as a sign of spiritual marriage to him, out of which sometimes came a perfume. Along with her mystical visions and stigmata, like most contemplative saints, she was very practical and a good administrator. She died in 1590 at the age of sixty-eight and was canonized in 1747.

In the past, most consecrated women viewed themselves primarily as a "bride of Christ." There are many accounts of a mystical marriage of the soul and Christ, considered to be a sort of foreshadowing of the full union between the saint and the Bridegroom, following previous phases of purgation and illumination. Given the universal call to holiness, it is not good for the faithful to simply assume that they will never experience any supernatural event in their own lives. We should be open to such supernatural visitations and any spiritual gifts that God may want to bestow on us. Sometimes fear of the unusual, accompanied by a desire to be in control of every aspect of one's life, can be an obstacle to letting God work with us as he wills.

Prayer-Meditation

May the intercessory prayers of St. Catherine dei Ricci help to bring us into a passionate love relationship to Jesus, the Christ, who loved us so passionately as to die for us. May we let go of our own preconceptions of God and let him act in our own lives as he sees fit. Through Christ our Lord. Amen.

171 ✠

St. Mary Magdalen of Pazzi
1566-1607[50]

St. Mary Magdalen of Pazzi was born in Florence to one of the ruling houses in 1566. Devout from early childhood, she was placed in a convent at age fourteen, when her father was sent to govern in another city. Naturally, her parents expected a brilliant marriage, but she insisted on entering the

Carmelites, attracted by their practice of daily Communion.

Immediately upon her arrival she began to desire to suffer with our Lord as intensely as possible. This she experienced by voluntary penances, by involuntary pain in terrible illnesses, and in the spiritual aridity which followed her early raptures. This emptiness was accompanied by violent temptations of gluttony and sensuality. These torments lasted for five purifying years, followed by the comfort of peace in his divine presence and more raptures. At this time Mary Magdalen of Pazzi received many gifts of the Holy Spirit including reading of the thoughts of others, prophecies about the future, healing, and bilocation. The most famous passage from her sayings is: "O Love, love is not loved, not known by His own creatures. O my Jesus! If I had a voice sufficiently loud and strong to be heard in every part of the world, I would cry out to make this Love known, loved and honored by all men as the one immeasurable good."[51] Toward the end of her life, she became ill with dreadful headaches and paralysis. She died in 1607 and was canonized in 1669. Her body is incorrupt.

For Your Life

Our sanctification depends to a great degree, not on our own initiatives but on the manner in which we respond to whatever God sends to us in the way of crosses, exterior or interior. From St. Mary Magdalen of Pazzi we can learn how to give every moment of these sufferings as a love-offering to our crucified Lord.

Prayer-Meditation

From the words of St. Mary Magdalen of Pazzi during a painful illness: "See what the infinite love of God has suffered for my salvation. That same love sees my wellness and gives me courage. Those who call to mind the sufferings of Christ and who offer up their own to God through His passion find their pains sweet and pleasant."[52]

172 ✠

St. Rose of Lima
1586-1617[53]

*B*orn to a family of eleven children in Peru, Rose was of mixed Spanish and Indian descent. She was originally called Isabella, but when a rose blossom was miraculously suspended in the air above her cradle, she was nicknamed Rose. The beginning of the beautiful, but fragile, little girl's contemplative vocation started when she said that she was not able to recite fixed prayers before the crucifix at the nearby shrine, but would instead want to stare at the cross for long hours at a time. When in pain from illness, Rose would identify her sufferings with those of Jesus. Although her family was of Indian descent, they clung to their Spanish ancestry. They shared the elitist sentiments of their neighbors toward the more downtrodden Indians who lived almost like slaves. Rose began to feel a great sense of concern for the Indians who would not respond to the God of their cruel conquerors and still worshiped in a pagan manner. At an early age, Rose decided to dedicate herself to prayer and penance for these peoples.

Little Rose liked to spend many hours praying in the back of the garden far from the busy social life of the house. Often she would play with the child Jesus who came to her and swung in the cherry trees to keep her company. She was also gifted with visions of Our Lady and the infant Jesus smiling at her. Disliking the pastimes of her sisters and their friends, Rose built a little hut of leaves and branches as a hideaway and eventually got her mother to agree to let her stay there even at night. Even though her mother was alarmed by Rose's fanciful ideas, she would always have to give in when not only Rose but all the people of the town began to see a beautiful supernatural child walking by Rose's side who left silver footprints on the road.

Nevertheless her mother started to protest more strongly when Rose, chided by a brother for loving her beautiful long hair, cut it off and started wearing a crown of thorns made of tin and string under the kerchief she used to cover the shame of her short hair. Her mother was also upset that she stopped eating meat and fruit and even drinking cool water, as a penance to end the Spanish wars and for the conversion of the Indians. Worst of all it wrung her mother's heart to see that her frail daughter was sleeping in her hut for only two hours each night on a bed made up of broken crockery. But when the distraught woman sought out a Dominican priest to force her daughter to become normal again, the priest told her that Rose was most pleasing to God and would bring blessings to all of Lima.

After awhile the Indian people of the city began to notice this Spanish maiden who spent so much time in prayer at church. Timidly they approached the back of the garden of her house and soon she began to feed the poorest of the Indians and even bring the sick ones into rooms in the house vacated by her married sisters. She would always try to tell them about Christ, their Savior. Rose wanted to enter a convent, but since her mother could not bear to lose her, she finally became a Third Order Dominican. The child Jesus came to her and told her, "Rose of my heart, you are my little chosen Bride."

Rose died in 1617 at thirty-one. At her funeral Mass, thousands of people rushed from their homes to touch the body of the saint, resulting in many healing miracles. Thousands of Indians suddenly sought baptism. And her mother, who had been so reluctant to accept her daughter's life of penance, later in life became herself a nun! St. Rose of Lima is the patron saint of the Americas and of the Philippine Islands.

For Your Life

In our own times the sufferings of Native American peoples have not ended. Although many of them in the United

States are baptized Catholics, they sometimes receive only sporadic ministry of the sacraments since they are often scattered in small groups on large, remote reservations. We should have the heart of St. Rose of Lima for all victims of injustice and do whatever we can to reach out to them.

Prayer-Meditation

St. Rose of Lima, intercede for us that we may have the simplicity of little children so that God may love to visit us as he did you. Through Christ our Lord. Amen.

173 ✠

Blessed Mary Agreda
seventeenth century[54]

Mary Agreda, who died in 1665, was one of the most outstanding mystical women ever born in Spain. When she was thirty-five, as a cloistered nun of the Franciscan family, she received a vision from the Holy Spirit ordering her to write a history of the Mother of God based on visions and locutions. At first she refused because of humility, but ultimately she was persuaded to write, and allowed to be published, the famous four-volume work called *The Mystical City of God.*

Although originally mocked as an incredible fraud perpetrated by a crazy mystic, shortly after its appearance, in spite of initial censure, this four-volume work was given approval by many popes for inspirational reading by the faithful.[55] What is most exciting about *The Mystical City of God* is the lively manner of narration of God and interior sentiments in the life of the Mother of God. The Virgin Mary's life story seems to be real rather than fanciful because it depicts how she felt year by year as the astounding events in the life of her Son unfolded. Particularly moving to some readers are the accounts of her solicitude for the apostles and disciples after the ascension. In these accounts she displays herself as one constantly in the most excruciating interior suffering offered in intercession for the eager but weak members of the mystical body.

For Your Life

No human person was closer to Jesus than his mother. We need to come close to her as a model and intercessor. The salvation won by the blood of the Savior must not be lost to us out of carelessness or despair.

Prayer-Meditation

From the writings of Blessed Mary Agreda in the name of Jesus: "Poor, abandoned, ignorant sinners, great and small, sick and weak, and all the children of Adam, of whatever state, condition, or sex you may be; prelates, princes, and subjects, all over the entire world, come and seek a remedy from my liberality and infinite providence, through the intercession of her (the Virgin Mary) who gave humanity to the Word."[56]

174 ✠

St. Mariana of Quito
1618-1645[57]

Called "the Lily of Quito," Mariana Paredes y Flores was of Spanish ancestry. An orphan, she was lovingly cared for by an elder sister and brother-in-law. As a little girl she used to teach her younger nieces how to pray the Rosary and make the stations of the cross. She would concoct penances for herself with thorns and prickles. At first she dreamed of being a missionary to Japan or a hermit, but when these schemes were frustrated by her relatives, it was thought best that she live in a convent. When these plans were also thwarted by what seemed like special interventions of Providence, she was directed to continue to live at her brother-in-law's house, but as a solitary, going out only to the church.

Then began a life of penance of extraordinary proportions. Daily she wore chains, a wire girdle, and a hair shirt. She spent Fridays lying in a coffin, with thorns and spiked iron on her head. She never slept more than three hours at a time. She ate only bread and water. By the end of her life she omitted drink so as to imitate the thirst of Jesus on the cross. These austerities were accompanied by miracles and prophecies. When the city was threatened by an epidemic, she offered herself as victim for the sins of the people. Immediately the epidemic stopped and she became very ill. She died in 1645. The whole town considered her a saint who had saved them from death. She was canonized in 1950.

For Your Life

Some Christians are repelled by descriptions of such self-torture and would be scandalized should any member of their own families even so much as fast on bread and water once a week. It is natural to want to preserve in good health, the body, seen as a gift from God. On the other hand, it is also natural to want to suffer everything with the beloved. How many husbands and wives say to each other, "I wish I could take your suffering on myself." If this is true, why should not a cherished bride of Christ want to imitate her beloved, even to sharing his worst sufferings on the cross?

Prayer-Meditation

May the intercession of St. Mariana of Quito bring blessings of conversion to Latin America, especially, and to all of us so much in need of holiness. Through Christ our Lord. Amen.

175 ✠

Blessed Marie of the Incarnation (Acarie)
1566-1618 [58]

One of the most influential of the interior women of the Spirit is Blessed Marie Acarie. She was one of the first to see the importance of bringing to France the reformed Carmelite Sisters who had achieved high contemplation by the work and writings of St. Teresa of Avila. This idea came from supernatural visions she received from St. Teresa herself. Indeed, her whole life was full of visions and ecstasies.

Marie had wanted to be a nun, but since she was the only child to survive in her family, she was urged to obey her parents who wanted her to marry and have children. She was married to Peter Acarie, an aristocratic lawyer. They had six children, all of whom Madame Acarie, as she was called, raised to be saints. She was successful in this endeavor insofar as her three daughters became Carmelites and of her sons, one was a priest, and the others good laymen.

At one point the whole family was bankrupted when it was alleged that Peter Acarie was a traitor to the king. Madame Acarie defended her husband in court herself. Meanwhile, she helped all kinds of people with her widespread charities. Her activities included feeding the hungry, tending the sick, assisting old people, instructing those fallen away from the faith, and bringing several orders of religious into France. After the death of her husband, Marie did become a nun as a Carmelite lay Sister and take the name Marie of the Incarnation. She died at fifty-two years old and was beatified in 1791.

For Your Life

Madame Acarie represents a particular type of contemplative—the kind that is also extremely active in the world while yet being in close union with Jesus in mystical prayer. This shows us that we should not pigeon-hole people into married or mystics, contemplative or active. God likes to work with us in an individual manner, according to how willing we are to let him use our natural gifts for his purposes, so we will become transfigured by his love.

Prayer-Meditation

May the prayers of Blessed Marie of the Incarnation help bring about the reform of the many orders she involved herself with while on earth. May her prayers also lead women to their own unique vocations. Through Christ our Lord. Amen.

176 ✠

St. Margaret Mary Alacoque
1647-1690 [59]

Of the many saints, both women and men, who promoted devotion to the Sacred Heart, the most well-known of the women is St. Margaret Mary Alacoque, a seventeenth-century Visitation Sister. Margaret was born in 1647 in Burgundy, France, to a family of seven children. Her father was a well-to-do notary. When Margaret was young, her father died. It was found that he had been extravagant in his expenditures, leaving the family in such poverty that eventually they ended up as servants. This brought Margaret grief for she could not see how to help her mother in her troubles, and she was not allowed to go to Mass as often as was her desire.

At twenty-two she entered the Visitation convent of Paray-le-Monial. There she devoted herself to prayer and severe penances. One day when praying in the chapel, Margaret Mary heard the Lord inviting her to take the place of St. John the Evangelist close to his Sacred Heart and to spread such devotion so that all Catholics would know of his great love for them. It was a time when many French people were caught up in Jansenism, a heresy which emphasized God's judgment to the neglect of his mercy, so much so that many Catholics rarely frequented Holy Communion. Some church historians regard devotion to the Sacred Heart as the remedy of the Holy Spirit for Jansenism.

For eighteen months, Margaret continued to experience special revelations. When she described them to her superior, this nun thought that the experiences were not authentic. Devastated, Margaret became very ill. The superior thought that perhaps her doubts might be the cause and vowed that if Margaret recovered she would take it as a sign that her visions were valid. When Margaret, indeed, got better, her superior sent for some theological experts to judge her story. These rejected her story but later a Jesuit priest confirmed them and spread the devotion to the Sacred Heart in England. Eventually devotion to the Sacred Heart was spread by the preachings and writings of St. John Eudes and Blessed Claude la Columbière throughout the world. Since 1929 the feast of the Sacred Heart has been elevated to the highest rank.

For Your Life

Rejection by at least some of the people we love is a common experience, and one of the most painful. When agonizing over the way others refuse to receive and return our love, we can meditate on how Jesus himself longs that we might rience if we devoted ourselves more regularly to prayer and the sacraments instead of our frantic grasping for human love and the fleeting security this world provides.

Prayer-Meditation

From the last words of St. Margaret Mary: "I need nothing but God, and to lose myself in the heart of Jesus."[60]

177 ✠

St. Catherine Labouré
1806-1876[61]

C atherine was born in poor circumstances in Châtillon-sur-Seine, France in 1806. At twenty-four she entered the Sisters of Charity and was sent to the motherhouse at the Rue du Bac of Paris, now shrine of Devotion to the Miraculous Medal in honor of the Immaculate Conception. This shrine arose as a result of her visions.

When she received a series of visions of Our Lady who showed her the form of the medal, Catherine told her confessor only, and he arranged for approval from the archbishop. This medal is now worn in all parts of the world and is said to be miraculous because of the number of graces obtained through Mary's intercession. The prayer of Catherine imprinted on the medal reads: "O Mary conceived without sin, pray for us who have recourse to you!" It was only shortly before her death that her part in the reproduction of the pray for us who have recourse to you!" It was only shortly before her death that her part in the reproduction of the medal was made known, for she preferred to keep her visions secret from the others in the convent in order to live out her life humbly as door-keeper and tender of the chickens. St. Catherine Labouré died in 1876 and was canonized in 1947.

For Your Life

Sister Catherine Labouré would not have been canonized solely on the basis of her supernatural visions. Her self-effacing humility gives us a striking witness, especially for those gifted with graces who receive pleasure in being center-stage. At the same time, her sharing of the visions indicates that we are to prudently share what God has given to benefit the church. Having a regular confessor or spiritual director can be a great help in avoiding the dangers of vainglory or of a reticence brought about less by humility than by fear of ridicule.

Prayer-Meditation

Through the intercession of St. Catherine Labouré, may devotion to the Blessed Mother increase, and may the Miraculous Medal be worn by Catholics who are so led as a sign of our faith in her motherly love for us. Through Christ our Lord. Amen.

178 ✠

Blessed Josefa Naval Girbes
1820-1893[62]

*E*mbroidery and reading were the pastimes of Josefa, born in 1820 in a city near Valencia, Spain. Her parish priest taught her catechism. This combination of sewing, reading, and studying doctrine were to be joined in the life of Blessed Josefa in a most charming and holy manner. When grown, Josefa found it natural to teach young women embroidery. During these lessons, she drew them into her own habits by engaging in spiritual reading and conversation. She began teaching them basic catechism and then went on to lead them to the highest stages of prayer. She also prepared young women for either marriage or the convent. By the age of fifty-five Josefa had arrived at mystical union with God, having developed her spiritual gifts through prayerful reading of St. Teresa of Avila and John of the Cross. She died at seventy-one in 1893 as a Third Order Carmelite and was beatified in 1988.

For Your Life

In our century we have just as much need as in the times of Blessed Josefa to turn our workplaces and homes into centers for spiritual growth. At work, sitting around the lunch table or during breaks, why not witness to what the Lord is doing in your life and start the others thinking and sharing themselves? When visitors come to your home, why spend all the time watching television or chatting aimlessly? Some of that time could be spent in spiritual sharing and mutual counsel.

Bd. Josefa, intercede for us that we may be so filled with joy in the Lord that we will delight in sharing our faith with others in the ordinary circumstances of our lives. Through Christ our Lord. Amen.

179 ✠

Blessed Maria Fortunata Viti
1827-1922[63]

C alled Anna as a girl, the future Blessed Maria Fortunata was the daughter of a good Italian religious mother and a weak father who was both an alcoholic and a gambler. Her mother died at age thirty-six of a heart attack, leaving the nine children to the care of their father. Anna shouldered the burden of the care of the children and the household and made up her mind to always show respect for her father, even though he was so hateful. A prospect for bailing out the family came with the offer of marriage to a rich young man, but Anna felt called instead to enter a Benedictine cloister in Viroli. Although she was hardly literate, the Sisters wanted to prepare her to become a choir Sister, but she chose instead to remain as a lay Sister, doing the domestic chores of the convent.

Nonetheless, she began to have many visitors who sought her out for advice. She had the gift of reading their hearts and prophecy. She was also attacked by the devil and for some time there was concern lest these mystical phenomena be a sign of mental illness. Her contemplative experiences were not shared with the community. Only her confessor seemed to realize how holy she was. As a result he insisted that she keep a spiritual diary. She died peacefully at the age of ninety-five. The people of the area of Viroli began to visit her grave and gradually devotion to her spread all over the world. She was beatified in 1967.

For Your Life

In every parish there are probably humble souls scarcely recognized for their holiness since they are not in prominent positions. God is interested in the love in our hearts, not in our status. Blessed Maria also demonstrates how the trauma of growing up in an alcoholic family can be overcome by love and prayer.

Prayer-Meditation

From the words of Blessed Maria Fortunata Viti: "I was offered the choice of becoming a choir nun, and I would have loved to sing the praise of God. To me, these sisters are like God's angels. But I chose rather to be a lay sister, in order to have greater opportunity to practice humility."[64]

180 ✠

St. Bernadette of Lourdes
1844-1879[65]

St. Bernadette is one of the most well-known of women saints because of the famous movie, *Song of Bernadette*, based on the novel of the same title by Franz Werfel. The personality of Bernadette was unvarnished by education or sophistication. At first sight, she would seem to be the least likely girl to be singled out for such a spectacular religious experience as the seeing of apparitions of Our Lady.

Bernadette was the oldest of four children of a family living in extreme poverty in a slum at Lourdes after the father lost his job. Bernadette was always sickly, especially suffering from asthma. In spite of the conditions of her life, she was always joyful and loving to others.

On February 11, 1858, Bernadette and her friends were off gathering firewood. They had to cross over an icy river. Afraid of an asthma attack, Bernadette lingered behind. Suddenly in a natural grotto she saw a great light in which appeared a beautiful lady. For fifteen days the lady appeared and asked that Bernadette tell the people to do more penance for sins. Also she directed her to dig in the ground. From that spot came healing waters. She also asked that a chapel be built.

When Bernadette's parish priest asked what the name of the lady was, the answer given to Bernadette in the dialect of the region was that she was the Immaculate Conception. Since these words had never been heard by the girl before, it was considered by some to be an authentic sign that it was truly Our Lady speaking and not Bernadette projecting some notion of her own onto a hallucination. Since then many miracles have occurred at Lourdes. The shrine there is one of the most popular places of pilgrimage of the sick.

Bernadette's revelations were not greeted by everyone with equal enthusiasm. Soon Bernadette was subject to intensive investigations. Even when she became a nun, some of the Sisters treated her with harshness. She accepted all this and was known for her funny stories and mimicry of others. For example, when told by another Sister that she would never be canonized because she took snuff for her asthma, she replied, "Well, does that mean that because you don't take snuff you will be canonized?"[66]

The last words of this privileged woman when dying of painful bone tuberculosis were "J'aime" (I love). After Bernadette's death in 1879 her body was found incorrupt. She was canonized in 1933, in spite of the snuff!

For Your Life

It is certainly not given to everyone to see apparitions of the Virgin Mary, but we can follow the clear gospel-truth counsels of Our Lady given to the world through these visionaries. All the words spoken during Marian apparitions approved by the church call for more prayer and penance that we might become temples of Christ's peace radiating out to our troubled world.

Prayer-Meditation

St. Bernadette, intercede for us that we might open our heart to Mary's message of prayer, penance, and conversion during our own troubled times. Through Christ our Lord. Amen.

181 ✠

Blessed Mariam Baouardy
1846-1878 [67]

Mariam Baouardy of Galilee was born in what was then called Palestine to a Lebanese Greek-Melkite Catholic family. Mariam's birth was itself supernatural. Her parents had twelve sons, all of whom died in infancy. After the death of the twelfth, her mother decided to make a pilgrimage on foot to Bethlehem to beg the Virgin Mary for a daughter. This daughter was Mariam. After that they had a son, Paul, but both parents died suddenly, and Mariam was taken in by an uncle.

As a young girl Mariam was very dreamy and thoughtful, always looking for ways to be alone with God. She was not taught to read or write but only the duties of a future wife and mother. The family moved to Alexandria. When Mariam was thirteen, the Lord came to her in a vision and promised her that he would make it possible for her to be his instead of marrying. Her relatives instead betrothed her and decked her out in wedding clothing for the marriage. To avoid this fate Mariam cut off her hair and refused to be wed. The family punished her by making her work as a servant.

Seeing how badly she was treated, a former Muslim servant of the same family befriended her and brought her to his house to serve instead. However, his real plan was to convert her to Islam. When Mariam refused, he slashed her throat and left her in an alley to die. Later Mariam was to tell her mistress of novices that she had died and been taken to heaven but was told to return to earth. Then a mysterious woman who, she was convinced, was the Virgin Mary herself nursed Mariam for a month. The Virgin then brought her to a Franciscan church, telling her that in time she would become first a Sister of St. Joseph in France, then a Carmelite in France, in India, and finally that she would found a Carmelite monastery in Bethlehem.

For several years she treasured these promises in her heart, meanwhile working as a maid. She was deeply loved in all the houses she lived for her great joyful goodness. Nonetheless she was twice accused of theft and once thrown into prison until the real thief was found. At one of these houses she met a French woman who took her back to France where she did become a Sister of St. Joseph. There she was beloved for her joy, simplicity, and affection, but when she began to receive the first signs of the stigmata, it was thought better that she enter the Carmelites of Pau for greater seclusion.

As a Carmelite she insisted on taking charge of the most menial of tasks. Her favorite name for herself was not "the little flower," but "the little nothing." In the midst of chores, however, she would be taken up in ecstasies. She would be found rapt in a trance and singing spiritual songs in the laundry. What was most delightful was the way she would levitate, flying in the air to the top of the trees, balancing on thin branches as if she was a bird.[68] She would also write supernatural poetry of sweet, lyrical beauty. With the stigmata came also seasons of hell[69] during which she endured terrible interior sufferings.

Although still an illiterate peasant girl, she received prophecies so compelling that the letters she dictated to bishops and popes resulted in many initiatives including the founding of Carmels in India, Bethlehem, and Nazareth. She was greatly admired by French Catholic intellectuals such as Léon Bloy, Julien Green, and Jacques Maritain. Mariam died at age thirty-three and was beatified in 1983.

For Your Life

Mariam's life is a perfect illustration of the Beatitudes. She was persecuted in youth, and the purity and simplicity of her heart ["Blessed be the pure of heart, for they shall see God" (Mt 5:8)] seems to have attracted the Holy Spirit to shower graces upon her in the form of joyful affection for all people, animals, and nature.

Prayer-Meditation

From the dictated writings of Blessed Mariam: "The whole world is asleep, and God so full of goodness, so great, so worthy of all praise, no one is thinking of Him! See, nature praises Him, and man... who ought to praise Him, sleeps! Let us go, let us go and wake up the universe... and sing His praises."[70]

182 ✠

St. Raphaela
1850-1925[71]

St. Raphaela provides us with a sacred Cinderella story as we see her descend by sacrificial choice from being the daughter of a wealthy Spanish landowner to a housemaid. This took place over the course of seventy-four years.

Born in 1850, Raphaela's father died when she was only five. She and her siblings were taught by a priest at home. The turning point of the young girl's life was when this priest happened to notice how often she liked to admire herself in the mirror and startled Raphaela by asking her how she thought she would look a quarter of an hour after her death! This statement and the subsequent death of her mother when she was just nineteen convinced her that the purpose of life was to turn to God and seek his mercy for one's salvation.

The two daughters of the house, Dolores and Raphaela, loved each other but suffered much conflict. Dolores was the elder, the more forceful, and the more domineering, whereas Raphaela was a peaceful, quiet person. She was hurt when the silences she imposed on herself to avoid quarrels were interpreted as a sign of stupidity.

It was Raphaela who conceived of the successful plan of how to enter a convent against the will of their relatives. The plan was to visit a convent with some relatives, for purposes of general discernment of which order to enter, and suddenly disappear inside, leaving one of the Sisters to explain to the relatives that Raphaela and Dolores were staying for good.

None of the seemingly-available possibilities worked out, and Raphaela found herself not joining an order but starting one. After some difficulties with a bishop who wanted to rewrite their rule, the Sisters formed a community in Madrid called the Handmaids of the Sacred Heart.

Shortly after the founding of the community, Raphaela was unanimously voted superior. Some of the Sisters, however, thought they were smarter than Raphaela. With the help of Dolores, Raphaela was forced to resign her office. They exiled her to Rome so that she would not reveal their machinations to the other Sisters who loved her so much. Instead of defending herself, Raphaela accepted her new role in the Roman community where she had no status and worked at household chores. They had been told by her enemies that she was mentally incompetent. Seen all day by visitors dusting and sweeping, like a Cinderella, no one knew that she had been the actual founder of the order!

Eventually, Raphaela's sister Dolores repented. Raphaela forgave her and wrote to her with great kindness. Still Dolores always tried to pretend that she was the true founder and did not even come to her sister's funeral. During the last ten years of her life, Raphaela was lame because of a knee ailment. During the last three years of her life she was bed-ridden. She bore her suffering with such holiness that the Sisters began to realize whom they had in their midst. Never did she defend herself but died at seventy-four in great simplicity, offering all her pain in prayer. Her face radiated joy and light. Thousands came to honor her after her death. She was canonized in 1977.

For Your Life

Many times sisters in a family do not get along because of envy. The pain of being betrayed by a family member is very great. It is wonderful to see how St. Raphaela was willing to forgive her sister for virtually consigning her to a dust heap. Instead of resenting her, St. Raphaela accepted her lowly duties as a way of charity and humility.

St. Raphaela was a very practical as well as contemplative woman. Her sensible advice about taking care of one's health can remind prayerful Christians not to become so caught up in spiritual matters that we neglect the body, the instrument for good works with which God has blessed us.

Prayer-Meditation

From the sayings of St. Raphaela instructing her Sisters: "Take good care of yourself.... Have a good appetite. God does not want his spouses to look as though he fed them on lizards."[72]

183 ✠

St. Gemma Galgani
1878-1903[73]

B orn in 1878 in Lucca, Italy, Gemma had a difficult childhood. She was brought up by two aunts who tried to raise eight orphaned children of a bankrupt family. Gemma, the oldest girl, became the angel of the family, unselfishly taking care of everyone's needs. One morning Gemma astounded her aunts by appearing with stigmata on her hands and feet and a wound in her side. The wounds opened regularly on Thursday evenings to Friday afternoons for three years. In spite of these supernatural signs, the girl continued household work and was known as intelligent, healthy, and of sound judgment. In her prayer life, long before the stigmata, she had experienced locutions leading her to offer herself as a victim-soul to do penance for sinners because of an oncoming chastisement of the world.

A close friend who was sympathetic to the special gifts that Gemma had received from the Lord realized that Gemma would be subject to all kinds of curiosity and ridicule if left in her own uncongenial home environment.

She invited her to become part of their large family as a mother's helper. This same friend and others were advised by a Passionist Father, who became Gemma's spiritual director, to take down the words of Jesus and Mary that Gemma uttered during her ecstasies. Some of these concerned Gemma's intercession for sinners, followed by documented conversions. This same priest was an expert on fraudulent mystical phenomena and tested Gemma extensively. He gradually became so impressed, in spite of initial skepticism, that he later became her biographer.

After some time the wounds ceased to bleed, but this was replaced by greater interior trials and torments of the devil with whom she fought for the conversion of particular souls. She died on Holy Saturday of 1903.

For Your Life

Today many adults heroically care for foster children, just as Gemma was brought up by two aunts who cared for eight orphaned children. From the unusual mystical life of St. Gemma we may wish, ourselves, to be more willing to accept being victims of the sins of others, offering our sufferings up to Jesus for their salvation, as well as being willing to accept any interior path Jesus may wish for us.

Prayer-Meditation

From the letters of Gemma: "Oh, if all were to know how beautiful Jesus is, how amiable He is! They would all die of love. And yet how comes it that He is so little loved? Oh, it is time lost, to be with creatures! Our heart is made to love one thing only, our Great God.... Thou art all mine, especially Thy Heart. Yes, Thy Heart is mine, because Thou hast so often given it to me. But Thy Heart, Jesus, is full of light, and mine is full of darkness. When, oh when, shall I pass from this darkness to that clear light of my Jesus?"[74] "I have need of a great expiation especially for the sins and sacrileges by which ministers of the sanctuary are offending Me."[75]

184 ✠

Blessed Rafka Al-Rayes
1832-1914[76]

B orn in Himlaya, a small village of Lebanon, in 1832, Petronilla was part of a family of poor villagers, close to God and to each other. Petronilla was so close to her mother, that when she later could choose her own name as a contemplative nun, she picked her mother's name, Rafka or Rebecca. Petronilla's mother died when she was only seven, so the little girl decided that now she had two mothers in heaven, Rafka and Mother Mary.

When she grew up, Petronilla's confessor thought that she should become an active teaching Sister even though the girl felt deeply drawn to the contemplative life. Obediently she joined the Congregation of the Maries. She taught girls and also took care of seminarians. All who knew her revered Sister Petronilla as holy because of her great recollection of the constant presence of God and the fact that she was never known to speak an offensive word in all her life.

When her order was to be joined to another and many Sisters left in protest, Rafka had a holy dream where an old patriarch affirmed that she was to become a contemplative. When she became part of the Maronite convent of St. Simeon in 1871, she realized that it was precisely this saint who had appeared in the dream. From henceforth she would be called Sister Rafka.

Realizing that the full union with Jesus would mean great suffering, and reflecting that she had never had a moment of ill-health in all her forty years, the nun decided to offer herself as a victim of divine love in the manner of little Thérèse of Lisieux. Immediately after her consecration, Rafka experienced severe pain in the head and eyes. This led gradually to total blindness, accepted by her with tranquil humility. Her only fear was being a burden on the community. This she overcame by doing washing, baking, and weaving, and every other little thing that any Sister might need.

Rafka greatly inspired the other Sisters by her love of suffering and her many hours of contemplative prayer. She had memorized the liturgy of the hours and would spend lots of time at the side of her Sisters reciting Scripture and telling the lives of the saints. Later on she suffered from total paralysis as well as blindness.

Jesus came to her in a daily Eucharist which tasted to her of honey, so that she began to eat less and less normal food. Once she begged God to give her one hour of sight that she might enjoy the faces of her beloved Sisters. This was granted to her, and immediately afterwards a vision of heaven, more beautiful than any earthly sight. Rafka, the blind mystic, died in 1914. After her death some 2,600 alleged miracles occurred by the application of the dirt around her grave.[77]

For Your Life

Rafka chose suffering as a way of closer union to Jesus. All of us have physical or emotional handicaps which cause us suffering. If we accept them as given to us from the hands of Christ, we can learn how to make our sufferings valuable offerings.

Prayer-Meditation

From the words of Blessed Rafka: "The novice must get used to penance, patience, and humility. She must forget her family, her country, and all that is in this world. She must become blind to the world to be able to be united to God alone."[78]

About her imminent death: "I am not afraid. I have been waiting for my Lord for a long time. He is the one who has made me love death, and now my one desire is to go and be with Him."[79]

185 ✠

Sister Miriam Teresa
Demjanovich
1901-1927[80]

*T*he cause of a holy woman of the United States was introduced in 1980. Her name was Miriam Teresa Demjanovich. Her parents had immigrated to New Jersey from Slovakia. They were in the Eastern Rite Catholic Church. Miriam Teresa was born in 1901. Teresa, as she was called, was a happy child, the last of seven children. She enjoyed baseball, reading, and joking in the form of wit and also harmless pranks. She was so bright that she entered public elementary school at four and high school at twelve. Her interior life was hidden from those who knew her. After her mother's death she went to the College of St. Elizabeth where she received highest honors in literature. She next became a teacher in a high school. During all this time, though it was noticed she liked to pray for a long time in chapel, no one knew of the mystical graces she was receiving.

In 1925 she entered the Sisters of Charity in New Jersey. In the novitiate she was always kind and helpful. Only her spiritual director knew of her supernatural experiences, for she thought that doing God's will steadily was more important than such gifts. However, she was much misunderstood, her fidelity to the rule and to authority striking others as scrupulous. This caused her great mental suffering. This she offered for the salvation of souls. Soon her director was having her secretly write the conferences he was giving to all the Sisters. These were published after her death with the title *Greater*

Perfection and achieved world-wide distribution.

Sister Miriam Teresa became ill in 1926 with seemingly minor problems. It is thought that her early death in 1927 came because she had offered herself in sacrifice for the sanctification of active Sisters. After her burial, the spiritual director informed the Sisters that his conferences had been written by Miriam Teresa. They were shocked. Her director also told them that he thought she would someday be canonized. Her cause has been introduced.

For Your Life

The story of a priest making the words of a woman his own may seem a little shocking to modern sensibilities. Perhaps he knew that given the tendency to envy, her Sisters would accept the truths Maria Teresa had discerned more readily from a person of authority. We might see a parallel in the contemporary practice of parish team-ministry, in connection with which some priests write their sermons only after asking for the ideas of the team about the same scriptural passages. Nowadays, however, most men of the church would feel more of an obligation to publicly acknowledge such help with appropriate gratitude. As well, more women, whether Sisters, married women, or single women, are given scope for ministry by means of retreats, workshops, and lectures. Christian men and women alike are becoming familiar with such feminine witness and learning how to benefit from it.

Prayer-Meditation

From the sayings of Sister Miriam Teresa: "If all would only make use of the ordinary duties and trials of their state in the way God intended, they would all become saints."[81]

186 ✠

Sister Alphonsa of India
1910-1946 [82]

A nna Muttathupandatu, called Annakutti as a child, was the daughter of a doctor. She was brought up by an aunt after the death of her mother. They lived in a three-room cottage with a mud floor. The family were Syrian Catholics.

Annakutti went to the state school. She was a good student and also a very compassionate girl. Once a troublesome boy pushed Annakutti and a friend down a fence as they were crossing it. Annakutti's friend planned to report him for punishment, but the future saint reasoned with him saying that the little hurt they had experienced was but short, whereas this boy might have this on his record forever. Let us forgive him, as God has forgiven, she pleaded.

Although Annakutti had supernatural dreams about a Carmelite vocation, her aunt wanted her close by and dressed her for courtship. Soon she had many offers. Having read of saints in the past who had disfigured themselves rather than marrying, Annakutti decided to put her foot into a fire with the hope of laming herself. In fact, she fell in and was more seriously burned, but this did not deter her aunt from planning matches. Finally Annakutti's uncle gave in when she insisted that she preferred death to marriage.

Annakutti joined the Clarist Sisters of Malabar, Franciscan tertiaries, and was given the name Alphonsa after St. Alphonsus Liguori. She soon became very ill. She offered all her sufferings for the conversion of the world. Sometimes her pains were so intense that the other Sisters asked her if she didn't prefer to die. She insisted that she was glad to suffer for God. During times of less pain, she used to teach at the convent school. The children loved her greatly and often came to her for advice and intercession when she was bed-ridden. She also was gifted by the Holy Spirit with prophecy. She could also read and translate languages unknown to herself.

To the amazement of the Sisters, after her death thousands of people started visiting her tomb. Overcoming all class barriers, Hindus, Muslims, and Christians, "untouchables," and rich women knelt together to give thanks for her intercessions and to pray for others. Among the attested healing miracles were more than forty for clubfoot. Perhaps she will be the patroness for people with foot trouble since she had been willing to go lame rather than give up her vocation. The cause for her beatification has been opened in Rome.

For Your Life

Happily, in our time, few would have to go to the lengths of Sister Alphonsa to become a consecrated Sister. However, there are other obstacles equally difficult to overcome. Nowadays the Sisterhood is diminishing in number. No longer considered to be the best path for any devout young woman to take, there is more courage involved in entering an order. What is more, some Christian feminists opt for the single life in fear of becoming subordinate to male prelates. To enter an order requires, therefore, careful discernment with a desire to follow the Lord wherever he leads, sure of the joys of his intimate presence as his gift to all his special brides.

Prayer-Meditation

From the words of Sister Alphonsa: "Let the Lord do with me what He wills... for the benefit of a world which is marching to its ruin."[83]

Part Six

Sinners Turned Saints

187 ✠

St. Mary Magdalene
first century[1]

O f all the penitential saints, Mary Magdalene of the Gospels is surely the most well-known. In times of sexual temptation or longing for forgiveness, many Christians think of St. Mary Magdalene and the Lord's words to her and take heart to repent. When we reflect upon the life of Christ, among the most dramatic scenes are always those of Mary Magdalene washing the feet of Jesus with her tears, anointing him with precious ointment, standing beneath the cross, and being the first to see the Lord in his resurrected and glorified body.

When reflecting on the scene of Mary Magdalene approaching Jesus at the banquet of the self-righteous (Lk 7:36-50), it should be remembered that no women in those times participated in such dinners. Mary Magdalene was doubly courageous to enter. Her surrender exemplifies the saying of John the Evangelist that "perfect love casts out fear" (1 Jn 4:18). Indeed, seven devils had to be cast out of her (Lk 8:2).

In reflecting on the conversion of Mary Magdalene, Terri Vorndran Nichols, in *Woman to Woman* wrote, "Sexuality is a window to each person's very heart.... We are only happy with ourselves when we love as God loves... forever... fruitfully and faithfully... a total self gift.... Mary Magdalene's pattern of counterfeit loves must have weighed on her heart like a stone. She was a great deal like ourselves in our own sins—torn, divided, restless but caught in a web.... Had a multitude of biblical scholars scolded her, she would never have been moved to change. But the flesh and blood presence of Incarnate Love was like a blinding, beautiful light of hope.... (His was) the kind of unconditional love that frees a sinner to change."[2]

Mary Magdalene stood under the cross even when the apostles, save John, had fled in terror. She rushed to the tomb and saw the Lord in his resurrected body first. This is often viewed by Catholic women as a sign that though we are not called to the sacramental priesthood, we are called to intimacy with Jesus and to prophetic witness.

After the ascension of the Lord into heaven Mary Magdalene performed evangelical ministries and also was a penitential hermitess. Both the Greek and French peoples claim that she died in their countries.

For Your Life

We tend to think that serious sexual sins, especially when publicly known, are more shameful than other less visible ones such as long nurtured resentment, pride, judging others, or clinging to money when others are in desperate need. The story of Mary Magdalene reverses these assumptions. Yes, Mary Magdalene was a sinner desperately in need of both exorcism and forgiveness, but she let God's love touch her heart. The merciful love of Jesus became to her a hundred times more important than the vanity, power, and wealth she could derive from lustful passion.

Prayer-Meditation

St. Mary Magdalene, when we are assailed by temptations or have fallen into sin, intercede for us. May we rush into the arms of Jesus in prayer and receive the Sacrament of Reconciliation, letting God strengthen us to live chastely. Through Christ our Lord. Amen.

188 ✠

St. Afra
d. A.D. 304[3]

A fra was a prostitute from the region of Bavaria at the time of the persecution of Christians by Diocletian. During this terrifying period, a holy bishop fled to the house of Afra's mother. While in hiding, he converted Afra as well as her other companions. Once a Christian, Afra felt great contrition for her sins and tried to make amends in generosity to the poor, in prayer, and penance. When brought to trial as a Christian she proclaimed: "I was a great sinner before God; but I will not add new crimes." The judge told her that if she recanted her faith, her previous lovers would give her great sums of money. Refusing this offer, Afra was burned to death in fire. Before her execution she asked God that the fire which was to burn her body would save her soul from everlasting flames.

For Your Life

Nowadays many Christians scoff at the idea of hell. They take for granted that if they cannot be held to account for serious sins, they should have no worry about eternal life. This type of attitude was contrary to that of the saints and is contrary to church teaching. They thought of themselves as great sinners in need of penance and mercy. From the example of St. Afra let us be careful to confess our sins regularly and pray for a peaceful death in God's presence.

Prayer-Meditation

From the sayings of St. Afra at her trial: "Let this my body, which has been the instrument of so many sins, undergo every torment; but let my soul not be contaminated by sacrificing to demons."[4]

189 ✠

St. Mary of Edessa
fourth century[5]

The story of St. Mary was written by St. Ephraem of Edessa, a desert father much admired by St. Jerome. Mary was an orphaned niece of a hermit called Abraham. At age seven her father's friends brought her to Abraham in his hermitage cell. She stayed in the outer room of the poor dwelling. Through a window that adjoined the two rooms Abraham taught the little girl to pray the Psalter and to study Scripture. Mary loved this way of life and prayed to follow it always, free from the snares of the world. In this way the young girl and the old hermit dwelt together for twenty years.

There was an evil man who used to visit Abraham. When he saw the beautiful Mary through the window, he became inflamed with lust. He tempted her subtly through the words he spoke to her uncle. When she finally opened the window of her cell and came out to meet him, he raped her. Overwhelmed with grief, she was consumed by despair and fear. Feeling now unworthy to dwell in the presence of her saintly uncle Abraham, she fled from her cell into another city and ended up in a brothel. When Abraham realized that his beloved niece had left her cell, he entreated God in constant prayer that she might be restored and saved. He sent a friend to search for her. When he found out that she was living in a house of prostitution, he decided that he would seek her out in a disguise. Dressed in military clothing, his face covered by a large hat and a gold piece in hand, he went to the tavern of the city where Mary lived and asked the innkeeper to see this beautiful woman of whom he had heard so much.

So well did Abraham dissemble his true identity that he was able to dine with Mary, jest with her, and finally let her lead him into her bedroom. There he took her face into his hands and revealed himself saying, "Mary, my daughter, ... how didst thou fall from heaven's light into this pit?... Why, when thou didst sin, didst thou not tell me?... I would have done thy penance for thee.... For who is without sin, save God Himself?... It is I that will answer for thee to God at the Day of Judgment."[6]

Slowly he convinced her that the mercy of God was greater than her sin, reminding her of the Lord's love for the repentant Mary Magdalene. Laying her head at his feet, she wept all night and the next day followed him back to their cell. There she wept night and day until God showed her a sign that her penitence was accepted. After this crowds flocked to her for healing and many miracles came to pass through her intercession.

For Your Life

Many young girls are seduced by our culture, their own curiosity, and desire to be loved into a life of sexual sin. Many girls and women who are raped also hold themselves responsible. Their feelings of guilt and despair can lead them to plunge into serious sin. Providentially, God has inspired many other Christians to seek out just such young people through ministry to unwed mothers and teenage run-aways. Some also reach out to prostitutes and those in prison. Girls and women in these predicaments should never lose hope, and those who love them should be as zealous and forgiving as was Abraham to his niece, Mary.

Prayer-Meditation

From St. Ephraem: "O wise understanding of the spirit! An upright and wise and discreet and prudent man is made a reckless fool to snatch a soul from the jaws of the lion, and set free a captive bound... in its dark prison-house."[7]

190 ✠

St. Theodota
d. A.D. 318[8]

*T*heodota was a martyr of Bulgaria. Her death occurred during the persecution of Agrippa, who insisted that all the city give reverence to Apollo. Although previously a prostitute, Theodota had converted. When called before the judge for her refusal to offer pagan sacrifices, she answered that although she had been a sinner, she would never commit another sin. As a result of her courage, seven hundred and fifty Christians refused to comply with the pagan rules.

Theodota was thrown into prison. She prayed for the other Christians and was scourged and tortured further. During her agony she continued to pray, which enraged her tormenters who arranged that vinegar and salt be poured into her wounds and then her teeth pulled out. Finally she was stoned to death. As she was led out to her martyrdom, she prayed aloud, "O Christ, who showed favor to Rahab the harlot and received the good thief, turn not your mercy from me."

For Your Life

Unfortunately, many Christians today curse at the slightest discomfort and are unable to endure greater pain. It is true that annoyance and pain are never pleasures, but crosses to be borne. However, when confronting such sufferings we should offer them as Theodota did. We can offer them to Jesus for the perseverance of other Christians, as well as penance for our own past sins.

May the prayers of St. Theodota give us greater courage in the face of our painful trials. May she intercede that many may be converted from atheism, neo-paganism, and the pseudo-Christian cults that are so popular in our day. Through Christ our Lord. Amen.

191 ✠

St. Fabiola
d. A.D. 399[9]

*F*abiola was a strong woman of noble Roman class. She divorced her husband without revealing why, but it was known to St. Jerome, her adviser, that he had been a man of sexual vices. Fabiola married again, contrary to church law. When her second husband died, she became a penitent and generously endowed many churches, religious communities, and hospitals for ill people she herself found in the streets of Rome. Her hospital was considered the first Christian hospital of the West. She herself tended those with the most repulsive diseases. In A.D. 395, Fabiola made a trip to Bethlehem and lived in a hospice with St. Paula, where she studied the Scriptures. Later, when she returned to Rome, she continued to write letters to St. Jerome. Fabiola died in A.D. 400 and all Rome came to the funeral.

For Your Life

In our times a woman married to a husband like Fabiola's spouse would be able to get an annulment. As in the case of Fabiola, however, many Catholic wives get divorced and remarry without consulting church authority as to the validity of their first marriages. Some also receive Holy Communion, though remarried without the blessing of the church. Women who find themselves in severe marital difficulties should seek competent spiritual and sometimes psychological counsel, and if civil divorce is warranted, apply for annulment proceedings, after which remarriage will be permissible.

Prayer-Meditation

From a eulogy of St. Fabiola: "Fabiola, the glory of the Christians, the wonder of the Gentiles.... Whatever point I take pales in comparison with what she was like. Shall I tell of her fastings? Her alms are greater still. Shall I praise her humility? It is outstripped by the ardor of her faith. Shall I mention her studied squalor, her plebian dress, and the slaves' garb she chose in condemnation of silken robes?"[10]

192 ✠

St. Mary of Eygpt
fifth century[11]

We know most of the life of this extraordinary saint from the account of Abbot Zossima, a holy monk who found her in the desert during his own retreat. Here are some excerpts from the The Life of Hallowed Mother Mary of Egypt: "As he sang, not turning his eyes away from heaven, he saw on the right from where he stood a shadow as of a human body.... It was naked; its body black as if scorched by the fierce heat of the sun; the hair on the head was white as wool and not long.... On seeing it, Zossima, as if beside himself with great joy, began to run in the direction in which the vision was going away.... But when the apparition saw Zossima approaching from afar, it began to run quickly into the depths of the desert.

"When Zossima ran near enough for his voice to be heard, he began to shout, wailing with tears: 'Why are you running away from an old man, a sinner?... Stop and grant me a blessing for the sake of the Lord who despised no one.' (Finally he caught up with the figure who spoke in this manner): 'Father Zossima, forgive me for God's sake, I may not turn round and face you. I am a woman and naked, as you see.... But if you wish to fulfill one prayer of a sinful woman, throw me your coat, so that I can hide my woman's weakness, and turn to you and have your blessing.'

"As she prayed for him he saw her raised a cubit off the ground. Then after being assured that she was not a spirit of evil, he begged her to tell him her story.

"'Already when I was twelve, I renounced (my parents) and went to Alexandria.... I destroyed my virginity, how without restraint and insatiably I gave myself up to lust, it is shameful even to remember. For nearly seventeen years... I had an insatiable longing and an irresistible passion for wallowing in the mud.'

"Then, noticing that a pilgrimage was leaving for Jerusalem she offered her body instead of passage-fare on the ship. 'The holy day of the Elevation of the Cross came (in Jerusalem) and I was still chasing, hunting young men.' (A mighty power held her back from entering into the Church.) 'The word of salvation touched the eye of my heart, and showed me that the impurity of my actions obstructed my entrance. I began to weep and grieve, beating my breast and groaning from the depths of my heart.' (She prayed to Mary to let her enter in order to repent.)

"'Never again shall I defile this body with shameful fornication, but as soon as I see the Tree of the Cross of thy Son, immediately I shall renounce the world and everything that is in the world and shall go where thou... orders me to go and leads me.'"

"After seeing the true cross she returned to the icon of Mary and was told to enter the desert to do penance. She did remain in solitude doing penance for forty-seven years. For seventeen of these years she had frenzied desires for meat and fish, for wine and water, and for past lusts.

"'But immediately in tears I beat my breast and reminded myself of the vow.... I returned mentally to the icon of the Mother of God... and implored her to chase away the thoughts, assailing my unhappy soul.... I saw light, shining around me from all sides. And at last protracted peace would take the place of distraction.'"

She ate whatever could be found in the desert and was scorched in the sun and freezing in the night. "I feed and cover myself with the word of God, Lord of all." Not meeting any human being, God himself taught her the words of Scripture. She died after receiving the sacraments from the abbot.[12]

It may be wondered if anyone could read this account and maintain that the lives of the saints are dull!

For Your Life

Mary of Egypt in a most sensational way chose to avoid the occasion of her previous sins and to spend her life in penance. Although our vocations in life may be different and may entail much contact with the world, we are certainly called to flee from all contacts with entertainments, places, and people that lead us into sinful thoughts, words, and deeds. Many Catholics find in the Virgin Mary a help with sins against purity. Let us have recourse to her in temptation.

Prayer-Meditation

St. Mary of Egypt, teach us not to give in to despair no matter how heavy our sins may be. Intercede for all prostitutes, men who seek the services of prostitutes, and all others who indulge in sexual sin. Ask the Lord to send us special grace to find peace and hope, especially in our hour of temptation. Through Christ our Lord. Amen.

193 ✠

St. Pelagia of Antioch
fifth century[13]

The story of St. Pelagia is told by James, a deacon friend of bishop Nonnus. During a break in a council of bishops, Pelagia, an actress and harlot, passed by the place where the bishops were being instructed. She rode naked on a donkey except for being decked out in gold and pearls, and scented with perfumes. Most bishops turned away in horror, but Bishop Nonnus admitted that her great beauty had delighted him. He compared the amount of time this harlot spent adorning herself to the niggardly rationing of his own time in adorning his soul for Christ, the bridegroom!

That night the bishop had a dream concerning a filthy black dove that he plunged into the holy water font so that it rose out white as snow. The next day Nonnus preached to the people in a manner so full of the Holy Spirit that the pavement of the church became wet with the penitent tears of the congregation. By the hand of God, Pelagia came to the church that very day and was so convicted by the bishop's preaching that she came to deep repentance. She sought him out later, for she had heard stories from the Christians of the Samaritan woman and of Mary Magdalene. She begged him, in the presence of the other bishops, to baptize her without the customary delay of the catechumenate since she longed so fervently to be taken out of her sins. After exorcising her, the bishop baptized her, gave her the body of Christ, and sent her with a deaconess to the other catechumens.

Immediately she gave all her jewelry and riches to the poor through the bishop, who swore that none of it would go to the episcopal treasury but all to widows and orphans. Then she adjured her previous servants to renounce their evil way of life and follow her into the church. That having been done, she left her city secretly and went to the Mount of Olives in Jerusalem.

There she lived in a cell in such penance that she was found by pilgrims to be wasted and haggard with fasting. No one knew that she was a woman, for she went by the name of Pelagius. Only when she died and was anointed was it discovered she had followed a life of penance so severe that it was deemed that only men could endure it. "It was told abroad to all the people, and all the convents of virgins came, some from Jericho and some from Jordan... with candles and torches and hymns: and so the holy relics of her were buried, and the good fathers carried her to her grave."[14]

For Your Life

Much is made of feminine beauty. In itself such loveliness is not negative, but a worthy part of God's creation. Beauty, however, can be abused. Many girls and women are tempted to spend inordinate amounts of time adorning themselves, some in the pursuit of sexual conquest. It can be very difficult for a beautiful, sensual woman to understand that the church teaches women to be modest and simple in their clothing and features. Christianity requires the beauty of the love in the heart rather than external charm. Sometimes young women are ignorant of how they can lead boys and men into temptation by their dress and manner.

While it is wholesome and pleasing to God when feminine beauty is manifest simply and truly, a public display of exotic sensuality must be renounced for the sake of promoting genuine love and respect between women and men. Of course, such eroticism has its place in the intimate context of married love. In that setting, it can be a beautiful act of love to prepare oneself for the beloved.

Prayer-Meditation

From the writings of James of Antioch: "We ought always to return great thanks to our Lord who desireth not that sinners should perish in death, but would have all men [and women] turn in penitence to life."[15]

194 ✠

Blessed Michelina
d. 1356[16]

At twelve Michelina was married into a ducal family in Rimini, Italy. Left a widow at twenty with one son, Michelina continued with her worldly life of pleasure and amusement. A holy Third Order Franciscan recluse, Syriaca, begged alms from Michelina. This led Michelina to conversion. When her young son died, she also became a Third Order Franciscan, giving all her wealth to the poor and begging her bread.

Michelina's relatives thought she was mad. For a time she was confined as one mentally ill. She responded so gently to this treatment that her family decided she was crazy, but harmless. Once released, she resumed her Franciscan ways, adding a ministry to lepers and others with terrible afflictions. Michelina died in 1356 and was immediately venerated as a saint. In 1737 she was beatified.

For Your Life

We can never underestimate the effect that meeting a truly holy person can have, no matter how materialistic the one to be converted. Let us give holy witness ourselves and also introduce our friends to those whose influence would be beneficial to their spiritual lives.

Please intercede, St. Michelina, for all those who are trapped in vanities, that they may come instead to love simplicity and care of the needy. Through Christ our Lord. Amen.

195 ✠

St. Olga
tenth century[17]

S t. Olga is venerated by Russians, Ukranians, and other Slavic peoples as one of the first Christians of Russia. Her name is associated with that of her grandson, St. Vladimir, and they are compared to St. Helen and her son Emperor Constantine who allowed Christianity to flourish in the West. A princess, married to Prince Igor of Kiev, Olga followed the customs of her times in cruel retribution toward enemies. She had the assassins of her husband scalded to death and slew hundreds of their followers.

Olga was baptized in A.D. 957 in Constantinople. She then became a courageous ruler. Olga tried various means to convert her country, but the pagans rallied around her son who did not want to become a Christian. To remedy this problem, Olga sent a letter to Emperor Otto I to send missionaries to her land of Kiev. This attempt was unsuccessful, but Olga was the grandmother of St. Vladimir who was able to convert the Russian peoples.

For Your Life

Many people can identify with a past that contains episodes of violence—be it abortion, gang warfare, or unjust killing of the innocent in war. Once converted, many such Catholic Christians suffer enormous guilt, thinking perhaps their sins can never be forgiven. It is important to seek the healing that comes with the Sacrament of Reconciliation and with sincere penance. Some who have violent acts in their past feel called to reparation through good works aimed at alleviating problems that led to their own sins. They might do pro-life counseling, prison ministry, youth work, or work for peace.

Prayer-Meditation

St. Olga, intercede for us that we may never consider that the sins of our past make us unworthy for apostolic works. Let us go forward confident that God can use our repented sins as a means to reach others caught in similar patterns of wrongdoing. Through Christ our Lord. Amen.

196 ✠

St. Margaret of Cortona
1247-1297[18]

Margaret was born in an Umbrian village in Italy in 1247 to a poor family. Her mother died when she was seven. There was continual enmity between the little girl and her new stepmother who envied the beauty of her husband's daughter. Deprivation of motherly love can explain why Margaret began to seek attention outside her home. In her teen years she was seduced by the promise of love and wealth. She became the mistress of a wealthy nobleman who decked her out in luxurious garments with gold chains in her hair.

Yet Jesus reached out to her amidst her sinful life, gifting her even before her conversion with glimpses of himself in mystical prayer! When her lover was assassinated in a vendetta, his dog led her to his body. At the sight of the rotting corpse, she was brought to make a total commitment to Christ. Immediately she gave away all her jewelry, took her love-child by the hand, and went back to her home. However, Margaret's stepmother refused to let the sinful daughter return, at which point Margaret begged Jesus to be henceforth her master, father, spouse, and Lord.

Margaret set out on the road to Cortona, child in hand, seeking a life of penance among the Franciscans. (Eventually her son became a Franciscan.) When she begged the male Franciscans to give her a robe of penitence, the brother superior dismissed her saying, "My daughter, you are too young and too pretty." Some holy women of the town took her in, let her live in a hut-like cell, and entrusted her to the spiritual care of Brother Bevegnati who was to be her confessor and to write accounts of her life and visions. After making a general confession which took a week to complete, she had the joy of hearing Christ call her his daughter.[19]

Thus began a life devoted to the most terrible imaginable penances. Overwhelmed with sorrow at the pain her sins had caused Jesus at his crucifixion, she would run up to the roof of her cell in the night and cry out that the inhabitants of Cortona should exile so terrible a sinner from their midst. In the general atmosphere of piety of her day these and other deeds of Margaret—shaving off her hair and wearing tattered garments with a rope around her neck—were admired rather than ridiculed. However, even with ashes over her face, her beauty still disquieted those who met her, leading her to still more severe penances of fasting and mortification.

Although Margaret's prayer progressed from purgation to contemplation to spiritual marriage, with many moments of supernatural joy, her spirituality was always marked by tremendous self-hatred and distrust of the body that had led her into so sinful a life in her youth. Eventually her excesses of penance were to lead some church people to consider her mad or drunk and even her confessor to doubt her holiness.[20] Later he would repent of these doubts and be reconciled.

During the time Margaret's confessor left for another city, she was tormented by a demon in the form of a snake who would insinuate that her penances were a mistake since God would want from her only joyful praise. Mauriac, the famous French novelist who wrote her biography, insists that those who have never sinned in the flesh to the degree of St. Margaret simply do not realize how deep is the imprint of sin, even after conversion. Mauriac also notes how tragically beautiful, if astounding and sometimes repulsive, is the life of a penitent such as Margaret. Margaret died at the age of fifty worn out in body but her soul afire with love for her Savior.

For Your Life

Among fervent Christians are many whose past was filled with sin of one kind or another. They are often terrified by the revival of sinful impulses after they have united themselves to the Lord. Some whose sins are not public nonetheless suffer from secret sins. The life of St. Margaret of Cortona shows that it is God who rescues us, Christ who woos us to love him instead of idols. As we reflect on our lives year by year, we come to see that. Mercy is the attribute of God in which we hope the most.

Prayer-Meditation

From the sayings of St. Margaret: "Hide nothing from your confessor.... A sick man can be cured only by revealing his wounds."[21]

197 ✠

Blessed Angela of Foligno
1248-1309[22]

*B*orn in the town of Foligno, twenty miles from Assisi, in 1248, Angela married young and had seven children. By her own account an unusually sinful woman, in her late thirties, after a pilgrimage to the birthplace of St. Francis, she had a sudden and tremendous conversion and became a Third Order Franciscan. When all of her family died within a short time, probably of a plague, she decided to cloister herself from the world in poverty and self-inflicted penance. She desired to live in poverty, freed from bondage to the vanities of social life.

Gifted with many visions, Angela was filled with such fire and fervor that if she heard anyone even speak of God she would cry aloud with joy, to the embarrassment of her followers. These were mostly also Franciscans who gathered around her in her little cell-like house for prayer, penance, and service to the sick.

Even after experiencing great consolations, Blessed Angela went through periods of demonic affliction and hideous temptations, some to sins she had never even imagined in her youth. Eventually she came to see these torments were given to overcome the pride that followed upon such singular gifts of the Spirit.

Angela's account of her life in union with God are contained in *The Book of Divine Consolation,* the reading of which made her one of the most beloved and popular women mystical writers of Europe.

It is not wrong to beg God for signs of his love as long as we do not insist on the nature and timing of such signs. The penitent heart is in great need of healing. Every temptation, no matter how shameful, can be lifted up to our divine Lover in prayer and in penance so that he can fill our deepest desires and heal us of insecurity.

Prayer-Meditation

From the writings of Blessed Angela: "The Crucified One spoke unto me and said: 'When these my sons, who through sin have departed from my kingdom and made themselves sons of the devil, do return unto the Father, he has great joy in them and shows them his exceeding great delight in their return because of the pity which he has on their wretchedness.'"[23]

198 ✠

St. Catherine of Genoa
1447-1510[24]

*B*orn in Genoa in 1447, Catherine came from a noble family of viceroys. Although surrounded by luxury, at the age of eight, Catherine began to do penance by giving up her bed and sleeping at night on straw. She was a quiet and obedient child and received so many supernatural graces that by the age of thirteen she begged to enter a convent. This was not permitted to one so young. At sixteen she agreed instead with her parents who espoused her to Giuliano Adorno, a noble man of Genoa.

Her husband had a peevish and difficult temperament. He finally bankrupted the family by his imprudence. During the first ten years of their marriage, Catherine sought refuge for her unhappiness in feminine company, often of a frivolous sort, for which she did penance for the rest of her life. But nothing could overcome the deep melancholy that beset her because of the incompatibility of character and ways between herself and her husband.

Catherine's conversion took place when she went to confession to a holy priest, at the urging of her sister, a nun. The moment she entered the confessional, such a strong sense of her own faults and of the burning love of God came over her that she vowed to renounce the world and all sin. For days she could only utter profound sighs of contrition and love. Henceforth, wherever she was she would see the bleeding Sacred Heart of the Savior on the cross, suffering for love of us sinners. So impressed was she by these revelations that she begged, unsuccessfully, to be allowed to shout out her sins from the rooftops to the whole city. So much did she love Holy Communion that if deprived of it for even a day, she would suffer bodily pain. Always attending to her home duties, she spent six hours a day in prayer, often so rapt in divine love that she could not hear or see anything exterior.

At the same time, she devoted herself to the poor, especially to the sick, often handling the most disgusting objects in the process of providing a clean atmosphere to the ailing. She kissed the incurable, even at the risk of infection. From natural bad consequences, the Lord protected her. Since her way of life was so different from that of her husband, he finally agreed to live with her as brother and sister and allowed her solitude to follow the way the Lord was leading her. Eventually he became a member of the third order of St. Francis and died a holy death.

Many Catholics have found in devotion to the Sacred Heart of Jesus and family consecration, where all members of a family solemnly give themselves to the protection of the Sacred Heart, a wonderful means for overcoming loneliness, depression, and despair—sometimes in a similar situation of marital strife to that of St. Catherine. Let us always spend part of our prayer time responding to the love of the Sacred Heart for us.

Prayer-Meditation

From the writings of St. Catherine: "Learn what a task it is to purge a soul here below and restore her with no further purgatory to her pristine purity. And when it is God's will to elevate her to a high degree of glory, it becomes more especially necessary, not alone to purify her, but to make her pass through many cruel sufferings that she may gain merit by many and grievous penances."[25]

199 ✠

Eve Lavallière
1866-1929[26]

A woman penitent with a most fascinating history, Eve Lavallière was a French comedienne.

Born in 1866 in the French port of Toulon on the Mediterranean, Eugénie, later to be called Eve, experienced a turbulent youth because of her father. He was an alcoholic and also unfaithful to Eugénie's mother. He battered his wife in drunken rages and terrorized the household. Periodically, the mother and her two children would flee to relatives, but they would always return when the father begged them to do so. Even more painful for the little girl was the favoritism shown her brother. For her, there was only rejection. She was hardly surprised when she was blamed unjustly for infractions of others at school, later to be beaten when her parents refused to believe her protestations of innocence.

A respite came when Eugénie was sent to an excellent boarding school. Here she received not only kindness and understanding but also moments of profound spiritual joy, especially at the time of her First Holy Communion. On her return to her miserable family situation, the young girl found diversion by organizing playmates into a theater group. She herself wrote plays and songs and even designed costumes and sets.

Real tragic drama was to occur all too soon in this troubled family. When Eugénie's mother decided to leave her brutal husband for good, taking her daughter with her, the angry husband insisted on visiting. During an argument he became violent, shot his wife to death, and then committed suicide. Left alone at eighteen under such miserable circumstances, the girl went from relative to relative seeking some security. Having left the faith of her childhood, she gave way to despair, often thinking of suicide.

A stranger Eugénie met by chance was attracted to her beauty and invited her to join a theater group. During this time, she was set up as the mistress of the marquis. Fearing problems with the police if anyone knew he had corrupted a minor, he had her change her name to Eve Lavallière to avoid detection from her family. This had been the name of a famous consort of Louis XIV who ended her days as a penitent Carmelite nun!

Tiring of the marquis, Eve left for Paris where she got involved in musical comedy. Here she fell in love with a theatrical director and gave birth to a daughter. She broke off with him when she discovered he had several other intimate women friends, and continued herself to enjoy liaisons with a variety of men who paid well in financial favors for the pleasure of her company. She was also loved by the critics who considered her musical comedy to be lively and witty.

But off-stage Eve was miserable. In despair she decided three times to kill herself, each time deciding against it at the last moment.

Then one summer she was vacationing in a French village. The parish priest had the audacity to suggest that she attend Mass, sinner or not. Eve went only to mock the priest. When he visited her afterwards, she admitted that she had made a pact with the devil in exchange for the promise of twenty more years of youthfulness. Outraged, the priest insisted that she reform. Suddenly, Eve realized that if the devil were real so must be God and that she ought to follow God instead. The priest gave her a book about Mary Magdalene which she read with genuine contrition, sobbing with repentance.

After coming back to the sacraments, Eve insisted on leaving the theater forever and began to seriously consider joining the Carmelite Order. To prove her sincerity, she forced herself to give up the use of hair dye and make-up. Her attempts to enter the cloister were blocked; the nuns were afraid the publicity would be disruptive. Eve had poor health as well.

Returning to Paris, she sold all her wealth and gave the money to the poor. Then she settled in a small country village to devote herself to prayer and joined the third order of St. Francis. She also became part of a lay mission team nursing Arab children in French Tunisia. Always physically weak, she contracted an African fever. Back in France she suffered great physical agonies for a year and a half during which all her beautiful features were drastically marred. This she offered to God saying that she had sinned through her body and now wanted to expiate for those sins in her body. She died in 1929. Her cause for canonization is currently being advanced.

For Your Life

Struggles with depression and despair can cause agonizing sufferings, not only to those who have been wounded by the choice of sinful lifestyles but to good Christians as well. No matter what, though, we must never despair utterly. Instead, we should call on our Lord in prayer, begging his merciful forgiveness and asking for his healing.

Prayer-Meditation

Dear Jesus, as you pardoned Mary Magdalene, we ask you to embrace with merciful love all those who have vainly attempted to find love through sin. May we be instruments of your love to others, never despairing over their rejection of you, but like the priest who ministered to Eve Lavallière, may we be always eager to do anything to serve those in spiritual need. Through Christ our Lord. Amen.

200 ✠

Venerable Mother Maria Magdalena Bentivoglio
1834-1905[27]

A little known saint of the United States, born in Italy, is Venerable Mother Maria Magdalena Bentivoglio. She is here placed among the penitents, even though her sins were not as scarlet, but because she considered herself to be a penitent. Also her example may help to correct the mistake of thinking that all those who regret their past lives were involved in sexual sin.

Called Annetta as a baby, she lived in the castle of San Angelo in Rome, the twelfth of sixteen children born to a count. Her father was a papal general. Five of the children became religious. Although thoughtful, pious, and kind, Annetta was extremely mischievious and full of self-will. She once risked her life by trying to climb out of a second story window of a school in which she had been locked as a punishment. She also teased the saintly founder of the Religious of the Sacred Heart, Madeleine Sophie Barat, when she was visiting. Trying constantly to overcome her failings and being a very prayerful girl, she decided she wanted to become a contemplative. In 1864 Annetta entered the Poor Clares, with the name of Sister Maria Magdalena of the Sacred Heart of Jesus, because she identified with Mary Magdalene as a penitent. It was a daily martyrdom to try to control her strong will in the convent. In the early days she was so irritable that she was tempted to throw away her office book. She also confessed to hating the plain food of the convent.

In 1875 Pope Pius IX sent Mother Maria and one of her blood-relation sisters to the United States to start the first Poor Clare foundation. There they faced many trials. Each place where they had been told they were wanted, they were rejected on arrival. They were instructed to seek out any bishop who would want them, but had no money for travel, and a language barrier as well. Some bishops thought the pragmatic spirit of the United States was unsuited to supporting contemplatives. They settled down in Omaha where they begged for their needs and also were helped by a generous American benefactor. This man was in the habit of having the nuns pray for all the needs that came to his attention. Once he asked them to pray for a childless couple. After nine months came a telegram: "Twins born! Call off the Poor Clares."[28] There are now sixteen foundations of this branch of the Poor Clares all over America.

Mother Maria Magdalena never lost her joyful high spirits. She was in the habit of leaving notes at the feet of the statues of St. Joseph and St. Anthony for various prayer intentions. Once she cut out pictures of five young girls from a Sears catalogue and placed them at the feet of St. Anthony, praying that he would send some girls like these to the Poor Clares. That year five young women did come to enter the monastery! Mother Maria Magdalena died at seventy-one surrounded by supernatural light, the scent of perfume, and many reports of miracles. Her body is still intact. She was declared venerable in 1932.

For Your Life

The Poor Clares have a charism of joyful praise. During our times when many active orders have dwindled in numbers, the Poor Clares are always replete with vocations. Many lay people like to visit the Poor Clares to enjoy their happiness in the Lord and to ask for prayers for particular graces. We would do well to imitate Mother Maria Magdalena and the Poor Clares in their joyful praise of the Lord.

Prayer-Meditation

From the sayings of Venerable Maria Magalena Bentivoglio: "All my life I have asked God for crosses and now that He has sent them, why should I not be glad?"[29]

Notes

Part One
Young Saints

1. See *Devotions to St. Dymphna* (Boston, MA: Daughters of St. Paul, 1980)
2. See *Butler's Lives of the Saints*, Vol. III, edited, revised, and supplemented by Herbert J. Thurston, S.J. and Donald Attwater (Westminster, MD: 1956) pp. 400-401.
3. See *Butler's Lives of the Saints*, Vol. I, pp. 467-468.
4. See *Butler's Lives of the Saints*, Vol. III, p. 571.
5. See *Butler's Lives of the Saints*, Vol. III, pp. 26-27.
6. See *Secular Saints*, by Joanne Carroll Cruz (Rockford, IL: Tan Books, 1989) pp. 486-487.
7. Ibid., p. 487.
8. Ibid., pp. 658-659.
9. Ibid., pp. 296-298.
10. See "St. Germaine de Pibrac," by Dana Black in *Woman to Woman* by Ronda Chervin and Terri Vorndran Nichols (San Francisco, CA: Ignatius Press, 1988) pp. 112-114.
11. Ibid., p. 114.
12. See "Blessed Kateri Tekakwitha," an article by Terri Vorndran Nichols in *Woman to Woman*, pp. 43-49.
13. See *Lives of Saints*, edited by Fr. Joseph Vann, O.F.M. (New York, NY: John J. Crawley and Co., Inc., 1954) pp. 451-457.
14. Ibid., pp. 456-457.
15. See homily by John Paul II at her canonization, April 9, 1989 in *L'Osservatore Romano*, No. 46, April 17, 1989.
16. Ibid., p. 2.

17. Ibid., p. 2.
18. See *Light Love Life: Elizabeth of the Trinity—a Look at a Face and a Heart*, text and illustrations edited by Conrad DeMeester, O.C.D., translated by Sister Aletheia Kane, O.C.D. (Washington, D.C.: ICS Publications, 1987) and *Elizabeth of the Trinity: The Complete Works*, Vol. I (General Introduction, Major Spiritual Writings), translated by Sister Aletheia Kane, O.C.D., introduction and notes by Father Conrad de Meester, (Washington, D.C.: ICS Publications, 1984)
19. Ibid., *Complete Works*, p. 112.
20. See *Letter to the Martyrs*, by Helen Walker Homan (New York, NY: David McKay Co., Inc., 1951) pp. 25-47.
21. See *Modern Saints* by Ann Ball (Rockford, IL: Tan Books, 1983) pp. 182-185.
22. Ibid., p. 185.
23. See *God, the Joy of My Life: The Diary of Blessed Teresa of the Andes*, trans. and with a biography by Michael D. Griffin, O.C.D. (Washington, D.C.: Teresian Charism Press, 1989)
24. Ibid., p. 14.
25. Ibid., p. 20.
26. Ibid., p. 23.
27. Ibid., p. 121.
28. See "You Would Never Suspect" Boniface Hanley, O.F.M., *The Anthonian* (Paterson, NJ: St. Anthony's Guild, April 11, 1978) pp. 3-29.
29. See *Vatican Decrees on Jacinta and Francisco Marto*, Rome, May 13, 1989, from the Congregation for the Causes of the Saints.
30. See *Sister Maria Gabriella: A Life for Unity*, by Paul B. Quatrocchi, OCSO (New York, NY: New City Press, 1990)
31. See *Secular Saints*, p. 62.
32. See *Modern Saints*, pp. 396-405.
33. Ibid., p. 396.
34. Ibid., p. 396.
35. See *Secular Saints*, pp. 624-630.

Part Two
Motherly Saints

1 See *St. Anne: Grandmother of Our Saviour*, by Frances Parkinson Keyes (New York: Julian Messner, 1955)
2. See *Butler's Lives of the Saints*, Vol. III, p. 205.

3. See *Butler's Lives of the Saints*, Vol. IV, p. 267.

4. See *Butler's Lives of the Saints*, Vol. III, p. 205.

5. See *Secular Saints*, pp. 534-538.

6. See *Secular Saints*, pp. 560-562.

7. Ibid., p. 561.

8. Ibid., pp. 560-561.

9. Ibid., p. 272ff.

10. Ibid., p. 273.

11. See *Secular Saints*, pp. 517-520.

12. See *Secular Saints*, p. 3.

13. See *Secular Saints*, pp. 329-330.

14. Ibid., p. 330.

15. See *Secular Saints*, p. 351.

16. See *Secular Saints*, p. 209.

17. See *St. Dominic's Family*, by Sister Mary Jean Dorcy, O.P. (New Hope, KY: The St. Martin De Porres Lay Community and Rockford, IL: Tan Books, 1983) and *Butler's Lives of the Saints*, Vol. I, p. 14.

18. *Butler's Lives of the Saints*, Vol. III, pp. 553-554.

19. See *Secular Saints*, pp. 563-570. See article "Bd. Margaret of Castello" by Terri Vondran Nichols in *Woman to Woman* by Ronda Chervin and Terri Vondran Nichols (San Francisco, CA: Ignatius Press, 1988) pp. 123-125.

20. See *Secular Saints*, p. 226.

21. See *Butler's Lives of the Saints*, Vol. II, pp. 173-174.

22. Ibid., p. 174.

23. See *Secular Saints*, pp. 339-340.

24. See *Secular Saints*, p. 144.

25. See *Butler's Lives of the Saints*, Vol. I, pp. 529-533.

26. Ibid., p. 529.

27. Ibid., p. 530.

28. See *St. Angela of the Ursulines*, by Mother Francis d'Assisi, O.S.U. (Milwaukee, WI: The Bruce Publishing Co., 1951)

29. Ibid., p. 17.

30. Ibid., p. 127.

31. See *St. Louise de Marillac*, by Mildred Violet Woodgate (St. Louis, MO: B. Herder Book Co., 1942)

32. Ibid., p. 169.

33. Ibid., p. 74.

34. See *Bond of Perfection: Jeanne de Chantal and François de Sales*, by Wendy M. Wright (New York, NY: Paulist Press, 1985)

35. Ibid., p. 36.
36. Ibid., p. 145.
37. See *Marie of the Incarnation: Selected Writings*, edited by Irene Mahoney, O.S.U. (New York, NY: Paulist Press, 1989)
38. Ibid., pp. 9-10.
39. Ibid., pp. 138-139.
40. See *Butler's Lives of the Saints*, Vol. I, pp. 237-238.
41. See *Hands to the Needy: Blessed Marguerite d'Youville: Apostle to the Poor*, by Sister Mary Pauline Fitts, F.N.S.H. (Garden City, NY: Doubleday and Co., Inc., 1971)
42. Ibid., p. 267.
43. See "For the Poor Alone," Boniface Hanley, *The Anthonian*, (Patterson, NJ, 1984) pp. 3-29.
44. Ibid., pp. 27-28.
45. See *Modern Saints*, by Ann Ball (Rockford, IL: Tan Books, 1980, pp. 1-5)
46. See *Philippine Duchesne: A Woman with the Poor*, by Catherine M. Mooney, R.S.C.J. (New York, NY: Paulist Press, 1990)
47. Ibid., p. 114.
48. See "St. Elizabeth Seton" by Ronda Chervin in *Woman to Woman*, pp. 141-150.
49. Ibid., p. 149.
50. See *Modern Saints*, pp. 12-16.
51. See *Married Saints*, by Selden P. Delany (Westminster, MD: The Newman Press, 1950) pp. 246-253.
52. Ibid., p. 252.
53. See *Butler's Lives of the Saints*, Vol. II, pp. 525-526.
54. See *Vision to Mission: Marie Rose Durocher*, by Germaine Duval, S.N.J.M., trans. by Jeanne Peugnet, S.N.J.M. and privately published, from the French edition (Montreal, Quebec, Canada: Les Editions Bellarmin: 1982)
55. Ibid., p. 209.
56. See "A Daughter of St. Francis," Boniface Hanley, O.F.M. *The Anthonian* (Patterson, NJ: St. Anthony's Guild, 1987) pp. 3-30.
57. Ibid., p. 29.
58. See *Modern Saints*, pp. 146-154.
59. Ibid., p. 151.
60. See *Modern Saints*, pp. 86-100.
61. Ibid., p. 98.
62. See *Modern Saints*, p. 80.
63. Ibid., p. 82.

64. Ibid., p. 82.
65. See *Bettina*, a booklet by P. Valentino Macca, published by the Carmelite Sisters of St. Teresa of Florence, 1986)
66. Ibid.
67. See *Butler's Lives of the Saints*, Vol. IV, pp. 619-620.
68. Ibid., p. 619.
69. See *Sorrow Built a Bridge*, by Katherine Burton (Garden City, NY: Doubleday and Company, Inc., 1956)
70. Ibid., from the Preface.
71. See *Conchita: A Mother's Spiritual Diary*, edit. by M.M. Philipon, O.P., trans. Aloysius J. Owens, S.J. (New York, NY: Alba House, 1978)
72. Ibid., p. 231.
73. See *Modern Saints*, pp. 141-143.
74. See *Modern Saints*, pp. 125-131.
75. Ibid., pp. 127-128.
76. See *Modern Saints*, pp. 201-207.
77. Ibid., p. 202.
78. See "The Mary of Ant Town," Boniface Hanley, O.F.M., *The Anthonian*, (Patterson, NJ: St. Anthony's Guild, 1986) pp. 3-29.
79. See *St. Dominic's Family*, pp. 589-590.

Part Three
Martyrs

1. See *Butler's Lives of the Saints*, Vol. II, p. 217.
2. See *Butler's Lives of the Saints*, Vol. II, p. 296.
3. See *Butler's Lives of the Saints*, Vol. I, pp. 255-256.
4. Ibid., p. 256.
5. See *Butler's Lives of the Saints*, Vol. IV, p. 612.
6. See *Lives of Saints*, pp. 24-25.
7. See *Lives of Saints*, pp. 11-17.
8. Ibid., p. 15.
9. Ibid., p.14.
10. See *Butler's Lives of the Saints*, Vol. II, p. 404.
11. See *Letters to the Martyrs*, by Helen Walker Homan (New York: David McKay Co., 1951) pp. 25-47.
12. See *Butler's Lives of the Saints*, Vol. IV, pp. 487-489.
13. See *A Woman Sealed in the Tower: A Psychological Approach to Feminine Spirituality*, by Betsy Caprio (New York, NY: Paulist

Press, 1983)

14. See *Lives of Saints*, pp. 28-29.

15. See *Butler's Lives of the Saints*, Vol. IV, pp. 613-614.

16. See *Butler's Lives of the Saints*, Vol. IV, pp. 530-531.

17. See *Butler's Lives of the Saints*, Vol. IV, pp. 165-168.

18. See *Butler's Lives of the Saints*, Vol. III, pp. 88-89.

19. See *Secular Saints*, p. 567.

20. See *Butler's Lives of the Saints*, Vol. III, pp. 196-197.

21. See *Secular Saints*, p. 255.

22. Ibid., p. 255.

23. See *Butler's Lives of the Saints*, Vol. III, p. 228.

24. See *Mementoes of the Martyrs and Confessors of England and Wales*, by Henry Sebastian Bowden of the Oratory, edited and revised by Donald Attwater (London, England: Burns and Oates, Ltd, 1962) pp. 77-79 and *St. Margaret Clitherow*, by Shelagh Halley (London, England: Catholic Truth Society) (No date is given for publication of the pamphlet.)

25. In this note, the lives of two other women who were martyrs during this period will be briefly sketched. Blessed Ann Line was the widow of an exiled gentleman. She was continuously ailing but desired to become a martyr for the faith, thinking it unjust that only men were dying for the church. In 1601 she was sentenced to hanging for having secret, forbidden Masses said in her home. At the gallows she called out, "I am sentenced to die for harbouring a Catholic priest, and so far am I from repenting that I wish I could have entertained a thousand."

Blessed Margaret Pole was a noble woman whose entire life was a continual suffering for the faith. Her mother died when she was only five years old and this loss was followed immediately by the death in the Tower of her father. All her relatives were tried and executed for defending the faith. Henry VIII even responded to her renowned goodness by making her the godmother of one of his infant children, later to become Queen Mary. However, the opposition of Margaret Pole's own grown children to the king's pretensions in his disputes with Rome caused Henry finally to arrest the mother and behead her in 1541 at the age of seventy. (*Mementoes*, pp. 53-54, 126, 221-222)

26. See *Butler's Lives of the Saints*, Vol. III, pp. 437-438.

27. See *Butler's Lives of the Saints*, Vol. III, pp. 533-534.

28. See *St. Dominic's Family*, pp. 389-390.
29. See *Catholic Korea—Yesterday and Today* (1784-1984), edited by Rev. Joseph Chang-mun Kim and John Jae-sun Chung (Seoul, Korea: St. Joseph Publishing Co., 1984) pp. 64-71.
30. Ibid.
31. See *Butler's Lives of the Saints*, Vol. III, pp. 611-613.
32. See *Butler's Lives of the Saints*, Vol. III, pp. 59-62.
33. See *St. Dominic's Family*, pp. 566-568.
34. See *Modern Saints*, pp. 332-335.

Part Four
Prophetic Saints

1. See *Butler's Lives of the Saints*, Vol. III, pp. 38-39.
2. See *Helena*, by Evelyn Waugh (New York, NY: Doubleday Image Books, 1957)
3. See *Butler's Lives of the Saints*, Vol. III, pp. 145-146.
4. See *Butler's Lives of the Saints*, Vol. I, pp. 171-172.
5. See *Lives of Saints*, pp. 30-32.
6. See *Secular Saints*, p. 639.
7. See *Butler's Lives of the Saints*, Vol. IV, pp. 646-649.
8. Ibid., p. 646.
9. See *Saint Brigid of Ireland*, by Alice Curtayne (Dublin: Browne and Nolan, Ltd., 1934)
10. From a poem of Phyllis McGinley, *The Love Letters of Phyllis McGinley* (New York, NY: The Viking Press, 1951)
11. See *Saint Clotilda*, by Godefroi Kurth (London, England: R and T Washbourne, Ltd., 1913)
12. Ibid., p. 40.
13. See *Butler's Lives of the Saints*, Vol. I, p. 204.
14. See *Secular Saints*, p. 429.
15. See *Butler's Lives of the Saints*, Vol. I, pp. 470-471.
16. See *Secular Saints*, pp. 491-495.
17. Ibid., p. 493.
18. See *Mystics of the Church*, by Evelyn Underhill (Wilton, CT: Morehouse-Barlow, 1925, pp. 74-79 and also from *Butler's Lives of the Saints*, Vol. III, pp. 580-585)
19. Ibid., from *Mystics of the Church*, p. 76.
20. See *Butler's Lives of the Saints*, Vol. II, p. 579.
21. See *Butler's Lives of the Saints*, Vol. I, pp. 462-464.

22. Ibid., p. 463.
23. See *Revelations,* by Anthony Butkovich (Los Angeles, CA: The Ecumenical Foundation of America sponsored by Conrad Hilton, 1972)
24. Ibid.
25. See *Secular Saints*, pp. 348-350.
26. See *Catherine of Siena's Way,* by Mary Ann Fatula, O.P. (Wilmington, DE: Michael Glazier, 1989) and from *The Life of Catherine of Siena,* by Raymond of Capua (Wilmington, DE: Michael Glazier, 1980)
27. Ibid., p. 54.
28. Ibid., p. 111.
29. See "Joan of Arc," by Mary Neill in *Great Saints: Great Friends,* by Mary Neill, O.P. and Ronda Chervin, (Staten Island, NY: Alba House, 1989), pp. 59-68 and *Butler's Lives of the Saints,* Vol. II, pp. 427- 431.
30. From *Great Saints: Great Friends*, p. 64.
31. See *Butler's Lives of the Saints*, Vol. I, pp. 506-508.
32. See "St. Teresa of Avila" by Ronda Chervin in *Great Saints: Great Friends,* pp. 81-102.
33. Ibid., p. 85.
34. See *Mary Ward,* by Mary Oliver, I.B.V.M., introduction and epilogue by Maisie Ward (New York, NY: Sheed and Ward, 1959)
35. Ibid., p. 122.
36. See *The Life and Times of Marguerite Bourgeoys,* by Margaret Mary Drummond (Boston, MA: Guardian Angel Press, 1907)
37. Ibid., p. 2 of the Preface.
38. See *St. Dominic's Family,* pp. 493-495.
39. Ibid., p. 494.
40. See *Secular Saints,* p. 43.
41. Ibid., p. 46.
42. Ibid., p. 50.
43. Information for this article was taken from a leaflet of the Society for the Propagation of the Faith.
44. See *Moments of Decision: Profiles of Great Men and Women Saints* (Boston, MA: St. Paul Editions, 1986) pp. 291-299.
45. See *Butler's Lives of the Saints,* Vol. II, pp. 392-395.
46. Ibid., p. 394.
47. See *Modern Saints,* pp. 43-48.

48. See *Eugénie Smet: Mère Marie de la Providence*, adapted from the French by Caroline C. Morehand (London, England: Sands and Co., 1927)

49. Ibid., p. xiv.

50. See *St. Dominic's Family*, pp. 524-529.

51. See *Mary MacKillop: Faithful in the Dark*, by Srs. Pat Sealey, Evelyn Pickering, and Teresita Cormack (Strasbourg, France: Editions Sadifa, 1984) and *Mary MacKillop: A Woman Before Her Time*, by William Modystack (Dee Why West, Australia: Rigby Publishers, 1982)

52. See *Biblioteca Sanctorum* (Rome, Italy: John XXIII Institute of the Pontifical University of the Lateran, 1966) Vol. VII, p. 1027.

53. See "St. Frances Cabrini," by Terri Vondran Nichols, in *Woman to Woman*, pp. 249-253 and Modern Saints, pp. 247-253.

54. See *Katherine Drexel: Friend of the Neglected*, by Ellen Tarry (London, England: The Catholic Book Club, 1958)

55. Ibid., p. 185.

56. See *Edith Stein*, by Hugh Clarke (London, England: Catholic Truth Society, 1984)

57. Ibid., p. 6.

58. Ibid., p. 15.

59. See *Woman, Collected Works of Edith Stein*, Volume II (Washington, D.C.: ICS Publications, 1987) pp. 9, 10, 43, 52.

60. See *Edel Quinn*, by Frank Duff (Legion of Mary, Shepherdsville, KY: Publishers Printing House, 1959)

61. Ibid., pp. 19-20.

62. See *A Woman for Our Time*, by Spartaco Lucarini, trans. by the Daughters of St. Paul (Boston, MA: St. Paul Editions, 1974)

63. Ibid., p. 213.

64. See *Dorothy Day: A Biography*, by William D. Miller (New York, NY: Harper and Row, 1982)

65. Ibid., p. 6.

66. Ibid., p. 284.

Part Five
Interior Women of the Spirit

1. See *Secular Saints*, p. 691.

2. Ibid.

3. See *Butler's Lives of the Saints*, Vol. I, pp. 292-293.
4. See *Butler's Lives of the Saints*, Vol. III, pp. 170-171.
5. See *Butler's Lives of the Saints*, Vol. III, pp. 318-320.
6. Ibid., p. 318.
7. See *A Dictionary of Saintly Women*, Vol. I, by Agnes B.C. Dunbar (London, England: George Bell and Sons, 1904) pp. 381-383.
8. See *Butler's Lives of the Saints*, Vol. IV, pp. 245-246.
9. See *Butler's Lives of the Saints*, Vol. II, pp. 620-621.
10. See *Butler's Lives of the Saints*, Vol. I, p. 54.
11. See *Secular Saints*, p. 720.
12. See *Butler's Lives of the Saints*, Vol. I, pp. 415-416.
13. See *Butler's Lives of the Saints*, Vol. III, pp. 668-671.
14. Ibid., p. 670.
15. See *Butler's Lives of the Saints*, Vol. III, p. 171.
16. *Dictionary of Saintly Women*, Vol. I, pp. 394-395.
17. See *The Family that Overtook Christ*, by M. Raymond, O.C.S.O. (Boston, MA: St. Paul Editions, 1986)
18. See *Butler's Lives of the Saints*, Vol. II, pp. 377-378.
19. See *Francis and Clare: The Complete Works* (New York, NY: Paulist Press, 1982) pp. 169-234.
20. Ibid., p. 169.
21. See *Secular Saints*, p. 31.
22. See *To Heaven with Diana!*, by Gerald Vann, O.P. (Chicago, IL: Henry Regnery Co., 1965)
23. Ibid., p. 44.
24. Ibid., p. 27.
25. See *Revelations of the Women Mystics*, by José de Vinck (New York, NY: Alba House, 1985)
26. Ibid., p. 50.
27. Ibid., p. 9.
28. *Secular Saints*, pp. 332-334.
29. See *Butler's Lives of the Saints*, Vol. II, pp. 557-558.
30. See *Gertrud the Great of Helfta: Spiritual Exercises*, trans., introduction and notes by Gertrud J. Lewis and Jack Lewis (Kalamazoo, MI: Cistercian Publications, 1989)
31. Ibid., p. 38.
32. See *Butler's Lives of the Saints*, Vol. II, pp. 239-240.
33. See *Butler's Lives of the Saints*, Vol. II, pp. 581-583.
34. See *Secular Saints*, pp. 672-673.
35. See *The Mystics of the Church*, pp. 127-132 and *Butler's Lives of*

the Saints, Vol. 2, pp. 301-303.

36. From *Mystics of the Church*, p. 129.
37. See *Butler's Lives of the Saints*, Vol. IV, p. 224.
38. See *Our Own St. Rita*, by Rev. M.J. Corcoran, O.S.A. (New York, NY: Benziger Brothers, 1919)
39. Ibid., p. 38.
40. See *Secular Saints*, p. 436.
41. Ibid., p. 436.
42. See *Secular Saints*, pp. 299-300.
43. Ibid., p. 299.
44. See *Butler's Lives of the Saints*, Vol. I, pp. 536-539.
45. See *Butler's Lives of the Saints*, Vol. II, p. 350.
46. See *Butler's Lives of the Saints*, Vol. I, p. 325.
47. See *Secular Saints*, pp. 585-586.
48. See *Secular Saints*, pp. 499-501.
49. See *Butler's Lives of the Saints*, Vol. I, pp. 328-331.
50. See *Butler's Lives of the Saints*, Vol. II, pp. 416-419.
51. Ibid., p. 418.
52. Ibid., p. 417.
53. See *Rose of America*, by Sara Maynard (New York, NY: Sheed and Ward, 1943)
54. See *The Life of the Blessed Virgin Mary* (an abridgement of *The Mystical City of God*, by Mary of Jesus of Agreda), translated by Abbé Joseph Boullan (New York, NY: P.J. Kennedy and Sons, 1872) pp. 25-44.
55. Ibid., pp. 30-33.
56. Ibid., p. 33.
57. See *Butler's Lives of the Saints*, Vol. II, p. 401.
58. See *Butler's Lives of the Saints*, Vol. II, pp. 124-126.
59. See *Lives of Saints*, pp. 426-429.
60. Ibid., p. 429.
61. See *The Saints* edited by John Coulson (New York, NY: Guild Press, 1957) pp. 165-166.
62. See *Secular Saints*, pp. 377-378.
63. See *Modern Saints*, pp. 254-259.
64. Ibid., p. 256.
65. See "St. Bernadette," by Mary Neill, O.P. in *Woman to Woman*, pp. 117-130 and *Modern Saints*, pp. 71-77.
66. *Modern Saints*, p. 75.
67. See *Mariam the Little Arab*, by Amedée Brunot, S.C.J., trans. Jeanne Dumais, O.C.D.S. and Sister Miriam of Jesus, O.C.D.

(Eugene, OR: The Carmel of Maria Regina, 1984)

68. Ibid., p. 25.
69. Ibid., pp. 51-56.
70. Ibid., p. 22.
71. See *Modern Saints*, pp. 272-277.
72. Ibid., p. 277.
73. See *A Book of Unlikely Saints,* by Margaret T. Monro (London, England: Longmans, Green and Co., 1943) pp. 167-210.
74. Ibid., p. 181.
75. Ibid., p.208.
76. See *Rafka: The Blind Mystic of Lebanon,* by Most Rev. Francis M. Zayek, S.T.D., J.C.D. (Still River, MA: St. Bede's Publications, 1980)
77. Ibid., p. 59ff.
78. Ibid., p. 37.
79. Ibid., p. 55.
80. See *Modern Saints*, pp. 290-297.
81. Ibid., p. 292.
82. See *Modern Saints*, pp. 388-394.
83. Ibid., p. 391.

Part Six
Sinners Turned Saints

1. See "St. Mary Magdalene," by Terri Vorndran Nichols, in *Woman to Woman*, pp. 170-174.
2. Ibid., p. 172.
3. See *Secular Saints*, p. 9.
4. Ibid., p. 9.
5. See *The Desert Fathers,* by Helen Waddell (Ann Arbor, MI: The University of Michigan Press, 1977) pp. 189-201.
6. Ibid., p. 197.
7. Ibid., p. 201.
8. See *Secular Saints*, p. 697.
9. See *Secular Saints*, pp. 243-244.
10. Ibid., p. 244.
11. See *Little Pictorial Lives of the Saints* (New York, NY: Benziger Brothers, 1925) and from *The Life of Hallowed Mother Mary of Egypt*, pp. 67-83 and from *Secular Saints*, p. 513.
12. See *Life of Hallowed Mother Mary of Egypt*, pp. 80-83.

13. See *The Desert Fathers*, by Helen Waddell (Ann Arbor, MI: University of Michigan Press, 1977) pp. 173-188.

14. Ibid., p. 88.

15. Ibid., p. 177.

16. See *Secular Saints*, pp. 531-532.

17. See *Butler's Lives of the Saints*, Vol. III, p. 72.

18. See *Saint Margaret of Cortona*, by François Mauriac, trans. Bernard Frechtman (New York, NY: Philosophical Library, 1948)

19. Ibid., p. 67.

20. Ibid., p. 132.

21. Ibid., p. 50.

22. See *The Book of the Divine Consolation of Blessed Angela of Foligno*, revised, adapted, and modernized by Msgr. William J. Doheny, C.S.C., privately printed in Rome, Italy, 1950.

23. Ibid., p. 184.

24. See *The Spiritual Doctrine of Saint Catherine of Genoa*, compiled by her confessor, Don Cattaneo Marabotto (Rockford, IL: Tan Books and Publishers, 1989)

25. Ibid., pp. 244-245.

26. See "Because of Her Great Love," Boniface Hanley, *The Anthonian* (Patterson, NJ: St. Anthony's Guild, 1980), pp. 3-31.

27. See *Modern Saints*, pp. 193-200.

28. Ibid., p. 196.

29. Ibid., p. 196.

Bibliography

Ball, Ann. *Modern Saints.* Rockford, IL: Tan Books, 1983.

Biblioteca Sanctorum, Vol. VII. Rome, Italy: John XXIII Institute of the Pontifical University of the Lateran, 1966.

The Book of the Divine Consolation of Blessed Angela of Foligno. Revised, adapted, and modernized by Msgr. William J. Doheny, C.S.C. Privately printed in Rome, Italy, 1950.

Bowden, Henry Sebastian. *Mementoes of the Martyrs and Confessors of England and Wales.* Edited and revised by Donald Attwater. London, England: Burns and Oates, Ltd., 1962.

Brunot, Amedée, S.C.J. *Mariam the Little Arab.* Translated by Jeanne Dumais, O.C.D.S. and Sister Miriam of Jesus, O.C.D. Eugene, OR: The Carmel of Maria Regina, 1984.

Burton, Katherine. *Sorrow Built a Bridge.* Garden City, NY: Doubleday and Co., Inc., 1956.

Butkovich, Anthony. *Revelations.* Los Angeles, CA: The Ecumenical Foundation of America, 1972.

Butler's Lives of the Saints, 4 Volumes. Edited, revised, and supplemented by Herbert J. Thurston, S.J. and Donald Attwater. Westminster, MD: Christian Classics, 1956.

Caprio, Betsy. *A Woman Sealed in the Tower: A Psychological Approach to Feminine Spirituality.* New York, NY: Paulist Press, 1983.

Chervin, Ronda and Nichols, Terri Vorndran. *Woman to Woman.* San Francisco, CA: Ignatius Press, 1988.

Clarke, Hugh. *Edith Stein*. London, England: Catholic Truth Society, 1984.

Conchita: A Mother's Spiritual Diary. Edited by M.M. Philipon, O.P. Translated by Aloysius J. Owens, S.J. New York, NY: Alba House, 1978.

Corcoran, Rev. J. J., O.S.A. *Our Own St. Rita*. New York, NY: Benziger Brothers, 1919.

Cruz, Joanne Caroll. *Secular Saints*. Rockford, IL: Tan Books, 1989.

Curtayne, Alice. *Saint Brigid of Ireland*. Dublin, Ireland: Browne and Nolan, Ltd., 1934.

D'Assisi, Mother Francis, O.S.U. *St. Angela of the Ursulines*. Milwaukee, WI: Bruce Publishing Co., 1951.

Delany, Selden P. *Married Saints*. Westminster, MD: The Newman Press, 1950.

De Vinck, José. *Revelations of the Women Mystics*. New York, NY: Alba House, 1985.

Devotions to St. Dymphna. Boston: Daughters of St. Paul, 1980.

Dorcy, Sister Mary Jean, O.P. *St. Dominic's Family*. New Hope, KY: The Martin de Porres Lay Community, and Rockford, IL: Tan Books, 1983.

Drummond, Margaret Mary. *The Life and Times of Margaret Bourgeoys*. Boston, MA: Guardian Angel Press, 1907.

Duff, Frank. *Edel Quinn*. Legion of Mary, Shepherdsville, KY: Publishers Printing House, 1959.

Dunbar, Agnes B.C. *A Dictionary of Saintly Women*. Vol. I. London, England: George Bell and Sons, 1904.

Duval, Germaine, S.N.J.M. Translated by Jeanne Peugnot, S.N.J.M. *Vision to Mission: Marie Rose Durocher*. Privately published from the French Edition. Montreal, Quebec, Canada: Les Editions Bellarmin, 1982.

Elizabeth of the Trinity: The Complete Works. Vol. I. Translated by Sister Aletheia Kane, O.C.D. Introduction and notes by Fr. Conrad de Meester. Washington, D.C.: ICS Publications, 1984.

Eugénie Smet: Mère Marie de la Providence. Adapted from the French by Caroline C. Morehand. London, England:

Sands and Co., 1927.

Fatula, Mary Ann, O.P. *Catherine of Siena's Way.* Wilmington, DE: Michael Glazier, 1989.

Fitts, Sister Mary Pauline, F.N.S.H. *Hands to the Needy: Blessed Marguerite d'Youville: Apostle to the Poor.* Garden City, NY: Doubleday and Co., Inc., 1971.

Francis and Clare: The Complete Works. New York, NY: Paulist Press, 1982.

Francis M., S.T.D., J.C.D. *Rafka: The Blind Mystic of Lebanon.* Still River, MA: St. Bede's Publications, 1980.

Gertrud the Great of Helfta: Spiritual Exercises. Translated and introduced with notes by Gertrud J. Lewis and Jack Lewis. Kalamazoo, MI: Cistercian Publications, 1989.

The Joy of My Life: The Diary of Blessed Teresa of the Andes. Translated and with a biography by Michael O. Griffin, O.C.D. Washington, D.C.: Teresian Charism Press, 1989.

Halley, *St. Margaret Clitherow.* London: Catholic Truth Society.

Hanley, Boniface, O.F.M., *The Anthonian,* Patterson, NJ: St. Anthony's Guild, 1978, 1980, 1984, 1986, 1987.

Homan, Helen Walker. *Letters to the Martyrs.* Rockford, IL: Tan Books, 1983.

Keyes, Frances Parkinson. *St. Anne: Grandmother of Our Saviour.* New York, NY: Julian Messner, 1955.

Kim, Rev. Joseph Chang-mun and Chung, John Jae-sun. *Catholic Korea: Yesterday and Today.* Seoul, Korea: St. Joseph Publishing Co., 1984.

Kurth, Godefroi. *St. Clotilda.* London, England: R and T Washbourne, Ltd., 1913.

Light Love Life: Elizabeth of the Trinity—A Look at a Face and a Heart. Text and illustrations by Conrad De Meester, O.C.D. Translation by Sister Aletheia Kane, O.C.D. Washington, D.C.: ICS Publications, 1987.

Little Pictorial Lives of the Saints. (No editor given for this old book.) New York, NY: Benziger Brothers, 1925.

Lives of Saints. Edited by Fr. Joseph Vann, O.F.M. New York, NY: John J. Crawley and Co., Inc., 1954.

Lucarini, Spartaco. *A Woman for Our Time.* Translation by the Daughters of St. Paul. Boston, MA: St. Paul Editions, 1974.

Macca, P. Valentino. *Bettina.* A booklet published by the Carmelite Sisters of St. Teresa of Florence, 1986.

Marie of the Incarnation: Selected Writings. Edited by Irene Mahoney, O.S.U. New York, NY: Paulist Press, 1989.

Mary of Agreda. *The Life of the Blessed Virgin Mary.* An abridgement of the *Mystical City of God.* Translated by Abbé Joseph Boullan. New York, NY: P.J. Kennedy and Sons, 1872.

Mauriac, François. *Saint Margaret of Cortona.* Translated by Bernard Frechtman. New York, NY: Philosophical Library, 1948.

Miller, William D. *Dorothy Day: A Biography.* New York, NY: Harper and Row, 1982.

Moments of Decisions: Profiles of Great Men and Women Saints. Boston, MA: St. Paul Editions, 1986. (No editor's name is given.)

Mooney, Catherine M., R.S.C.J. *Philippine Duchesne: A Woman with the Poor.* New York, NY: Paulist Press, 1990.

Modystack, William. *Mary MacKillop: A Woman Before Her Time.* Dee Why West, Australia: Rigby Publishers, 1982.

Monro, Margaret T. *A Book of Unlikely Saints.* London, England: Longmans, Green and Co., 1943.

Oliver, Mary, I.B.V.M. *Mary Ward.* Introduction and Epilogue by Maisie Ward. New York, NY: Sheed and Ward, 1959.

Quattrocchi, Paul B., O.C.S.O. *Sister Gabriella: A Life of Unity.* New York, NY: New City Press, 1990.

Raymond, M., O.C.S.O. *The Family that Overtook Christ.* Boston, MA: St. Paul Editions, 1986.

Raymond of Capua, Bd. *The Life of Catherine of Siena.* Wilmington, DE: Michael Glazier, 1980.

Sealey, Sister Pat, Evelyn Pickering and Teresita Cormack. *Mary MacKillop: Faithful in the Dark.* Strasbourg, France: Editions Sadifa, 1984.

Tarry, Ellen. *Katherine Drexel: Friend of the Neglected*. London, England: The Catholic Book Club, 1958.

Underhill, Evelyn. *Mystics of the Church*. Wilton, CT: Morehouse-Barlow, 1925.

Vann, Gerald, O.P. *To Heaven with Diana!* Chicago, IL: Henry Regnery Co., 1965.

Vatican Decrees on Jacinta and Francisco Marto. Rome, Italy: Congregation for the Causes of the Saints. May 13, 1989.

Waddell, Helen. *The Desert Fathers*. Ann Arbor, MI: The University of Michigan Press, 1977.

Waugh, Evelyn. *Helena*. New York, NY: Doubleday Image Books, 1957.

Woodgate, Mildred Violet. *St. Louise de Marillac*. St. Louis, MO: B. Herder Book Co., 1942.

Wright, Wendy. *Bond of Perfection: Jeanne de Chantal and François de Sales*. New York, NY: Paulist Press, 1985.

Alphabetical Listing
of Entries

Special Sufferings

Note to Reader: This index is organized so readers can locate saints who endured particular sufferings. Readers are encouraged to locate saints with whom they share particular sufferings, so they can identify with the saints and ask for their intercession.

Abusive or Unfaithful Husbands

Physical Abuse
St. Rita of Cascia

Verbal Abuse
Bd. Anna Maria Taigi
St. Godelieve
St. Monica

Infidelity
St. Elizabeth of Portugal
Bd. Margaret d'Youville
Bd. Paola Gambera-Costa

Battered by Relatives or Others (Martyrs Listed Separately)

St. Adelaide
Bd. Agostina Pietrantoni

Eve Lavallière
St. Germaine de Pibrac
St. Godelieve
St. Jeanne de Lestonnac
St. Jeanne Marie de Maillé
St. Joaquina
Laura Vicuna
Bd. Maria Bagnesi
Bd. Mariam Baouardy

Demonic Temptations

St. Angela of Foligno
St. Catherine of Bologna
St. Catherine of Genoa
St. Catherine of Siena
St. Elizabeth of Schönau
St. Eustochium of Padua
St. Gemma Galgani
Bd. Helen dei Cavalcanti
St. Margaret of Cortona

Bd. Maria Fortunata Viti
St. Syncletia

Disabled

St. Angela Merici
St. Germaine de Pibrac
St. Lutgardis
St. Margaret of Castello

Disappointing Children

St. Clotilda
Cornelia Connelly
Eve Lavallière
St. Louise de Marillac
St. Matilda
St. Monica

Divorced

Mother Alphonsa Hawthorne
Cornelia Connelly
Dorothy Day
St. Fabiola

Early Death of Children

Mother Alphonsa Hawthorne
Bd. Angela of Foligno
St. Clotilda
Cornelia Connelly
Concepción Cabrera de
    Armida, (Conchita)
Bd. Dorothy of Mantua
St. Elizabeth Seton
St. Frances of Rome
St. Joaquina
Bd. Marguerite d'Youville
St. Matilda
St. Melania the Younger

Bd. Michelina
Praxides Fernandez

Extreme Poverty

Bd. Agostina Pietrantoni
St. Bernadette of Lourdes
Dorothy Day
St. Germaine de Pibrac
St. Margaret Bourgeoys
St. Margaret of Castello
Bd. Maria Gabriella
St. Maria Goretti
Bd. Maria Fortunata Viti
Bd. Marie of the Incarnation
    (Acarie)
Venerable Pauline-Marie
    Jaricot
St. Soledad

Forced into Exile

St. Adelaide
Mother Angela Truszkowska
St. Arthelais
St. Clotilda
St. Elizabeth of Hungary
Bd. Jeanne Marie de Maillé
St. Joaquina
Bd. Kateri Tekakwitha
Sister Marina
St. Melania the Younger
St. Pulcheria
St. Rose of Viterbo
St. Susanna

Gravely Ill

St. Alpais
Sister Alphonsa of India

Sister Amparo Carbonell
St. Angela Merici
Mother Angela Truszkowska
St. Arthelais
St. Bathildis
St. Bernadette of Lourdes
St. Catherine dei Ricci
St. Catherine of Siena
Edel Quinn
Bd. Elizabeth of the Trinity
St. Elizabeth of Schönau
Eve Lavallière
St. Gorgonia
Bd. Isabella of France
Venerable Jacinta Marto
St. Julia Falconieri
St. Julie Billiart
St. Louise de Marillac
St. Lydwine
Mother Margaret Hallahan
Margaret Sinclair
Bd. Maria Bagnesi
Bd. Maria Gabriella
St. Maria Mazzarello
Venerable Maria Teresa
  Quevedo
St. Mariana of Quito
Bd. Marie Rose Durocher
St. Mary Magdalen of Pazzi
Nano Nagle
Bd. Paula Frassinetti
Bd. Rafka Al-Rayes
St. Raphaela
St. Romula
Satoko Kitahara
St. Syncletia
Bd. Teresa of the Andes
St. Teresa of Avila
Teresa Valse Pantellini
St. Thérèse of Lisieux

Imprisoned

Bd. Beatrice da Silva
Venerable Jacinta Marto
St. Joan of Arc
Bd. Mariam Baouardy

In-Law Problems

St. Adelaide
St. Elizabeth of Hungary
St. Elizabeth Seton
St. Godelieve
St. Helen of Skovde
St. Jeanne de Chantal
Bd. Jeanne Marie de Maillé
St. Ludmila
Bd. Marguerite d'Youville
Bd. Michelina
St. Pulcheria

Loss of Father or Mother

Mother Alphonsa Hawthorne
Sister Alphonsa of India
St. Angela Merici
St. Colette
St. Dymphna
Bd. Elizabeth of the Trinity
St. Elizabeth Seton
Eve Lavallière
Bd. Frances Scherviers
St. Gemma Galgani
St. Germaine de Pibrac
St. Humbeline
St. Jeanne Marie de Maillé
St. Jeanne de Chantal
Bd. Kateri Tekakwitha
Laura Vicuna
St. Louise de Marillac

St. Margaret of Cortona
St. Margaret Mary Alacoque
Mother Margaret Hallahan
Venerable Marguerite
  Bourgeoys
Bd. Marguerite d'Youville
Bd. Maria Bagnesi
Bd. Maria Fortunata Viti
Bd. Maria Gabriella
St. Maria Goretti
Bd. Mariam Baouardy
St. Mariana of Quito
Bd. Marie Rose Durocher
Bd. Marie of the Incarnation
  (Acarie)
Sister Miriam Teresa
  Demjanovich
St. Pulcheria
St. Radegunde
Bd. Rafka Al-Rayes
St. Raphaela
Bd. Sibyllina Biscossi
St. Susanna
St. Syncletia
St. Teresa of Avila
Bd. Sister Teresia Benedicta
  (Edith Stein)
St. Thérèse of Lisieux

Married Unhappily

Mother Alphonsa Hawthorne
Bd. Castora Gabrielli
St. Catherine of Genoa
Cornelia Connelly
St. Fabiola
St. Godelieve
Bd. Marguerite d'Youville
St. Monica
St. Radegunde

St. Rita of Cascia
Bd. Zedislava Berka

Mental Illness or Judged so by Enemies

Bd. Eustochium of Padua
St. Margaret of Cortona
Bd. Michelina
Bd. Maria Fortunata Viti
St. Raphaela

Murdered (as Confessors of the Faith or for Moral Integrity)

St. Afra
St. Agatha
Bd. Agatha Kim
Bd. Agostina Pietrantoni
Sister Amparo Carbonell
St. Anastasia
Bd. Antonia Messina
St. Barbara
Sister Carmen Moreno
St. Catherine of Alexandria
St. Cecilia
St. Dymphna
Sts. Flora and Mary
St. Helen of Skovde
St. Joan of Arc
Laura Vicuna
St. Lucy
Bd. Lucy de Freitas
Lugartha Lee Yu-Hye
St. Margaret Clitherow
Bd. Margaret of Louvain
Bd. Margaret Ward
St. Maria Goretti
Bd. Mariam Baouardy

Sister Marina
Bd. Mary Hermina Grivot
Sts. Maura and Brigid
St. Natalia
Sts. Nunilo and Alodia
Sts. Perpetua and Felicity
St. Susanna and Companions
Bd. Sister Teresia Benedicta
(Edith Stein)
St. Theodota
St. Winifred of Wales

St. Jeanne de Lestonnac
St. Louise de Marillac
Bd. Margaret of Castello
Venerable Marguerite
Bourgeoys
St. Mariana of Quito
Mary Ward
St. Rose of Viterbo
Bd. Teresa de Gesu, Jornet y
Ibars
Mother Thecla Merlo

Opposition of Church Authorities to Their Hopes and Dreams

St. Elizabeth Seton
St. Joan of Arc
Mother Margaret Hallahan
Bd. Marguerite d'Youville
Sister Mary MacKillop
St. Mary Magdalena
Bentivoglio
Mary Ward
St. Philippine Duchesne
St. Raphaela
St. Teresa of Avila

Parents not Married

St. Bridget of Ireland
Bd. Eustochium of Padua
Henriette Delille
Bd. Sibyllina Biscossi

Rejected by Religious Orders

St. Clare
Bd. Eugénie Smet

Ridiculed for Their Piety
(Other than Martyrs)

Bd. Agostina Pietrantoni
Bd. Angela of Foligno
St. Bernadette of Lourdes
St. Catherine of Genoa
St. Catherine of Siena
St. Clelia Barbieri
St. Elizabeth of Hungary
St. Elizabeth Seton
St. Frances of Rome
Venerable Jacinta Marto
Bd. Jeanne Marie de Maillé
St. Joan of Arc
Bd. Kateri Tekakwitha
St. Margaret of Cortona
Bd. Marguerite d'Youville
St. Mary Magdalene
Mary Ward
St. Matilda
Sts. Nunilo and Alodia
St. Rose of Lima
St. Susanna
St. Teresa of Avila
Bd. Teresa Maria of the Cross
(Bettina)
Bd. Zedislava Berka
St. Zita

Separated from Children

Cornelia Connelly
St. Jeanne de Chantal
Bd. Marie of the Incarnation
(Acarie)

Subject to Extreme Sexual Temptation

Bd. Angela of Foligno
St. Catherine of Siena
St. Margaret of Cortona
St. Mary of Edessa
St. Mary of Egypt
St. Mary Magdalene
St. Mary Magdalen of Pazzi
St. Pelagia of Antioch

Threatened by Incest

St. Dymphna
Laura Vicuna
Sister Susanna
St. Winifred of Wales

Threatened with or Victim of Rape

St. Agnes
Bd. Antonia Mesina
St. Joan of Arc
St. Maria Goretti
Bd. Pierina Morosini
St. Zita

Widowed

St. Adelaide
St. Anastasia

Bd. Angela of Foligno
St. Bathildis
St. Birgitta of Sweden
Bd. Castora Gabrielli
St. Clotilda
Concepción Cabrera de
Armida (Conchita)
Bd. Dorothy of Montau
St. Elizabeth of Hungary
St. Elizabeth Seton
St. Etheldreda or Audrey
St. Eulalia
St. Frances of Rome
Bd. Helen dei Cavalcanti
Bd. Ida of Boulogne
St. Jeanne de Chantal
St. Jeanne de Lestonnac
Bd. Jeanne Marie de Maillé
St. Joaquina
St. Jutta
St. Louise de Marillac
Bd. Lucy de Freitas
St. Ludmila
Bd. Marguerite d'Youville
Bd. Marie of the Incarnation
(Acarie)
St. Matilda
Bd. Michelina
St. Monica
St. Olga
St. Paula
Praxides Fernandez
St. Rita of Cascia

Acknowledgments

The author and the publisher wish to express their gratitude to the following authors, editors, and publishers whose publications have proven very helpful in researching background information for entries in Treasury of Women Saints.

Ann Ball. *Modern Saints.* Rockford, IL: Tan Books, 1983.

Butler's Lives of the Saints, 4 volumes. Edited, revised, and supplemented by Herbert J. Thurston, S.J. and Donald Attwater. Westminster, MD: Christian Classics, 1956.

Joanne Carroll Cruz. *Secular Saints.* Rockford, IL: Tan Books, 1989.

Sister Mary Jean Dorcy, O.P. *St. Dominic's Family.* New Hope, KY: The Martin de Porres Lay Community, and Rockford, IL: Tan Books, 1983.

Lives of Saints. Edited by Fr. Joseph Vann, O.F.M. New York, NY: John J. Crawley and Co., Inc., 1954.